Learning and Everyday Life

Written by world-renowned social anthropologist, Jean Lave, with an afterword by Brazilian anthropologist Ana Maria R. Gomes, this book weaves together ethnographic accounts of work and learning, apprenticeship and everyday life, through a critical theory of practice. Each chapter explores in different ways the proposition that learning is a collective, transformative process of change in the historically political complex relations of everyday life. At the same time, the book demonstrates the changing character of Lave's own research practice over two decades. Lave addresses work practices and everyday life and discusses the problem of context and decontextualization. Analyzing two decades of ethnographic studies of craft apprenticeship, she explores teaching as learning and examines the reciprocal effects of theories of everyday life and learning.

JEAN LAVE is Professor Emerita at the University of California, Berkeley. She is a social anthropologist and critical theorist. Her books include one of the most cited works in the social sciences *Situated Learning: Legitimate Peripheral Participation* (with E. Wenger, Cambridge, 1991) as well as the prize-winning *Understanding Practice* (with S. Chaiklin, Cambridge, 1993).

Learning and Everyday Life

Access, Participation, and Changing Practice

Jean Lave
University of California, Berkeley

Afterword by
Ana Maria R. Gomes

CAMBRIDGE
UNIVERSITY PRESS

University Printing House, Cambridge CB2 8BS, United Kingdom

One Liberty Plaza, 20th Floor, New York, NY 10006, USA

477 Williamstown Road, Port Melbourne, VIC 3207, Australia

314–321, 3rd Floor, Plot 3, Splendor Forum, Jasola District Centre, New Delhi – 110025, India

79 Anson Road, #06–04/06, Singapore 079906

Cambridge University Press is part of the University of Cambridge.

It furthers the University's mission by disseminating knowledge in the pursuit of education, learning, and research at the highest international levels of excellence.

www.cambridge.org
Information on this title: www.cambridge.org/9781108480468
DOI: 10.1017/9781108616416

First published 2019

Printed in the United Kingdom by TJ International Ltd, Padstow Cornwall

A catalogue record for this publication is available from the British Library.

Library of Congress Cataloging-in-Publication Data
Names: Lave, Jean, author.
Title: Learning and everyday life : access, participation and changing practice / Jean Lave, University of California, Berkeley ; afterword by Ana Gomes.
Description: Cambridge, United Kingdom ; New York, NY, USA : Cambridge University Press, [2019] | Includes bibliographical references.
Identifiers: LCCN 2018043477 | ISBN 9781108480468 (hardback) | ISBN 9781108727433 (paperback)
Subjects: LCSH: Educational anthropology. | Learning–Social aspects. | Educational sociology.
Classification: LCC LB45 .L39 2019 | DDC 306.43–dc23
LC record available at https://lccn.loc.gov/2018043477

ISBN 978-1-108-48046-8 Hardback
ISBN 978-1-108-72743-3 Paperback

Contents

Acknowledgments

This book has grown, changed, and taken shape in its travels between the Instituto de Estudos Avançados Transdiciplinares at the Universidade Federal de Minas Gerais and the Slow Science Institute in Berkeley; through encounters with participants in the Brazilian Danish Workshop on Learning in Practice in Belo Horizonte (2013) and Copenhagen (2017); and in meetings in San Francisco, in Mexico City and in St. Andrews. So, we are indebted to students in the PhD program at UFMG, including Xakriabá teachers and researchers, and especially colleagues Maria Cristina Gouvêa and Eduardo Mortimer. We must also note students and colleagues from Aarhus and Roskilde universities and the Danish Pedagogical University in Denmark, brought together by leaders of the Brazilian Danish Workshop, Dorte Kousholt, and Line Lerche Moerk, to thank them for many intense and thoughtful discussions about our work, and many memories of good fellowship. Our colleague and friend Elsie Rockwell first took an interest in our project as it sprouted in 2011 in Belo Horizonte. She encouraged its development and improvement both through a meeting at DIE-CINVESTAV in Mexico City in 2013 and by her searching and provocative reading of our manuscript. Gill Hart has patiently and ruthlessly read draft after draft – for which the book is very much the better in every respect. Peter Skafish had a very similar effect on the Introduction. Anthropologist Janet Keller, a long-time colleague, friend, and extraordinary editor, welded our first attempt at a two-language endeavor into a coherent draft. Without her we could not have continued on to finish the project. Lucy Suchman's perspicacious reflection on the manuscript has been extraordinarily helpful in bringing it together. Two generous anonymous readers for Cambridge University Press gave us useful and interesting ideas for improving the manuscript – as has our editor, Andrew Winnard, Executive Publisher, Language, Linguistics, Anthropology at Cambridge University Press. Jacob Liming, has applied remarkable intellectual and technical sophistication to the preparation of the manuscript. Our heartfelt thanks to one and all.

Introduction

The Long Life of Learning in Practice

The seven essays brought together in this book trace a trajectory of critical theoretical and ethnographic research as it has grown and changed over many years. My work as a whole attempts, it has been said, to excavate the politics of knowledge that inform theories of learning, and to reconceive learning in/as transformation, and as itself always a cultural/historical practice. This began with a conception I proposed years ago of learning as "situated in context." It has continued into my recent attempts to work out a dialectical notion of learning as "changing participants' changing participation in (humdrum, complicated, conflictual) everyday practice." The essays show how those ideas have changed in the process of moving, first, from my early ethnographic work on apprenticeship and everyday math practices, to a very different view of trajectories of changing participation in the practices of everyday life; second, from the idea that there are island-like contexts (plural) in which persons thus situated engage in "the same" activities differently, to that of participation in social practice of persons moving in complex relations through and across the contexts of their everyday lives (everyday lives now understood as produced with others in historical, political relations); and, third, from an inkling that these are contradictory processes to a deeper appreciation of the dialectical relations of which they are composed.

It probably is not a surprise, then, that I do not believe "learning" is an individual or psychological phenomenon. I worry about the theoretical, ethno-graphic and political implications of work in fields that claim "learning" as central to their disciplines (e.g., education, psychology). By reducing learning to individual psychological processes they thereby ignore the conflicting forces and relations that change participation in always-changing social practice. Educative disciplines and institutions that limit themselves to such reductions do not have the critical analytic power to conceive of learners and learning in such transformative terms. As for anthropologists, they too largely share the common sense view of learning, which is to imagine that "learning" is already accounted for in notions of teaching. Or they just avoid the subject altogether, assuming that it is not part of their remit. My own view is that anthropologists who ignore that learning is, as this book contends, an effect and source of

1

social change, do so at their peril. But it is rare that those interested in social change – whether as interaction, or institutionalized local practices, or epochal struggles – feel compelled to seek, again, a *transformative* rather than reproductive conception of learners learning.

So, whether because of their politics or their (lack of) social theoretical formation, or both, researchers in the social sciences tend to think of learning only as the means for reproducing a stable social order. This is an unfortunate view, given the integral role that learning plays in undermining, upsetting, reordering – *changing* – the social processes that compose social life. Each essay in this book can be read as a response to this state of affairs. If I were to summarize my approach here (as elsewhere), I might distill it into these six points:

1) Try to formulate critical arguments against problematic customary psychological, educational, sociological practices that underwrite reduced and decontextualized conceptions of learning. Such arguments are difficult to make – but they are needed for the forseeable future for others who will in turn change and pass them on.
2) Insist that a *critical* social theoretical formation, and not just political will, is urgent and necessary in order to pursue change. Show why this is so as concretely as possible.
3) Recognize at the same time that a critical theoretical formation is never adequate by itself, but always only part of critical encounters between the analytic terms and questions addressed in historical/ethnographic research projects, and the assumptions and theoretical claims that underlie them. At best, each should inform and also change the other.
4) There are, of course, many brilliant exceptions to my hyperbolic complaints, so find colleagues who share in the same struggles from similarly critical perspectives and try to join with them and change my work in response to their work.
5) On the basis of the above, work toward an encompassing, dialectical understanding of learning as an integral part of the condition of possibility for social life in all its political–economic, historical, and processual particularities.
6) Recognize that these tasks are worth spending a lifetime on, because learning, which always embodies possibilities for change, always embodies possibilities for transformative change. It is part of – and essential to – revolutionizing future practice.

This critical "agenda" sums up the impetus that led me to write these essays. But there is also another, more immediate reason for gathering them together here. This book has taken shape in collaboration with anthropologist Ana Gomes at the Federal University of Minas Gerais. I began to write about the situatedness of learning around 1980, a decade before the publication of *Situated Learning* (1991); and even that book has had a longer life than many of its current readers. Thinking about the age of this work led us to wonder how, in communicating among generations of researchers, it would be possible to show what has happened as both my work and the times have changed – and Ana suggested that this collection of essays might help.

But there is more to it than that. I found Ana Gomes and the anthropologists with whom she works in Belo Horizonte engaged in close studies of everyday life and learning in their city. I was intrigued by the way in which they were looking at participants' everyday engagements in practice, and following them through and across the multiple contexts that compose those everyday lives. These anthropologists are also participants in struggles to transform relations between the hegemonic educational apparatuses of the Brazilian state, UFMG, and new indigenous visions of educational practice. These initiatives are emerging as indigenous people and anthropologists have invented new state and local organizations to provide the kinds of spaces they need in which to work together, reinvented relations between universities and indigenous communities, and remade anthropological participation in indigenous community practices as well; both parties are engaged in new forms of co-production of their shared ethnographic practice. (Ana Gomes explores these challenges in her Afterword. You might want to read that next.) The impetus for this book came, then, from finding that my ideas about learning in and as changing practice resonate with and inform their work. Their radical vision of ethnographic relations and political action make me feel that this book is worth sending out into the world.

Ana and I collaborated in choosing the essays, bringing together work that explores interrelated research questions, the sometimes divergent collective conversations that nourished them, and the particular intellectual movements that in different ways allowed me to write them in the first place. Though the essays came together as a whole as we selected and assembled them, they can also be read in almost any order. I have accordingly provided a separate introduction for each of them, and will only say a brief word about them here.

The first essay (Chapter 1), "The Savagery of the Domestic Mind," (1981), was for me an opening salvo on a cluster of issues common to early anthropological concerns with rationality and "the primitive mind" and to psychological theories of learning (and experimental method). Ethnographic research on everyday math practices provided the empirical resources for joining the debate. This essay serves as a point of departure for exploring the book as a whole. The second and third essays open out to questions of theory – and then practice – provoked by discussions that followed from *Situated Learning* (1991): "The Problem of Context" (Chapter 2) asks what a variety of our theoretically sophisticated colleagues were debating about conceptions of situation, context, practice, learning, and activity; and "Ethnographies of Apprenticeship" (Chapter 3) reviews a large body of ethnographic studies of craft practice and apprenticeship, wondering how (or if) they contextualized learning in illuminating ways. Ana proposed the fourth essay (Chapter 4) as an antidote to common complaints that I rarely discuss teaching. Even there the title serves notice that it explores "Teaching as Learning in Practice." In that spirit, the following essay (Chapter 5), "Production Schools," explores the subtle and contradictory power of an extraordinary Danish school that operates as a matter of course with the assumption that teaching is a complex practice of learning. The final two essays reflect changing theoretical developments in ways that bring them closer to the present. "Everyday Life" (Chapter 6) explores different ways in which "the everyday" is conceived with respect to learning, for sooner or later every theory of learning makes claims about the everyday life of which it is part. This question (along with broader theoretical debates around "everyday life"), looms increasingly larger in my work, as the relation between them is ubiquitous and yet often conceived in confused ways that demand clarification. Finally, I wrote the last essay for this book (Chapter 7) to bring it to an end with (something close to) a point of arrival. It begins with my own critical review of *Situated Learning* as a prelude to exploring relations between Gramscian theory of practice and critical psychology on the conduct of everyday life.

The essays indeed reflect a long arc of change in the theoretical and ethnographic projects they explore. Read in sequence, they demonstrate what I mean by saying, as I often do, that we are all apprentices to our own changing practice. In fact, every ethnographic project I have undertaken has felt like a preamble to the one before and has ended with an inevitable sense that yet another project is needed; surely an active process of apprenticeship to past and future work.

Theoretical development, too, is similarly open ended: Think of one's theoretical formation as being like an ethnographic project. A field research project is many years in the making, involving years in the field, years of analysis and writing, and years of talking with others about it. The same can be said about the exploratory and transformative intentions animating the process of theoretical formation. It is a very long-term project; it changes over time, and is a situated practice – it is situated, that is, as part of *other* practices. It is an ongoing process of collective discussion and puzzling over difficult theoretical texts, and of ethnographic inquiry, analysis, and critique. (It is in part, also, its institutional, intellectual, political, scholarly contexts, and relations.) But perhaps the most important, and most difficult, step is the labor of getting one's theoretical understanding and related ethnographic inquiry to meet "in the middle" and challenge each other – so that neither stays the same.

Coming to take a critical stance toward conventional theorizing is probably a matter first of coming to recognize that our common sense understandings of the world and their epistemological and ontological presuppositions are the very same ones that frame conventional academic theorizing. They will, if taken for granted, lead to the diagnosis of only the problems and visions of change confined to, and defined by, that framework in the first place.

Ana Gomes recently co-edited a special issue of *Horizontes Antropologicos* on Culture and Learning (Gomes et al. 2015). She began with a diagnosis of common anthropological assumptions about culture and learning in Brazil. (They are the same ones I took with me to begin the research on apprenticeship among Liberian tailors in the 1970s.) She observes that they stand between two widely shared traditions. One is a venerable theory of cultural transmission. The other is borrowed from cognitive psychology, notable for its rationalist, individual, and behaviorist assumptions. They both issue from the same positivist, empiricist theoretical problematic that informs the common sense of the discipline as well as our lives more broadly.

It took quite an extended struggle to break with the theoretical traditions that Ana Gomes identifies even today, and that included both conventional distinctions between "formal" and "informal" education, and common assumptions about learning. As soon as I began fieldwork in tailors' workshops in Monrovia I found evidence that Vai and Gola tailors' apprentices were learning a lot (as, obviously, the master tailors to whom they were apprenticed must also have done), but I could not see it happening. I was faced with a deeply frustrating question about *how* apprentices were learning to tailor. And that was not even the complete question. More honestly I was caught up in asking "how are the apprentices learning to tailor – if they are not being taught by teachers, as pupils?" How could I find out how to characterize what was going on, since the only conceptual tools at hand when I started came from those theories that "knowledge gets transmitted," on the one hand, and "mental activity leads to internalized knowledge," on the other? How was I going to inquire into how the apprentices learned to become master tailors if ethnographic inquiry made it amply clear that what I was seeing could not be explained in school-centric theoretical terms? First, recognizing the limitations of the conventional theory clearly grew out of experiencing the limitations of ethnographic inquiry as well as vice versa.[1] Further it takes work to come to inhabit a theoretical problematic other than "the usual." And figuring out, and figuring out how to articulate, an alternative theoretical stance – a theory of *practice* – has clearly been crucial in

---

[1] Lave (2011) speaks to the disconcerting challenges posed by the ethnographic inquiry in Liberia to commonplace theory – and the development of social practice theory, including the notion of "situated learning" as well.

responding to the challenges raised both by my ethnographic work and by the constricting claims of common sense theory.

The variety of theory of practice which I have been working with, and trying to extend my grasp of, began to become clearer to me in the early 1990s, when reading Marx's work with a group of colleagues, while also struggling to make better sense of the tailors' project. Marx's theory of praxis has been fought over and enriched in generations of scholarly debate. There are crucially diverse Marxist theoretical stances – a hugely complex field of scholarly and political debate that has taken place for over a century and a half. This domain is easily ignored when "Marxism" is reduced to a single, politically convenient stereotype: That is, a fixed, dogmatic "theory" about a political–economic system, capitalism, that would be one pole in a grand dualism where the economic "base" completely determines everything else – merely "superstructure" – in collective and individual history in a teleological, linear fashion. Clearly that's not the strand of Marxist theory running through Marx's Theses on Feuerbach; Gramsci's philosophy of praxis; the dialectical method of Bertell Ollman (1976, 2003); the work of Henri Lefebvre (1991, 2000); Stuart Hall's reading of the *Grundrisse* (2003); or Paul Willis's ethnography of working class learning (1977). I have slowly learned from these and other thinkers, all of them working within Marx's theory of praxis, a relational, dialectical conception of material, historical processes and practices. This critical theory does indeed reject common sense assumptions about those dual divisions that we register as mind and body, subject and social world. Ollman tells us that rather than being related in just one way, as is the case when something is either one thing or its opposite – e.g., individual or social, mental or manual, produced or reproduced – a dialectical relation is a matter of "*both and.*" It is precisely that Marxist insight that makes it possible to articulate that culture is not just something to be learned. Culture produces learning, even as learning always produces culture, in relations that are themselves cultural and historical; those relations make *culture/learning* what it is. In other words, those relations (which are multiple and contradictory, i.e., composed of many relations) are, together and at the same time, also a relation – call that relation "learning in/as practice."[2]

---

[2] "Things as their relations" is a difficult idea to grasp. But to introduce the idea here, Ollman helps:

> The philosophy of external relations, which reigns in both the common sense and learned discourse of our time, holds that there are both "things" ... and relations, but that they are logically independent of each other. Thus, in principle, the relations between two or more things can undergo dramatic changes and even disappear altogether without affecting the qualities by which we recognize these things and with which we define the terms they refer to.

Ollman's characterization of relations expresses in a more formal way theoretical insights that developed gradually as the questions I worked on changed. What I can do here is trace those evolving theoretical questions over the years as they shaped the essays, beginning with the ethnographic project on craft apprenticeship in Liberia. That project had the effect of generating unanticipated, field-inspired pressures to rethink dualist premises about "formal and informal education." It was crucial in coming to see learning as a relation – "situated learning" – because it brought me face to face with questions about participants' access, through each other, to participation, in ongoing practice.

But craft apprenticeship arguably also had limitations as a resource for changing theory. A Vai tailors' workshop was not a school but it nonetheless involved an intentional educational practice; apprentices were there to learn a trade while they were taking part in it. That raised questions for me about learning in circumstances that were not educational in an institutional sense. My subsequent ethnographic project, on math practices in everyday life, pushed me toward questions about learning as everyday participation in ongoing practice. This reframed the theory project to ask: *How* is learning part of the moving, cross-contextual, profoundly interconnected, conduct of everyday life?

In turn this led me to grapple with the concept of "everyday life." Conventional theoretical claims about "everyday life" are saturated with assumptions about learning and schooling – learning, in common sense and academic educational theory is treated as movement away from "the everyday" toward (high-) cultural knowledgeability and the extra-ordinary. (This argument is laid out in the essay "Everyday Life" [Chapter 6]). Differently theorized notions of everyday life – not as a thing in itself but as people participate in it, and thus as "the conduct of everyday life" – made it possible to arrive at a radically different view. Critical psychologists argue that everyday life quintessentially involves movement across a series of contexts and their ongoing practices, as participants engage with sundry others who are part of those contextual engagements (Dreier 2003, 2008a, 2008b). So, the question "how does learning happen?" changed for me through iterative transformations, to another that takes learning-in-practice to be constituted as participants, changing, move across and deal with, and among, the contexts in which they participate.

In contrast, the philosophy of internal relations holds that what others take to be a "thing" that may or may not undergo change and may or may not have relations with other things is itself both a "process" and a "relation" ... What was a thing for the philosophy of external relations becomes a relation evolving over time (or a process in constant interaction with other processes). (Ollman 2015: 10)

Eventually, I came to realize that even transformative struggles for broader, radical social change are made in everyday practice. I am thinking, again, of the many-sited everyday practices that compose new initiatives for indigenous education in Brazil. In another register, 18-year-old participants in Danish Production Schools come to understand that they are there, not for the purpose of accumulating scholasticized "knowledge," but rather (as they engage in their work with others in the school's workshops to produce things used and valued by others, and contribute in other ways to collective projects at the school) in order to develop a stronger grasp on their own future possibilities – what Henri Lefebvre identifies in virtually the same words, as the basis of revolutionary change.

In bringing this Introduction to a close I would like to respond to at least one among the common ways this work has been misunderstood over the years. Yes, learning is always a political project, a collective endeavor, situated in everyday practice and a key to future transformative change. Yet a reader who works through the essays might wonder why I keep the focus on learning when I do not take it to be a project in theorizing mind or brain or individual subjects. Does not all this talk about "practice," she might ask, amount to a behaviorist claim that we (must) bracket out what goes on in minds because we can only infer internal processes from external inputs and outputs (stimuli and responses)? In general, my response comes in the form of another question: How can you have a theory of mind or brain that does not situate them in the world of which they are a constitutive part – in changing practice? A theory of mind or cognition as a thing-in-itself will not get you to an understanding of how unemployed coal miners' wives and daughters join their evangelical church in forming a Tea Party group, nor account for tensions between apprenticed young women and men struggling to transform and hold on to traditional masculine arrangements for working in bakeries in Denmark. Starting instead with either of those scenarios puts you in a position to ask questions about what and how participants as incoherent persons, with multiple partial identities – contradictory, emotional, thought-embodied beings – are made in practice, through practice; as *they* make themselves in practice. These are questions about history, power, relational being and conflict – not questions about "the mind" or an individual mind, or different "kinds of minds." Thought, thought forms, self-reflection, and critique are *part, but only part,* of ongoing social practice, just as are participants struggling for coherence and collective meaning-making, for their identities and lives. My penchant for saying that "it is (only) learners who learn" is a way of arguing against claims that human existence is completely determined, or inevitable, or unchangeable, and that the powers of inculcation and repression guarantee this. In my view it is altogether too well kept a secret that as people engage in "learning" (that is, as changing participants engaged in changing participation in everyday changing practice) – they do inhabit possibilities for transformative social change.

This introduction has been an account of political struggles over the theory and practice of learning in and as practice. A dialectical theory of praxis embodies these struggles in several different respects. It situates ethnographic studies of learning in political relations in the historically made and present world and refuses to dissemble or hide them. It recognizes that every project is necessarily incomplete and partial. "Partial," it should be carefully noted, never justifies bracketing off narrow bits of social life, picking them apart from their participation in making and being made in the world. Instead it is a way of asserting the crucial nature of simultaneous attention to political/economic historical configurations of forces and their relations in and through everyday life. In contradictory ways they are part – past, present, and future – of possibilities for bottom-up transformations of everyday life's practices.

1   The Savagery of the Domestic Mind

* * * * *

The "Savagery of the Domestic Mind" was written for a session of the American Association for the Advancement of Science on the anthropology of science (Nader 1996). The "Savagery" chapter draws its argument from the theoretical/empirical project laid out in *Cognition in Practice: Mind, Mathematics, and Culture in Everyday Life* (1988). This book was based, not on the Liberian project on apprenticeship, but on the next research project, on mathematical practices in everyday life activities. I had written a book manuscript on the research in Liberia shortly after the fieldwork came to an end. This first attempt ended with a clear sense that I did not know how to articulate theoretical objections or write within an alternative theoretical framework. I also set it aside on grounds of the empirical, especially linguistic, limitations of the Liberian project. Instead I began a new research project in Orange County, California. That project, nicknamed the Adult Math Project, occupied several years in the early 1980s (with Michael Murtaugh [1985b] and Olivia de la Rocha [1985]). *Cognition in Practice* was intended as ground-clearing preparation for trying again to develop the argument of the manuscript on apprenticeship.

Cognition in Practice set the context for the theoretical and empirical analysis of everyday mathematical practice in the anthropology of the late nineteenth and the first half of the twentieth centuries. Anthropologists were arguing not so much about scientific practice as about the nature of rationality, couched as debates about science and magic, oral and literate cultures, civilized and primitive minds. Along with Durkheim and Mauss (1903) and the late nineteenth-century social Darwinists, Levy-Bruhl (1910) was a key figure during this period, important from my perspective because his arguments had inordinate effect on Vygotsky, Luria, Bartlett, and Evans-Pritchard among others, and thus on Soviet psychology, activity

The first draft of this chapter grew out of a series of conversations with Steven Shapin. Laura Nader deserves thanks not only for bringing together examples of the anthropology of science in *Naked Science: Anthropological Inquiry into Boundaries, Power and Knowledge* (1996), but for organizing an anthropological presence at the meetings of the American Association for the Advancement of Science in the first place. Thanks especially to Paul Duguid for a thoughtful critique at the right time and to Shawn Parkhurst for his perspicacious suggestions, which led me to revise the chapter yet again. This article was translated into Portuguese in 1996 by Angela Maria Moreira in an issue of *Revista Critica de Ciêncas Sociais.*

10

theory, British psychology, and anthropology.[1] This historical lineage of debate was central to the tensions between the fields of psychology and anthropology in the 1980s – and still dominates these fields when they touch on learning, thinking, or school/education (Lave 1988: 76–93). Further theoretical inspiration came from new work by sociologists of science examining science as its own everyday practices (cf. Latour and Woolgar 1979). They raised questions of great interest to the Adult Math Project, for if science is everyday practice, what do we mean when we talk about "the everyday" as a foil, as something that in dualist parlance is "not science?"

The Anthropology debates and early social studies of science came together in the book (and in "The Savagery of the Domestic Mind") in two ways. First, it was possible to confront arguments about mind, science, rationality, and mathematics with instructive differences among quantitative practices of shoppers in grocery stores, dieters in their kitchens, and subjects in psychological experiments (and also on paper and pencil tests, the latter instantly categorized as "school math" by participants in the project).

Second, this chapter intertwines discussions of two sets of "subjects." One set included people whom social scientists investigate in studies of cognitive processing, problem solving, learning, and cognitive development. The other set contained the social scientists themselves as they engaged in everyday practices of cognitive research. The question was, how do the experimental practices of cognitive research help to generate apparently mathematically incompetent jpfs (just plain folks [Lave 1988: 191]) who are not only demonstrably competent in assembling relations of quantity (if you are willing to look carefully at their everyday practices) but who also embody incoherent and contradictory beliefs about mathematical competence (as do the social scientists who, after all, are also jpfs).

Treating the social scientists and their "subjects" as equally the focus of analysis of everyday practice is a concrete way to engage in a major aspect of critical theory – this move was central to the Liberian research as well, and it has shaped in one way or another virtually everything I have done since. Theory of praxis takes critique seriously, because, among other things, theorists grow their theories through their everyday practices and that includes their own research practices.

Sometime between *Cognition in Practice* (1988) and *Situated Learning* (1991) the concept that confined "learning" to (categorically unsituated) abstraction as merely a cognitive process of acquiring and internalizing "information" was so evidently in conflict with notions of the situatedness of human activity including learning, that it felt both impolitic and misleading to continue relying on the term. We were (arguably are) living in an historic period in which cognitivist ideology wields enormous hegemonic institutional power and, at the same time, offers deeply

---

[1] The continuous proliferation of new translations, editions, and reprints stands as testimony to the durability of Levy-Bruhl's dualistic thought. The French original, *Les Fonctions Mentales dans les Sociétés Inferieures,* was translated by Lilian Clare to the gentler title, *How Natives Think,* in 1926, was republished in 1986 through Princeton University Press, and a facsimile of the original translation was made widely available in 2015. Beyond this, a quick glance at the table of contents of most American cognitive psychology textbooks is further proof that the categories and tradition of Levy-Bruhl's reductive cognitive anthropology is alive and well in contemporary thought.

inadequate explanatory power with which to confront lived (as opposed to hypothetical) practices of learning. Vaguely defined claims about "cognition" and narrow research on "mechanisms" to improve learning together help limit and prevent critical social analysis of education-wrought inequities by making it all too easy to read political historical failure as individual cognitive failure. Theory of practice takes social-historical struggles and practices with respect to changing participation in changing practice as constitutive of explanations of learning. "Cognition" has stopped appearing in my attempts at comprehensive conversations about learning.

Two other reflections on this project come from a more contemporary perspective: In the Adult Math Project we concentrated on expert grocery shoppers and dieters, asking how they grocery shopped, dieted, and managed household finances (looking at the different ways they dealt with quantitative relations in different contexts). This was therefore not yet a study of changing practice nor an inquiry into how participants learned to engage skillfully in practice. And finally, I miss a focus on how the work and learning of participants was shaped in particular ways by the social events, political conflicts, economic, and cultural struggles of the epoch in which they were living.

I learned the hard way in working on this project about how difficult it is to articulate and document arguments that question dominant, education-based theories of learning. The issues are still with us. And for those interested in *Situated Learning*, much of the thinking that went into that book developed through *Cognition in Practice*.

* * * * *

Sociologists and anthropologists of science have begun to study scientific knowledge production in laboratories and elsewhere as everyday practice. This work raises questions about what we mean by "everyday practice." It encourages questions about what becomes of "everyday" everyday practice when science is thus reconceived. And it provokes opposition from many, in part because views of science as everyday practice contest conventional claims: The prevailing belief among scientists and non-scientists alike is that whatever science may be it is most definitely "not-everyday." Such a belief defines "science" in opposition to the "not-science" otherwise known as "everyday life." Philosophical traditions and scientific discourses ascribe to scientists specialized, value-neutral, and powerful thinking and to their work an exceptional character, inevitably helping to reinforce the hegemonic role of science and underlining distinctions between real scientists and the rest – the "others" who are not scientists.

Anthropologists of science find themselves in a tough position, threading their way through varied conceptions of everyday practice that spring from their research on the practice of science, from scientists' understanding of themselves and their work in opposition to "the everyday," and from the traditions of Western thought that undergird the practice of science.

In the early 1980s, my students and I undertook a study of everyday mathematical practices in Orange County, California (de la Rocha 1985; Murtaugh 1985a, 1985b; Lave 1988). Our main concern was to explore interconnected American cultural practices that generate and sustain core conceptions about rationality. Rather than investigating laboratory science practices, we observed people engaged in daily activities in supermarkets and kitchens – as they shopped for groceries, cooked meals, dealt with quantitative relations while learning the Weight Watchers dieting program, and managed their household finances. This offered us an unusual perspective – that of "just plain folks" (jpfs) – on what is often labeled "everyday problem solving" in laboratory studies of cognition or research on learning in schools. The differences between these perspectives of lab studies and jpfs raised strategic questions about characterizations of "the everyday" and "the inferior other." Both concepts have contributed to ideologies of science and scientific thinking.

Our project differed from the growing body of research on physical scientists in their laboratories in other respects as well. Many disciplinary practices juxtapose "science" and "everyday life" (Lave 1988: 4), including discourses on the mind, cognition, representation, problem solving, logic, mathematics, the expert, scientific thinking, and the effects of schooling. Among the social sciences, cognitive science has been an especially important site for the production of claims about the everyday world and its relations with "scientific" knowledge. Cognitive studies depend on, and produce, contrasting views of what are called "scientific" and "other" forms of thinking. Indeed, the study of functional modes of thinking in this century has been persistently based on an imagined conception of the thinking of "the other," considered the inferior. "The inferior other" is deeply embedded in Western thought: in the practices of more traditional psychologies and cognitive science, in laboratory experiments and computer simulations, and in schools.

Schooling complicates the story. It is difficult to address claims about thinking, knowing, and learning without analyzing the school practices that are supposed to produce good thinkers, knowers, and learners. For the last century, at least, schooling has been a mediating institution in which relations among (1) social science theorizing about everyday life, (2) living everyday lives, and (3) the practices of science are mutually implicated in one another. Schooling is a major institutional form in which the claims of cognitive scientists about "scientific" and "everyday" thinking are confirmed (as well as inculcated). Schooling itself often is made to stand in for "science" as the opposite pole to everyday life.

The everyday practices of cognitive scientists leave little room to notice, much less to explore, the practices of those typically designated as "the other." When we began our study we had all of Orange County to ourselves except the

Cognitive Science Laboratory at the university. Why so little company? To witness the practices of jpfs requires venturing outside the university into (other) places where "everyday" knowledge is constituted in activity, in situ. To do this requires assuming that ways of thinking and forms of knowledge are historically and socioculturally situated phenomena. Cognitive theory in particular and Western thought much more generally has assumed quite differently. Learning, thinking, information processing, and knowledge representations are taken to be universal ahistorical processes by which all individual humans operate and have always operated. Two consequences are worth noting. First, with views like this cognitive scientists have no incentive to venture beyond the laboratory and, second, distinctions between scientific thinking and the thinking of "the other" are thus naturalized and universalized.

Claims about the nature of mind, mental processes, and powerful thought have often, in the past, confusingly assumed the mathematical nature of all three (de la Rocha 1985; Lave 1988). (Current rejections of rule-governed models of mind in favor of associationism and intuition – e.g., Dreyfus and Dreyfus [1986] – propose changes in the value assigned to mathematical structures of mind but not to the terms of the debate.) These models take the mind itself to be mathematically structured, take mathematics as the structure of thought processes, and take the mathematical content of reasoning (or mathematical intuition) to be the most powerful content of most exemplary – read scientific – thinking. Thus, mathematical practices, especially mathematical practices in nonschool settings, offer a promising venue for exploring theoretical issues concerning science, the everyday, and the thinking of "the other."

I have outlined three ways in which our "anthropology of science" has differed from more typical studies in the field. Rather than studying biomedicine or physics, we chose to study social science approaches to mind and mathematics; rather than studying scientists in their laboratories, we investigated domestic practices (though against a background of school and psychology laboratory practices). And that meant that our research and this chapter address intertwined American cultural practices involving two sets of "natives." One set are the people whom social scientists investigate (in studies of cognitive processing, problem solving, learning, and cognitive development). The other set are the social scientists themselves (as they engage in the everyday practices of cognitive research).

The following section introduces the domestic quantitative practices of jpfs. The section after that explains why we describe these practices as "assembling and transforming relations of quantity in ongoing activity" rather than interpreting and evaluating them in terms of scholastic math puzzle solving. Next we turn to the other subjects of our research, the scientists of mind, exploring the dialectical process by which scientists' theorizing about the mind depends upon assumptions about the "civilized mind" to generate characteristics of the "primitive mind" and vice versa, so that in the end each is defined by how it is not the other. The following section describes how practices of empirical cognitive research similarly generate superior and inferior others. In the last section we take up where and how the dialectics of competent and incompetent rationality are absorbed into the practices of jpfs.

The Math Problem in Everyday Life

Here is a fairly typical example of mathematical activity by jpfs in the supermarket. The example is intended to illustrate the difficulty of translating everyday math practice into conventional thinking about math problem solving.

The following was observed during a grocery-shopping expedition. A shopper was standing in front of a produce display. She spoke as she put apples, one at a time, into a bag. She put the bag in her grocery cart as she finished talking.

There's only about 3 or 4 [apples] at home, and I have 4 kids, so you figure at least two apiece in the next three days. These are the kind of things I have to resupply. I only have a certain amount of storage space in the refrigerator, so I can't load it up totally ... Now that I'm home in the summertime this is a good snack food. And I like an apple sometimes at lunchtime when I come home. (Murtaugh 1985b: 188)

In the end the shopper bought nine apples. For analysts of mathematical practices this example poses several problems that a conventional math "word problem" does not. There are several plausible answers – 9, 13, 21. It appears that the problem was defined by the answer at the same time an answer was developed during the problem, and that both took form in action in a particular, culturally structured, setting – the shopper's local supermarket. The shopper's engagement with quantity did not lead to a pause for formal calculation, yet relations between inventory, family apple consumption, budget, and sack size were all reconciled in action.

There was quite a substantial body of research on mathematics in everyday practice at the time this chapter was written. It started with Gay's and Cole's *The New Mathematics in an Old Culture* (1967); my research on tailors in Liberia; and Posner's (1979) and Petitto's (1979) work with farmers, tailors, and cloth merchants in Côte d'Ivoire. Sylvia Scribner (1982) and her associates carried out a path-breaking study of math practices among blue collar workers in a commercial dairy in Baltimore, followed by research focused on CAD-CAM production practices. Carraher (1982; 1983), Carraher, Carraher, and Schliemann (1982) in Brazil studied market-vendor children at work in open-air markets selling garden produce and in school. They also compared master carpenters to trade school carpenters' apprentices and made a study of the math practices of bookies taking bets on the national lottery "numbers" game. Geoffrey Saxe (1988) studied Brazilian children's activities selling candy on the street and learning math in school, and Hutchins (1993) was following US Navy navigation teams on a helicopter transport ship.

Two robust findings appear in all of this work. The same people deal with relations of quantity in quite different ways in different situations. On the one hand, when engaged in everyday activity they are remarkably accurate in their calculations – even by the (arguably irrelevant) standards of school math practices. Participants in our grocery shopping research averaged 98 percent accuracy in their calculations in the supermarket. Market vendors in Recife in Brazil who had spent very little time in primary school were 99 percent accurate. Dairy workers in Baltimore, with an average of a sixth-grade education, made no errors when observed at their work of assembling wholesale orders for dairy products. On the other hand, the same people did much less well on tests designed to be comparable with problem solving in supermarket, open-air produce market, or commercial dairy. This finding suggests that things are different enough "out there" to pose some interesting questions for conventional cognitive theorizing about everyday mathematical practice.

The discontinuity in performance between work and test settings suggests that even mathematical problem solving is situationally specific activity. Other sources support this claim: For instance, people's educational biographies (i.e., how much schooling they have had and how long ago), predict test scores but do not predict everyday performance differences between individuals, which in any case hardly exist. In the end, however, it is the apple example and many like it that provide the more interesting empirical evidence for the situational specificity of everyday math. They show that math seems part of the flow of activity; that math activity is quite different in different settings and with it the assembly and transformation of quantitative relations.

The Transformation of Quantitative Relations in the Resolution of Quandaries

De La Rocha's (1985) study of Weight Watchers provides rich, complex, situated examples of the transformation of quantitative relations in everyday practice. She followed the activities of nine women, all new members of the dieting program, as they incorporated new measurement practices into their meal preparation over a period of weeks. The diet program emphasized meticulous control of portions of food consumed. Thus, it promised to generate many opportunities for calculation in the kitchen, and she hoped to see attempts at new kinds of math activity in a setting far removed from school.

De la Rocha carried out repeated, intensive interviews with each dieter, including an exploration of the participants' biographies as dieters. She spent lots of time with them as they prepared meals in their kitchens. At the end of the six-week observation period, nine women took part in a variety of arithmetic-testing activities. The participants also kept diaries of all food items consumed each day. De la Rocha conducted interviews about the process of dieting, asking how each person learned the Weight Watchers' system of food portion control and about the specific procedures she used in weighing and measuring each item.

There was lots of measuring and calculating activity. All dieters calculated portion sizes for about half the food items they prepared, on average, across the six weeks. This statement requires some qualification, however. First, some dieters calculated considerably more often than others. Second, dieters measured and calculated more at the beginning of the new program than near the end. We were especially interested in the "disappearance" of math over time. Third, having carefully coded the measuring and calculating activities of the dieting cooks in the preparation of hundreds of food items, de la Rocha showed that none of several factors that might plausibly account for differences between the cooks' measuring patterns did so. Factors that did not explain their uses of arithmetic included their age, the number of children living at home, the dieters' years of education, the amount of weight they hoped to lose, the amount of weight they had already lost, and their scores on the arithmetic tests.

De la Rocha's analysis of the dieters' accounts of their lives and diets offers insight into the quandaries that compel dieters to engage in the transformation of quantitative relations. Begin with American culture writ large. It encompasses some serious problems of quantity. The abundance of food products in the United States, the ideology of consumption, and fascination with the self-mastery reflected in a slim physique have provoked an obsession with body weight and its control. For most plagued by it, "excessive" weight is a profound blight deeply affecting self-image. Although weight can be remediated by dieting, it is only with great difficulty and often for brief intervals. In translating the determination to lose weight into practical action, the dieter faces the dilemma posed by a strong desire to alter the "distortions" of the body and a craving for the solace and pleasure of food. Dieting is an arduous process that requires not just one decision, but a continual struggle in which the question of self-denial arises many times each day over many months and even years. Inconsistent commitment leads to backsliding, or to the end of a diet cycle and resulting feelings of failure and depression. From interviews about their history as dieters, it appeared that participants in the project had relatively long-term, consistent resolutions to these dieting dilemmas. Some espoused the view that meticulous control of food portions was the way to control weight. Others expressed their approach to dieting as "so long as you feel hungry you must be losing weight." Each of them put their resolutions to these dilemmas into practice: long-term dieting styles clearly shaped measurement activity differently. Methodical dieters used arithmetic measurement and calculation techniques on nearly two-thirds of the food items they recorded in their food diaries; the "go hungry" dieters measured only a quarter of the food items.

Gaining control over food intake is the central quandary of dieting. But attempts to control food portions come into conflict with other concerns of the dieters. The more elaborate the steps to gain control of quantity, the greater the conflict with putting food efficiently on the table. While the dieter calculates, the family and the evening meal wait. The conflict between dieting rules and efficient food handling appeared most directly to generate the dieters' arithmetic "problems" and clearly shaped the long-term shift from more to less calculation over time. All the dieters responded to this conflict in two ways: by generating reusable solutions to recurring math problems and by finding ways to enact solutions as part of ongoing activity.

One simple example illustrates both. Initially, to find the correct serving size for a glass of milk the dieter had to look up the correct amount in the Weight Watchers' manual, get out a measuring cup, a drinking glass, and the carton of milk; pour the milk into the measuring cup and from the cup into the glass; then wash the measuring cup and later the glass. This procedure was shortly transformed into getting out the glass and milk and pouring the milk into the glass to just below the circle of blue flowers, knowing that this would be one cup of milk. This is just one among a myriad of examples, for the cooks invented hundreds of units of measurement and procedures for generating accurate portions (de la Rocha 1985). In the process they made it possible to do less and less measurement and calculation over time. But they continued losing weight at the same rate, so presumably no relevant accuracy was lost.

Importantly for the dieting cooks, math problem solving is not an end in itself. Procedures involving quantitative relations in the kitchen are given shape and meaning by the quandaries that motivate their activity; school math knowledge does not constrain the structure of their quantitative activity, and it does not specify what shall constitute math problems. It is the specific character of action-compelling conflicts that generally determine what will constitute a "problem-in-need-of-solution."

Other characteristics emerged as typical of "everyday" math practice. People are efficacious in dealing with problems of number and space in everyday settings. Their math activity is structured into and by ongoing activity and its settings – its structure unfolds in a situated way. So people do not stop to perform canonical, school-taught math procedures and then resume activity. In the supermarket and kitchen shoppers and cooks have more than sufficient resources of mathematical knowledge to meet the mathematical exigencies of their activities. They almost never arrive at wrong answers because they are clear about the meaning of the quantitative relations they are trying to interrelate and what a ballpark solution should look like. Also, having a strong sense of the meaning of what they are doing, they are able to abandon problems they recognize they cannot solve in the time, and for the purposes at hand. Many relations of quantity have closer relations with other aspects of activity than with each other. For example, people frequently go straight from a relation of quantity ("The price is higher this week") to a decision: "Forget it!" Thus, there are many more relations of quantity than there are well-formed "arithmetic problems." Generating problems for themselves, shoppers and cooks also change those problems, resolve them, transform them, or abandon them as well as solve them. At the same time, quantitative quandaries that do not have solutions but only partial resolutions constitute almost all of what is seen as "problematic" in ongoing activity. People are walking histories of their own past calculations, but not of procedures for solving problems. Old results, "answers" if you will, are carried around, but procedures are invented on the spot, as part of situated ongoing activity. Finally, the kinds of activities we investigated do not provide a curriculum for school mathematics: the "assembly and transformation of quantitative relations" is not school-like in any sense.

What I have not conveyed in telling the story of the Weight Watchers study, and summing up some of the ways in which math is different "out there," is the extreme difficulty of capturing "what is going on" in everyday math activity in something like its own terms. The language and assumptions of math-cognition studies, formal mathematics, and closed-system puzzle/problem-solving processes are not easy to exorcise. They presume that everyday practice is simple, erroneous, routine, particular, concrete – in short, inferior. These assumptions furnish an important contrastive set of meanings to the (assumed) character of the thinking of experts and scientists.

This observation has led me to inquire into the practices and beliefs of the second set of natives under discussion here, those engaged in the theory and practice of cognitive studies – including anthropologists as well as psychologists.

The Absent Mind of the Civilized Savant

Given the long history of attempts to distinguish "the primitive mind" from the "civilized" one, we might plausibly expect that psychologists and anthropologists would have established two essential resources for their inquiries: a canonical set of categories pinning down just what the superior, scientific mind consists of, and an intimate acquaintance with some relevant "natives." Nothing could be further from the truth. Assumptions about each type enable claims about the other, as "superior" minds are constructed with respect to putative "inferior" ones, and vice versa.

The work of Lucien Levy-Bruhl offers a classic example of how this works. He published a book in 1910 whose title has been translated *How Natives Think*. A more literal translation would be "The Mental Functions in Lower Societies." It has been widely influential throughout the century and the 1926 edition was reprinted in 2015. Levy-Bruhl claims that a set of mental functions divides the thinking of "civilized" people from the thinking of "primitive" people. Primitive people are in his terms non-rational, have no interest in logic, and have no concern with the law of negation, the proposition that if something is A it cannot be $-A$ at the same time. "Natives" think concretely, and thus create shallow trees, categorical structures with many terminal taxa, rather than deep hierarchical structures of classification. They participate directly in the world and hence cannot think logically about it. They cannot abstract from nor generalize about their experience. They lack, in short, the distance from the world that "powerful thinking" requires. How can the enmeshed natives survive to function at all? Levy-Bruhl speculates that they have superb memories for detail, a point that Frederick Bartlett tried to substantiate several decades later in Africa.

We must ask where Levy-Bruhl discovered those mental functions. Clearly it is not direct acquaintance as he never traveled far abroad. It could be that he derived his arguments from scientific treatises, philosophical or empirical, detailing the characteristics of civilized minds. But he says not: "As far as the mentality peculiar to our society is concerned, since it is only to serve me as a state for comparison, I shall regard it as sufficiently well defined in the works of philosophers, logicians and psychologists, both ancient and modern, without conjecturing what sociological analysis of the future may modify in the results so obtained." (1926: 19) If Levy-Bruhl did not draw his inspiration from either the subjects of his claims or his colleagues, he must have fallen back on the common "wisdom" of his time. The civilized mind is elusive although it is vital to such a comparative enterprise. The detailed picture of the primitive mind that emerges in his work seems as much a specific resource for characterizing the "superior other" as the reverse.

Levy-Bruhl's work was taken up directly by L. S. Vygotsky in Russia, E. E. Evans-Pritchard (whose work on the Azande shows up with unusual frequency in cognitive psychology texts), Frederick Bartlett and others. Cognitive psychology texts still take up the opposites of items in the list of primitive mental characteristics (cf. Rumelhart and McClelland 1988; Anderson 1990). The meaning of "good thinking" is dependent on its implicit contrast with the thinking of unspecified (primitive) others.

In a century of debate about superior and inferior minds, "science" and "scientists" have been the matter-of-course foil for the "primitive." Lévi-Strauss in *The Savage Mind* (1966), invents neolithic "science" in contrast to the (unspecified) modern variety. With it, he contrasts the scientific versus the mythical, abstract thought versus intuition, and the use of concepts versus the use of signs. Jack Goody, in *The Domestication of the Savage Mind* sums up: "In the simplest terms, [this] is a contrast between the domination of abstract science ... as against the more concrete forms of knowledge ... of 'primitive' peoples." (1977:148) Cognitive psychologists tout Einstein, great chess players, and famous mathematicians as heroes for school children whom they hope to teach to think similarly. Scientism pervades all levels of educational research.

The categories against which common conceptions of the scientist and scientific thinking play include marginal, powerless or stigmatized categories in Western society – the lower classes, women, children, criminals, the insane, and, of course, the primitive. But the central focus is not the same today as in 1910. The contrast between civilized and primitive thought was the major preoccupation of the early anthropologists (among others). The more salient contrast today is between the everyday thinking of "ordinary" folks and scientists. Bartlett, for instance, spoke of everyday thought in contrast to scientific thought: "By everyday thinking I mean those activities by which most people, *when they are not making any particular attempt to be logical or scientific*, try to fill up gaps in information available to them." (1958: 164, italics mine). Here is C. R. Hallpike on the same subject: "Rather than contrasting primitive man with the European scientist and logician, it would be more to the point to contrast him with the garage mechanic, the plumber, and the housewife in her kitchen." (1979: 33) He calls attention to the interchangeability of women with those engaged in manual labor and with primitive man. Each represents "the inferior other" satisfactorily in opposition to the white, European, bourgeois, male scientist.

Barnes (1973) has argued that the historical and artifactual basis of the vague characterization of "civilized" "scientific" thought lies in an antiquated empiricist philosophy of science. He speaks of its role in anthropology in the 1970s, and the analysis is equally apt for cognitive studies today:

Attempts to understand or explain preliterate systems of belief have frequently led anthropologists to compare them with ideal "rational" models of thought or belief ... It is clear that the form of many anthropological theories has been partially determined by the ideal of rationality adopted and in practice this ideal has usually been presented as that which is normative in the modern natural science, that is to say modern anthropological theory has been profoundly influenced by its conception of ideal scientific practice. (Barnes 1973: 182)

That is, imagined ideal forms of scientific practice have furnished normative beliefs about the nature of civilized/scientific thought. These depend in turn on definitions of the inferior other. Contemporary ethnographic studies of the practice of science (whether grounded in phenomenological or social practice theories) clearly call into question such conceptions. They also challenge broad claims about what constitutes high and low forms of thinking, theorizing about learning, and educational practice.

Such challenges are urgently needed: Consider the contrast between our description of Weight Watchers resolving problems in their kitchens and another interpretation of their activities. This exchange occurred in the context of debates about proper relations between math as it is taught in school and as it arises in everyday life. The following is a published description of an encounter that occurred with yet another Weight Watcher dieter during the Adult Math Project:

We posed a problem of quantity to new members of Weight Watchers in their kitchens. The dieters were asked to prepare their lunch to meet specifications laid out by the observer. In this case they were to fix a serving of cottage cheese, supposing that the amount allotted for the meal was three-quarters of the two-thirds cup the program allowed. The problem solver in this example began the task muttering that he had taken a calculus course in college. Then after a pause he suddenly announced that he had "got it!" From then on he appeared certain he was correct, even before carrying out the procedure. He filled a measuring cup two-thirds full of cottage cheese, dumped it out on a cutting board, patted it into a circle, marked a cross on it, scooped away one quadrant, and served the rest. Thus, "take three-quarters of two-thirds of a cup of cottage cheese" was not just the problem statement but also the solution to the problem and the procedure for solving it. The setting was part of the calculating process and the solution was simply the problem statement, enacted with the setting. At no time did the Weight Watcher check his procedure against a paper and pencil algorithm, which would have produced $3/4 \times 2/3 = 1/2$ cup. Instead, the coincidence of problem, setting, and enactment was the means by which checking took place. (Lave 1988:165)

This example has achieved a certain fame in circles where the nature of cognition is debated. Brown, Collins, and Duguid (1989) quoted accurately and then discussed "the cottage cheese problem" and Palincsar, a cognitive and educational researcher, replied. Her comment illustrates how researchers produce claims that, e.g., dieting cooks are "inferior others."

[T]he article [Brown et al. 1989] cites with approval the example of some poor soul at (sic) Weight Watchers confronted with the challenge of measuring three-fourths of two-thirds of a cup of cottage cheese. The dieter mounded a pile of cottage cheese, separating first three-quarters of a cup (sic) and then taking two-thirds of that to arrive at the required half-cup of cottage cheese. The authors regard the dieter's ineptitude with fractions as giving rise to an inventive solution ... Instead, it was an act of desperation, born of ignorance. I question whether it was learning at all. Where does this so-called solution lead? Nothing has been learned that could be generalized.

The domestic savage is alive and well – an impoverished soul inept at fractions and unable to generalize – if only in the mind of the cognitive researcher.

Out to Lunch: The Mind of the Other

I have suggested that the theoretical characterization of the "civilized," "scientific" mind seems to have been constituted in the process of imagining "the mind of the other." There is also a huge body of empirical research investigating cognitive processing and problem solving. How can this apparently direct empirical investigation of mental activity avoid uncovering the "real thing" – the concrete content of different kinds of mind-in-practice? And how do cognitive researchers generate inferior others, and, if only by implication, their superiors as well?

First, their research is predominantly experimental, designed deductively from idealized normative models of good thinking rather than from a knowledge of actual practice. In the late 1970s Rommetveit characterized such investigations as inquiries into "negative rationality." Thus, cognitive researchers begin with ideal models of how people should think. For example, Gentner and Stevens point out in their book on "mental models" that they have studied physics problem solving rather than marriage because no normative models of ideal problem solving exist in the latter case (1983). Experimentation would be impossible without such models, they argue. As Rommetveit (1978) points out, any investigation designed to explore evidence of "ideal" problem-solving activity is sure to reveal the shortcomings of its subjects. That is, experiments devised to reveal forms of thought that reflect normative assumptions (which do not accurately reflect any actual social practice), can only reveal what are interpreted by researchers as "deficiencies" (see Lave 1988: chapter 5). This process creates and confirms a conception of the inferior other and thus affirms the ideal model. At the same time, producing the nonideal thinking of jpfs (the subjects in experiments) for careful inspection by the scientist is part of the process by which "scientific thinkers" generate themselves and their models.

The content of normative models of the logical, rational, representational, and generalizing mind has its own effect on the production of inferior others. It helps to preserve the indirect characterization of the civilized mind by idealizing the separation of thought from action. Rationales for mathematics offer a case in point by viewing mathematics as abstract structure (as the pejorative reading of the cottage cheese example shows). Good mathematical thinking should have the power to extract and formalize structure from concrete particulars. In this view, mathematics is conceived as a move away from situated (read "particular") forms of experience. When everyday math practice involves quantitative relations as a seamless part of its situated unfolding, investigations based on normative models of formal math and scientific thinking interpret this as evidence of the inferior character of everyday mathematical practice, without reference to the intentions of actors; the activity they are engaged in; the located, situated meaning of what they are doing; or how they are doing it. Seamless (though highly effective) everyday math practice suggests to researchers pursuing an understanding of mathematical "thinking" that everyday practice can and should be colonized in the name of formal mathematics.

The Situated Dualism of Mathematical Practice

There are other reasons why social science investigations of everyday activity "confirm" but do not analyze the meaning of inferior otherhood. If the "inferior other" is a myth, it is a myth so deeply incorporated into cultural practices that all of us know how to become its exemplars. Not all the time: the same persons address quantitative relations in very different ways with very different effects when engaged in activities as competent selves and when engaged in activities as inferior others. This is, of course, one way to sum up the findings of the Adult Math Project about the different performances of jpfs in different settings.

Mathematicians know how to display competent incompetence – they make "modest" jokes about being unable to add, subtract or reconcile their checkbooks. Incompetence at arithmetic in everyday life by nonmathematicians is something else again. We discovered in the Adult Math Project that even denying that someone's math practice is being subjected to a "scientific" gaze causes it to dissolve into displays of schoolish practices less competent than they would be otherwise. We wondered how jpfs learned to collude in their identification as incompetent others. Schools are certainly deeply implicated, as they legitimize certain kinds of knowledge and selectively eliminate certain kinds of students. I once carried out a small research project with one of my students in a third grade math class in a bicultural, bilingual school in Santa Ana, California (Hass 1986; Lave 1991). The children liked math and their teacher. When doing "seat work" in a group around a table, they engaged in much sub-rosa mathematical activity together. They hid their use of reliable, familiar counting procedures for solving problems, knowing that the teacher disapproved, in order to create the appearance of competence at procedures for multiplication that the teacher had just introduced. We could see a painful distinction being made in practice, one the children were quite conscious of, between "real math" and "what I do because I'm no good at math." This distinction was generated and elaborated in the organization of school math instruction, not in the division of children's lives between school and the "everyday" of home.

On the other hand, the idiom of math and displays of utilitarian rationality are very commonly employed – but incompetently – to assert the competent self. There are vivid examples in the supermarket research. One example concerned an experienced grocery shopper who picked out a package of noodles of a particular size, a choice she had made many times in the past for multiple substantive reasons given the way she cooked. She noticed while shopping with the anthropologist that her choice was not the "best buy." Clearly she felt herself called into question as a competent shopper. She tried to redeem her sense of competence by criticizing her usual choice and promising to choose the more economical package "next time" (even though it would not suit her purposes if she did) (Lave 1988: 160–4). This suggests that for jpfs as well as for scientists, certain kinds of "competence" are equated with the "superior" thinking of utilitarian rationality. It further suggests that this unquestioned belief must often lead to incompetent and inappropriate displays of "rationality" by those not entitled to the real thing.

Conclusions: The Place Value of Other and Self

Research on science as everyday practice has led us to questions about cultural–political relations among sciences of mind, domestic life, and schooling. I have tried to show (through examples involving domestic relations of quantity on the one hand, and cultural practices of research about the mind on the other), that much hinges on assumptions about the exceptional nature of scientific activity and the unexceptional nature of the daily activity of jpfs.

I have tried to show that there are other ways to characterize relations between the quantitative practices of jpfs and mathematicians. For instance, we observed in the Adult Math Project, jpfs assembling and transforming relations of quantity in the ongoing activities of domestic life in efficacious ways that served remarkably well the purposes for which they were invented. They were not merely pathetic imitations of scholastic mathematics. Scholastic mathematics, dropped into these activities, would have destroyed their purpose and possibility. It seems reasonable to conclude that scholastic mathematics is but one practice among others – but one blessed with an ideological power not given to complementary practices.

This essay has also called into question dual categories of "good" and "bad" thinking, scientists and jpfs, laboratory life and everyday activities, by exploring the manner in which these categories are constituted. Rather than static bracketing, which simply separates two things, I have tried to show that dual categories are generated dialectically. That is, they involve several simultaneous kinds of relations at the same time. Polar social categories such as "primitive" and "civilized" minds are mutually dependent constructs, elaborated together in "scientific" discourse. Each is a part of the other (*pace* Levy-Bruhl's law of negation), and is thus embedded in the identities and practices of jpfs and scientists alike. The cultural resources to perform both competent and incompetent calculative rationality inhabit all concerned, though not with homogeneous political effects.

Polar social categorization is a political relation since high and low categor-ies of thinking and thinkers are not equal nor symmetrical (see Stallybrass and White 1986). Science and scientists dominate the definition of superior and inferior thinking, and scientists have a stake in sustaining the view that dual divisions separate people into the two categories. Jpfs do not hold the high ground in this respect and participate in as unreflecting ways as the scientists in the dominant characterizations of the "inferior other." Further, "sciences" of the rational suppress the recognition of the political character and conse-quences of their assumptions and activities.

This inquiry into the production of inferior others, and with it the scientific mind, calls contemporary everyday practices into question in several different respects: "primitive" unconcern for the law of negation seems to be a pre-requisite for analyzing polar categories in dialectical terms; mathematicians are just plain folks; just plain folks are virtuosi at sizing up quantitative relations; and sociologists and anthropologists of science, speaking reasonably, offer arguments for disturbing the tidy divisions of high versus low rational orders. We are all more successful at playing our parts in the cultural politics of the world we inhabit than we are in understanding them.

2   The Problem of Context and Practices of Decontextualization

* * * * *

This chapter was inspired by *Situated Learning*. It grew out of questions about the meaning of "situated" in situated learning, or "context" in context embedded activity, or settings of practice. These terms substituted all too easily for one another in casual conversation. And clearly in different theoretical lineages they had different meanings, depending on underlying assumptions about the nature of persons' engagements with/in the world and on how that world can be known.

Seth Chaiklin and I organized what we called "the context conference" in 1987 to explore different theoretical traditions with respect to conceptions of "situation" and social context. (Chaiklin and Lave 1993). We invited as participants colleagues we knew had irreconcilably different conceptions of "context" – coming from ethnomethodological, structuralist, behaviorist, and historical materialist theoretical problematics. How could we talk with each other? The first time we met, for several days, Seth and I asked everyone not to give prepared papers, but to talk at length about how they had come to hold the theoretical assumptions and do the work they do. Those descriptions of years of scholarly development were disarming. It is hard to be disrespectful (whether you agree or not), knowing the serious processes of producing such a life's work. We met again six months later with papers in hand that reflected our (still irreconcilable) differences but in ways that were open to critical discussion.

The participants reflected theoretically on notions of context read through their ethnographic studies which included many different kinds of situated participation in ongoing social life. Some focused on everyday work practices, (e.g., the development of medical practices for primary care, the work of navigating a helicopter transport ship) and some focused on everyday activities in settings of institutional education (e.g., the evaluation of university exams in Denmark; teachers' directives in school classrooms). This division did not affect the commonalities and differences of the participants about concepts of *context*. But it did lead to questions about how they understood *learning* where learning was on the one hand part of, but not the institutional target, of ongoing activity, and

This essay was first published as "The Practice of Learning," the introduction to Chaiklin and Lave, *Understanding Practice: Perspectives on Activity and Context* (1993).

on the other hand where the focus was on practices in educational institutions with their attendant confusions of teaching with learning.

Understanding Practice explored these differences. The present chapter makes clear that different theoretical problematics contain very different understandings of "context" or "situation," ranging from common notions of inert containers holding social life without influencing its context or vice versa, to the relational constitution of praxis in which neither context nor activity can be reduced to the other, nor at the same time are they separable. They make each other in dialectical relations of world and persons, so are neither wholly subjective nor wholly objective in character. An ethnomethodological view takes the "contexts" of social life to be produced intersubjectively, invoked and produced in and through social interaction.

In working on this chapter I found that concepts of context(s) of practice were part of another relation besides the relation between context and activity at the heart of our project. Very frequently a pair of terms cropped up together: "contextualization" in a dualist opposition to "decontextualization." I often encounter claims that, while some persons and activities may be situated in/as practice, many are surely *not* situated – by virtue of being abstract, general, universal, virtual, theoretical, or otherwise distant in space or time. But from my theoretical perspective – including my historical relational understanding of concepts of "context" – all those cultural artifacts and claims are themselves situated practices – practices of decontextualization. Further, they are dependent on what we, with historical/cultural particularity, mean when we invoke and wield this (and other) dualist couplets. Every chapter in this book grapples in one way or another with these issues.

* * * * *

The Problem with "Context"

If it is not possible to discuss learning in practice without drawing directly or indirectly on its contextual character, it is surely worth considering seriously just what that might mean. This chapter explores assumptions and relations lurking in different theoretical traditions with respect to notions of social context and situation and a socially constituted world. Seth Chaiklin, Steinar Kvale, and I decided to take up the issue with a heterogeneous group of scholars and organized a two-part conference that convened in April and again in August 1987 in which the participants came together to consider what we initially called "the context problem." Together, we eventually combined to produce *Understanding Practice* (1993). All of us were involved in research on socially situated activity. We were concerned about conventional limitations on various approaches to the study of activity. In particular, we wished to explore questions about the "socially constituted world" – the contexts of socially situated activity – which our work often seemed merely to take for granted. My job was to write the introduction to the book, to bring together what we had learned from and with each other, as we explored our theoretical differences through the empirical/theoretical contributions of a bakers' dozen of participants.

I had tried in previous research to understand how math activity in grocery stores involved being "in" the "store," walking up and down "aisles," looking at "shelves" full of cans, bottles, packages and jars of food and other commodities. My analyses were about shoppers' activities, sometimes together, and about the relations between these activities and the distractingly material, historically constituted, subjectively selective character of space–time relations and their meaning. Seth Chaiklin and I knew that other people conceived of the problem in quite different terms. These were old, but still perplexing questions (cf. Bartlett 1958; Barker 1963, 1968; Goffman 1964; Birdwhistell 2010 [1970]; and more recently Rommetveit 1987, 1988; Haraway 1988; Hanks 1990a, 1990b; Dannefer 1992; Goodwin and Duranti 1992). The time seemed appropriate for further inquiry into understandings of activity-in-context, given that theoretical approaches to the study of situated activity, and hence to its situations, had fairly recently become surprisingly diverse and increasingly informed by rich empirical research. The traditions behind the work of the conference participants included activity theory, critical psychology, Barker's ecological psychology, cognitive anthropology, and ethnomethodology. The contributors include psychologists, sociologists, and anthropologists from Sweden, Denmark, Finland, France, Switzerland, and the United States.

We met first without prepared papers in hand. Participants used their time to talk about how they had come to inhabit the (quite different) theoretical problematics that informed their research, as we set out to establish the grounds for a serious discussion of different approaches to the study of situated activity. We re-assembled several months later to discuss papers drafted in the interim. We then worked for two years more to develop the papers in ways that reflected the impact of these interchanges on our research.

Why would a diverse group of students of the human condition participate over months, and even years, to try to understand each other's perspective? Seth Chaiklin and I initially proposed the following rationale: Theories of situated everyday practice insist that persons acting and the social world of activity cannot be separated (cf. Minick 1985). This creates a dilemma: Research on everyday practice typically focuses on the activities of persons acting, although there is agreement that such phenomena cannot be analyzed in isolation from the socially material world of that activity. But less attention has been given to the difficult task of conceptualizing *relations* of persons acting and the social world. Nor has there been sufficient attention to rethinking the "social world of activity" in relational terms. Together, these constitute the problem of context.

The conference participants agreed to this set of priorities, with the obvious proviso that relational concepts of the social world should not be explored in isolation from conceptions of persons acting and interacting and their activities. That proviso gradually took on a more central meaning and, as a result, our conception of the common task crystallized into a double focus – on context and to our surprise learning. A focus on one provided occasions on which to consider the other. If context is viewed as a social world constituted in relation with persons acting, both context and activity seem inescapably caught up in ongoing change. And thus characterized, changing participation and understanding in practice – the problem of learning – cannot help but become central as well.

It is difficult, when looking closely at everyday activity as the authors did, to avoid the conclusion that learning is ubiquitous in ongoing activity, though often unrecognized as such. Situated activity always involves changes in knowledge and action (as Keller and Keller [1996] argue in *Understanding Practice*) and "changes in knowledge and action" are central to what we mean by "learning." It is not the case that the world consists of newcomers who drop unaccompanied into unpeopled problem spaces. People in activity are skillful at, and are more often than not engaged in, helping each other to participate in changing ways in a changing world. So, in describing and analyzing people's involvement in practical action in the world, even those authors whose work generally would be least identified with educational foci (Keller and Keller 1993; Suchman and Trigg 1993[1]) are in effect analyzing peoples' engagement in *learning*. We have come to the conclusion, as McDermott (1980) suggests, (see also Lave and Wenger 1991) that there is no such thing as "learning" *sui generis*, but only changing participation in the culturally designed settings of everyday life. Or, to put it another way around, participation in everyday life may be thought of as a process of changing understanding in practice, that is, as learning.

Learning became one focus of our collective attention, even where unintended, partly because of our concern with everyday activity as social and historical process, and with the improvisational, past-and-future-creating character of mundane practice; partly, also, because those of us whose research has touched on educational questions had come to insist on denaturalizing the social processes that unfold within educational institutions by turning them into analytic objects. So whether the participants approached the problem of context through its temporal dimension as activity (or practice), or whether

---

[1] Suchman and Trigg: "Our objective here is to view the work of designing intelligent machines as a specific form of social practice" (Chaiklin and Lave 1993: 145). Keller and Keller (1993) explore in detail what it is one needs to know or believe in order for a house blacksmith to craft a colonial style skimming spoon.

they looked at institutionalized educational contexts, learning had become a central issue.

In the next section a brief description of the chapters in *Understanding Practice* provides an opportunity to show how they developed around the issues of context and learning. Next, I shall explore at greater length issues concerning the character of learning as situated activity, especially its heterogeneity – the various scopes of social processes (of learning) simultaneously enacted in everyday settings, and their open-ended character. The point is to show how the meaning of "learning" in the research discussed in these chapters differs in significant ways from conventional views of learning. But what, given unconventional conceptions of learning, becomes of the concept of context? The fourth section lays out the views of "context" that assume changing understanding and situated practices to be part and parcel of the lived social world. The discussion of context suggests a problem, however: Conventional theories of learning and schooling appeal to the decontextualized character of knowledge and forms of knowledge transmission, whereas in a theory of situated activity "decontextualized learning activity" is a contradiction in terms. These two very different ways of conceiving of learning are hardly compatible. Nonetheless, a belief that the world is divided into contextualized and decontextualized phenomena is not "merely" an academic speculation that can be discarded if we find it theoretically inadequate or incomplete. This dualistic view of the world has a lively presence in our everyday lives. This dilemma motivates two developments in *Understanding Practice*. On the one hand its chapters reflect a growing sense of responsibility for historical explanation of the mainstream conventional theoretical tradition. It is not accidental that conventional theory is treated as part of the activity we were studying, rather than as a contrastive object to be discarded (cf. Chaiklin's concluding chapter, "Understanding the social scientific practice of *Understanding Practice*"). On the other hand, much of the analysis in the book focuses on the mechanisms by which decontextualization practices are generated in situated ways in everyday life.

Craftwork Learning and Social Production

Traditionally, learning researchers have studied learning as if it were a process contained in the mind of the learner and have ignored the lived-in world (see Lave 1988). This disjuncture, which ratifies a dichotomy of mind and body, sidetracks or derails the question of how to construct a theory that *encompasses* embodied mind and lived-in world. It is not enough to say that some designated cognitive theory of learning could be *amended* by adding on a theory of "situation," for this raises crucial questions about the compatibility of particular theories (cf. Soviet psychologists' discussion of the "match"

between psychologies and sociologies in the 1920s (Davydov and Radzhi-
kovskii 1985: 49). Nor is it sufficient to pursue a principled account of
situated activity armed only with a theory of cognition and good intentions.
Without a theoretical conception of the social world one cannot analyze
activity in situ. A more promising alternative lies in treating relations among
person, activity, and situation as they are *given* in social practice, itself viewed
as a single encompassing theoretical entity. It is possible to detect such a trend
in most if not all of the research traditions represented in *Understanding
Practice* – all of the chapters work toward a more inclusive, intensive, development of the socially situated character of activity in theoretically
consistent terms.

While cognitive theory divides the learning mind from the world, theories of
situated activity do not separate action, thought, feeling and value, and their
collective, cultural-historical forms of located, interested, conflictual, meaningful activity. The idea of learning as cognitive acquisition – whether of facts,
knowledge, problem solving strategies, or metacognitive skills – seems to
dissolve when learning is conceived as the construction of present versions
of past experience for persons acting together (Kvale 1977; Hutchins 1993;
Cole, Hood, and McDermott 1994). And when scientific practice is viewed as
just another everyday practice (Latour and Woolgar 1979; Latour 1987; Suchman 1987; Lave 1988), it is clear that theories of "situated activity" provide
different perspectives on "learning" and its "contexts."

Participants in the conference agreed, on the whole, on four premises
concerning knowledge and learning in practice.

1. Knowledge always undergoes construction and transformation in use.
2. Learning is an integral aspect of activity in and with the world at all times.
   That learning occurs is not problematic.
3. *What* is learned is always complexly problematic.
4. Acquisition of knowledge is not a simple matter of taking in knowledge;
   rather, things assumed to be natural categories, such as "bodies of knowledge," "learners," and "cultural transmission," require reconceptualization
   as cultural, social products.

David Pear argues that to explore the meaning of "knowledge" you must
begin with what is not knowledge (1972); we took up this strategy as well.
Chapters in the first part of *Understanding Practice* (1993) are about work,
which is usually assumed to be something other than learning. A number of
other chapters are about failures to learn, which is also usually assumed to be
something other than learning. If learning is taken to be an aspect of everyday
practice, however, distinctions between learning and work or learning and
failure to learn dissolve, posing new questions about how and why such
distinctions are produced in the first place.

Several themes that emerge in a first group of chapters concerned with what we dubbed *craftwork* help to reformulate the meaning of learning.[2] They are about adults engaged in culturally, socially, historically defined forms of ordinary, productive activity.[3] "Learning craftwork" includes Hutchins' study of the careers and work practices of navigators on a US Navy helicopter transport ship. Engeström presents his research on changing medical practice in public clinics in Finland, and Dreier discusses his research on therapist–client relations. The work of artificial intelligence practitioners, viewed as craft practice, is the focus of Suchman and Trigg's chapter, while the craft of blacksmithing is the topic of Keller and Keller's. Fuhrer examines the uncommon hazards of unfamiliar activity for newcomers to a career placement center who are trying to track down information about jobs. The settings for these studies lie outside conventional educational institutions and away from the usual research populations of children and other academic novices. They focus on prosaic everyday practices.

It should be said that their conceptions of craftwork bear little resemblance to the small-scale problem solving tasks typical of cognitive learning research (memorizing nonsense, syllogism problems, etc.): Forging a cooking utensil, or taking part in the work of a national university examination committee, are substantial, meaningful forms of activity. In all cases the work described takes on meaning from its broader interconnections with(in) other activities.

Authors in the second group of studies in the book, "Learning as Social Production," (re)conceptualized what might be meant by learning-in-practice. They address the question, "if people learn in activity in the seamless way suggested by investigations of situated activity, how does this come about?" They begin by shifting from terms such as *learning* (given its traditionally narrow connotations) to concepts more akin to *understanding* and *participation in ongoing activity*. *Understanding* is assumed to be a partial and open-ended process while at the same time there is structure (variously conceived) to activity in the world. Thus structured, the indeterminacy and open-endedness of understanding are *not* viewed as infinite or random. Finally, authors argue that knowledge and learning will be found distributed throughout the complex structure of persons-acting-in-setting. They cannot be pinned down to the head

---

[2] This included chapters by Edwin Hutchins (Learning to Navigate); Yrjö Engeström (Developmental Studies of Work as a Testbench of Activity Theory: The Case of Primary Care Medical Practice); Ole Dreier (Re-searching Psychotherapeutic Practice); Charles Keller and Janet Dixon Keller (Thinking and Acting with Iron); Lucy A. Suchman and Randall H. Trigg (Artificial intelligence as Craftwork); and Urs Fuhrer (Behavior Setting Analysis of Situated Learning: The Case for Newcomers).

[3] Bruno Latour participated in the conference, but did not prepare a chapter for the book. This choice of terms was made in part in order to connect with Latour's designation of *science* as craftwork.

of the individual or to assigned tasks or to external tools or to the environment, but lie instead in the relations among them.

Paradoxically, learning may appear easy in the studies of "craftwork," whereas it often seems nearly impossible to learn in settings dedicated to education. But appearances are deceptive: Studies in the second half of the book suggest that it is as easy to learn to fail in school as it is to learn to navigate a ship. On the other hand, the first group of studies shows that what people are learning to do is difficult, complex work. The learning is not a separate process, nor an end in itself. If it seems effortless it is because in some sense it is invisible.

If learning-in-practice is ubiquitous, what are we to make of educational institutions, formal methods of learning and teaching, and of failure to learn? The cluster of studies that compose "Learning as social production" explore different approaches to the analysis of institutionalized education, to learning identities *as a process*, to learning identities *as products*, to teaching, and to participants' beliefs about knowledge and the everyday world. These chapters focus on how institutional arrangements (such as schools) generate "learners," "learning," and "things to be learned" – in practice. They analyze the processes by which these products of situated activity are socially produced.[4]

These studies focus on Western cultural institutionalized arrangements for learning and failing to learn. Success and failure at learning are viewed, not as attributes of individuals, but as specialized social and institutional arrangements. There is a strong emphasis on the problematic and differentiated character of what gets learned. This depends on the subjective and intersubjective interpretation of the how and why of ongoing activity. National examination systems, placement processes for children nominated for special education, and learning disabilities are analyzed respectively by Kvale, Mehan, and McDermott as what might be called rituals of legitimation or degradation and exclusion. (Latour's analysis of the centralization of control achieved through the mathematization of science offers a complementary analysis of institutional arrangements for producing knowledge and legitimacy (1987). Likewise, Levine focuses on the social organization of mild mental retardation, arguing that it is the product of a cultural process of ritualized exclusion of some in the name of a normality that, once turned into a goal, becomes unobtainable (Levine and Langness 1983). Levine and Minick trace

---

[4] Steinar Kvale (Examinations Reexamined: Certification of Students or Certification of Knowledge?); Hugh Mehan (Beneath the Skin and between the Ears: A Case Study in the Politics of Representation); R. P. McDermott (The Acquisition of a Child by a Learning Disability); Harold G. Levine (Context and Scaffolding in Developmental Studies of Mother-Child Problem-Solving); Roger Säljö and Jan Wyndhamn (Solving Everyday Problems in the Formal Setting: An Empirical Study of the School as Context for Thought); Norris Minick (Teacher's Directives: The Social Construction of "Literal Meanings" and "Real Worlds" in Classroom Discourse).

the changing meanings of tasks for learners and teachers alike, and build a rich picture of the situated character of knowing, doing, and learning identities for all those involved.

Their work provides evidence of the *sociocultural* production of failure to learn (Kvale; Levine; McDermott; Mehan; Minick; Säljö; and Wyndhamn). They focus on how people learn identities, how they identify the situated meaning of what is to be learned, and explore the specific shaping of people's identities as learners. Thus, Levine insists on the sociocultural construction of retardation within the family in terms compatible with Mehan's analysis of a school system's construction of educationally handicapped children. He shows how parents restrict the experience of developmentally delayed children and are silent to them about the general and extended meanings of everyday activities, a theme that resonates through other chapters as well. Kvale argues that university comprehensive exams are, from one perspective, tests of students, measuring what they have learned or failed to learn. At the same time, the national system is the means by which representatives of academic disciplines, acting in examination committees, establish what will constitute legitimate academic knowledge and what lies outside its boundaries. Students who fail (and perhaps the most successful as well) are the sacrificial lambs whose fates give material form to legitimate knowledge. Further evidence that school accomplishments (including failure) are situated and collective is to be found in demonstrations that a child's "handicap" may be reformulated when it turns out to be incompatible with class scheduling requirements (Mehan, Hertweck, and Meihls 1986), and in McDermott's argument that learning disabilities acquire the child, rather than the other way around. McDermott argues that people are so knowledgeably experienced in detecting, diagnosing, highlighting, and otherwise contributing to the generation of such identities that the society produces its quota of nonactors, or flawed actors, as they participate in the everyday world. As for identifying the meaning of things-to-be-learned, understanders' "conceptions," Säljö and Wyndhamn (1990) (also Säljö 1982) demonstrate the different meanings students assign to a single task when the task is embedded in different situations. Minick explores early attempts of primary-school teachers to induct children into a distinctive form of school discourse. These scholars provide evidence that tasks are viewed differently, and responded to differently, with characteristic variations in success and failure, when things to be learned are situated differently.

Relations with Theory Past: Some Paradoxes and Silences of Cognitive Theory

Silences and paradoxes are generated in any theoretical problematic: questions that cannot be asked and issues for which no principled resolution is possible.

At least four such issues trouble traditional cognitive theory. They concern those conventional divisions alluded to earlier, between learning and what is not (supposed to be) learning. Resolutions to these difficulties have been anticipated in the four premises concerning knowledge and learning in practice mentioned earlier. The problems include, first, an assumed division between learning and other kinds of activity. Second, both the invention and reinvention of knowledge are difficult problems for cognitive theory if learning is viewed as a matter of acquiring existing knowledge. Third, cognitive theory assumes universal processes of learning and the homogeneous character of knowledge and of learners (save in quantity or capacity). This makes it difficult to account for the richly varied participants and projects in any situation of learning. Finally, there is a problem of reconceptualizing the meaning of erroneous, mistaken understanding in a heterogeneous world.

First, how is "learning" to be distinguished from other human activity? Within cognitive theories it has been assumed that learning and development are distinctive processes, not to be confused with the more general category of human activity. This involves two theoretical claims that are in question here: One is that actors' relations with knowledge-in-activity are static and do not change except when subject to special periods of "learning" or "development." The other is that institutional arrangements for inculcating knowledge *are* the necessary, special circumstances for learning, separate from everyday practices, such as those described as "craftwork." The difference may be at heart a very deep epistemological one, between a view of knowledge as a collection of real entities located in heads, and of learning as a process of internalizing them, versus a view of knowing and learning as engagement in changing processes of human activity. In the former case it is "learning" that becomes a complex and problematic concept, whereas in the latter case it is "knowledge" that is problematic.

A second, related issue concerns the narrow focus of learning theories on the transmission of existing knowledge, while remaining silent about the invention of new knowledge in practice. Engeström argues that this is a central lacuna in contemporary learning theory (1987). Certainly, any simple assumption that *transmission* or *transfer* or *internalization* are apt descriptors for the circulation of knowledge in society faces the difficulty that they imply *uniformity* of knowledge. They do not acknowledge the fundamental imprint of interested parties, multiple activities, and different goals and circumstances, on what constitutes "knowing" on a given occasion or across a multitude of interrelated events. These terms imply that humans engage first and foremost in the reproduction of given knowledge rather than in the production of knowledge-ability as a flexible process of engagement with the world. Engeström's conceptualization of how people learn to do things that have not been done before elaborates the idea that zones of proximal development are collective, rather than individual, phenomena and that "the new" is a collective invention in the face of felt dilemmas and contradictions that impede ongoing activity and impel movement and change.

Further, part of what it means to engage in learning activity is expanding what one knows beyond the immediate situation, rather than involuting one's understanding "metacognitively" by thinking about one's own cognitive processes. Critical psychologists (e.g., Dreier 1980, 1991; Holzkamp 1987, 1991) insist on the importance of a distinction between experiencing or knowing immediate circumstances ("interpretive thinking," "restricted action") and processes of thinking beyond and about an immediate situation in more general terms ("comprehensive thinking," "extended, generalized action"). Together, in a dialectical process by which each helps to generate the other, they produce new understanding.

Doing and knowing are inventive in another sense: They are open-ended processes of improvisation with the social, material, and experiential resources at hand. Keller and Keller's research illustrates this: The blacksmith's practices as he creates a skimming spoon draw on rich resources of experience, his own and that of other people, present and past. But his understanding of the skimmer also emerges in the forging process. He does not know what it will be until it is finished. At one point he spreads one section of the spoon handle for the second time but goes too far and, in evaluating the work, finds it necessary to reduce the width of the handle again. "It is as though he has to cross a boundary in order to discover the appropriate limits of the design" (Keller and Keller 1993: 139). The work of researchers in artificial intelligence appears to have the same character: Suchman and Trigg describe it as "a skilled improvisation, organized in orderly ways that are designed to maintain a lively openness to the possibilities that the materials at hand present" (1993: 146). And "analyses of situated practice ... point to the contingencies of practical action on which logic-in-use, including the production and use of scenarios and formalisms, inevitably and in every instance relies" (1993: 173).

Fuhrer emphasizes the varying emotional effects of the improvisational character of activity. These effects are perhaps most intensely felt by newcomers, but he equates newcomers' predicaments with those of learners in general. He insists that in addition to cognitive and environmental dimensions, there is an emotional dimension to all learning. He argues that:

To some degree, all individual actions within everyday settings, especially those of newcomers, are somewhat *discrepant* from what is expected; the settings change continuously. Most *emotions within social situations*, such as embarrassment, audience anxiety, shyness, or shame follow such discrepancies, just because these discrepancies produce visceral arousal. And it is the combination of that arousal with an ongoing evaluative cognition that produces the subjective experience of an emotion. (1993: 186)

Given these considerations, Fuhrer raises the question of how people manage and coordinate "the various actions that arise from cognitive, social, and environmental demands or goals." Old-timers as well as newcomers try to carry out the usual activities in given settings, but they are also trying to address many other goals, among which are impression management and "developing interpersonal relations to other setting inhabitants. Thus, the newcomers *simultaneously pursue several goals* and, therefore, they may simultaneously perform different actions" (1993: 194).

The third issue, the assumed homogeneity of actors, goals, motives, and activity itself was frequently challenged in our discussions, replaced with quite different assumptions that emphasize their heterogeneity. I believe this view is new to discussions of learning. It derives from an intent focus on the multiplicity of actors engaged in activity together, and on the interdependencies, conflicts, and relations of power so produced. These views are elaborated in *Understanding Practice* by several authors: Keller and Keller argue that, "the goal of production is not monolithic but multifaceted" (1993: 130) and is based on considerations aesthetic, stylistic, functional, procedural, financial, and academic as well as conceptions of self and other, and material conditions of work (1993: 135). Dreier proposes that different participants' interpretations are based on different contextual social positions with inherent differences in possibilities, interests, and perspectives on conflicts arising from different locations. Suchman and Trigg describe artificial intelligence research as a socially organized process of craftsmanship consisting of "the crafting together of a complex machinery made of heterogeneous materials, mobilized in the service of developing a theory of mind" (1993: 144). And McDermott proposes that "by institutional arrangements, we must consider everything from the most local level of the classroom to the more inclusive level of inequities throughout the political economy (preferably from both ends of the continuum at the same time)" (1993: 273). These statements refer to a wide variety of relations, but each challenges research on knowing and learning that depends implicitly on a homogeneity of community, culture, participants, their motives, and the meaning of events.

The heterogeneous, multifocal character of situated activity implies that conflict is a ubiquitous aspect of human existence. This follows if we assume that people in the same situation, people who are helping to constitute "a situation" together, know different things and speak with different interests and experience from different social locations. Suddenly assumptions concerning the uniformity of opinion, knowledge, and belief become, on the one hand, matters of common historical tradition and complexly shared relations with larger societal forces (whatever these might mean – now an important question) and, on the other hand, matters of imposed conformity and symbolic violence. Analysis focused on conflictual practices of changing understanding in activity is not so likely to concentrate on the truth or error of some knowledge claim. It is more likely to explore disagreements over what is relevant; whether, and how much, something is worth knowing and doing; what to make of ambiguous circumstances; what is convenient for whom, what to do next when one does not know what to expect, and who cares most about what. There are always conflicts of power, so mislearning cannot be understood independently of someone imposing her or his view. There is, of course, and at the same time, much uniformity and agreement in the world. The perspectives represented here differ about whether this is always, or only much of the time, a matter of one party imposing assent, subtly or otherwise, on others.

The fourth and final issue concerns "failure to learn." In mainstream theorizing about learning this is commonly assumed to result from the inability or refusal on the part of an individual to engage in something called "learning." The alternative view explored earlier is that not-learning and "failure" identities are active normal social locations and processes. This generates further questions, however: If failure is a socially arranged identity, what is left to be said about the making of "errors?" Given that several of the authors provide novel construals of failure to learn, question the meaning of "consensus," and call attention to the deficiencies of claims that knowing unfolds without conflict and without engaging the interests of involved participants, does the term *error* still have meaning? The answer depends on whose socially positioned point of view is adopted, and on historically and socially situated conceptions of erroneous action and belief. Several research projects described in *Understanding Practice* develop powerful ways of conceptualizing socially, historically situated "nonlearning" or "mislearning." They discuss nonlearning activities that occur when embarrassment is too great or that result from anxiety, from the social delegitimation of learning or the learner, and from the retarding effects of denying learners access to connections between immediate appearances and broader, deeper social forces, or access to concrete interrelations within and across situations (e.g., Levine). Mehan explores the discoordination of voices in interactions between school psychologist, teacher, and parent, who speak in different "languages"– psychological, sociological, and historical. Engeström locates unproductive encounters between patients and physicians in the mismatch among historically engendered discourses – thus, in practice, among the biomedical and psychosocial registers or voices the physician and patient use for communicating about medical issues.

Hutchins' analysis raises questions about the location of error making in historical systems of activity and in relations among participants. He describes what it is possible for novice navigators to learn in practice in terms of task partitioning, instruments, lines of communication, and limitations and openness of access for observing others, their interactions, and tools. He argues that these define the portion of the task environment that is available as a learning context for each task performer. This constitutes the performer's "horizon of observability." The density of error correction (which helps to make learning possible) depends on the contours of this horizon.

In sum, the assumptions proposed here amount to a preliminary account of what is meant by *situated learning*. Knowledgeability is routinely in a state of change rather than stasis, in the medium of socially, culturally, and historically ongoing systems of activity, involving people who are related in multiple and heterogeneous ways, whose social locations, interests, reasons, and subjective possibilities are different, and who improvise struggles in situated ways with each other over the value of particular definitions of the situation, in both immediate and comprehensive terms, and for whom the production of failure is as much a part of routine collective activity as the production of average, ordinary knowledgeability. These interrelated assumptions run deeply through the work presented in *Understanding Practice*.

Context as Situated Activity

Common concerns – theories of person-activity-world and their intrinsic heterogeneity, and a commitment to the investigation of everyday practice in detail – by no means determine a single theoretical position on the question of "context." Roughly speaking, there are two major viewpoints represented in *Understanding Practice*, built upon these commonalities but differing in their conception of the relations that constitute the contexts, or perhaps more precisely the contextualization, of activity. One argues that the central theoretical relation is historically constituted between persons engaged in socioculturally constructed activity and the world with which they are engaged. Activity theory is one representative of such theoretical traditions. The other focuses on the construction of the world in social interaction; this leads to the view that activity is its own context. Here the central theoretical relation is the inter-subjective relation among coparticipants in social interaction. This derives from a tradition of phenomenological social theory. These two viewpoints do not exhaust the positions taken by authors here, but cover the majority.

Analysis of "context" in the activity theory perspective begins with historically emerging contradictions that characterize all concrete social institutions and relations. Unlike some other traditions inspired by Marxist principles, activity theory emphasizes the non-determinate character of the effects of objective social structures. Differences in the social location of actors are inherent in political-economic structures, and elaborated in specific sociocultural practices. Differences of power, interests, and possibilities for action are ubiquitous. Any particular action is socially constituted, given meaning by its location in societally, historically generated systems of activity. Meaning is not created through individual intentions; it is mutually constituted in relations between activity systems and persons acting, and has a relational character. Context may be seen as the historically constituted concrete relations within and between situations. As Engeström puts it: "Contexts are activity systems. An activity system integrates the subject, the object, and the instruments (material tools as well as signs and symbols) into a unified whole ... [that includes relations of] production and communication ... distribution, exchange and consumption" (1993: 67). Dreier argues that: "The immediate situation has particular connections with the overall societal structure of possibilities and actions that produce and reproduce the concrete social formation ... So even the immediate "internal" connections of any situation are societally mediated in a concrete and particular way." (1993: 114)

Minute actions are by no means the constitutive elements of "interaction" in social constructionist approaches either. *Understanding Practice* contains rich descriptions of the unfortunate *effects* of beliefs that "meaningful activity" is composed, building block fashion, out of operations (see Suchman and Trigg's description of the artificial intelligence researchers' approach to action, Mehan's description of the assumptions and procedures of school psychologists, and Levine's chapter and his research more generally on approaches to mental retardation).

Säljö and Wyndhamn offer a good example of relations among actions, operations, meaning, and systems of activity (though they might not use these terms). They describe how children's engagement in action (finding the correct postage for a letter from a postal table) is realized through different operations (e.g., calculating amounts of postage to several decimal places, or instead determining which is the right-priced stamp) in different settings (math classes, social studies classes, and in the post office) in which the situated "sense" of the task differs. The meaning of the postal task cannot be defined independently from the activity within which the problem is posed, and the children's assumptions about what are the relevant premises for action.

The conception of "context" in the phenomenological perspective, in contrast with that typical of activity theories, begins with the premise that situations are constructed as people organize themselves to attend to and give meaning to figural concerns against the ground of ongoing social interaction. Silence, erasure, the construction of boundaries, and collusion are constitutive here (e.g., Latour and Woolgar 1979; and, in *Understanding Practice*, Suchman and Trigg; McDermott; and Mehan). The figure – ground metaphor highlights the key relation of context and meaning – both determined by the relation and determining of it. McDermott argues that "context is not so much something into which someone is put, but an order of behavior of which one is a part" (see also McDermott 1980). He draws on Birdwhistle's view of context:

I like to think of it as a rope. The fibers that make up the rope are discontinuous; when you twist them together, you don't make them continuous, you make the thread continuous. . . . The thread has no fibers in it, but, if you break up the thread, you can find the fibers again. So that, even though it may look in a thread as though each of those particles are going all through it, that isn't the case. (1993: 274)

Mehan points out that a social constructionist research tradition is concerned with

how the stable features of social institutions such as schooling, science, medicine, politics and the family are both generated in and revealed by the language of the institution's participants. . . . [P]eople's everyday practices are examined for the way in which they exhibit, indeed, generate, the social structures of the relevant domain . . . Inferences about social structure are permissible only when the workings of the structure can be located in people's interaction. (1993: 243–4)

The major difficulties of phenomenological and activity theory as seen from the viewpoint of the other will be plain: Those who start with the view that social activity is its own context dispute claims that objective social structures exist other than in their social-interactional construction in situ. Activity theorists argue, on the other hand, that the concrete connectedness and meaning of activity cannot be accounted for by analysis of the immediate situation. Thus, Dreier points out a widely held assumption that the context of activity is the immediate surround of specific persons' actions – that the context of action is the "characteristics of the immediate interaction and/or of the participating personalities" (1993: 110). Much of his chapter is devoted to argument concerning how this view distorts not only therapeutic relationships but also the analyses typically carried out by social scientists who study therapeutic and other kinds of face-to-face relations, as it erases historical processes, both large and small.

The chapters by Suchman and Trigg and by Mehan represent innovative responses from phenomenological researchers to criticisms of the self-contained, ahistorical character of much of that tradition. In fashioning cross-contextual, transitive analyses of the complex projects they investigate, they raise questions about the ground against which meaning in particular contexts is configured, a ground that goes beyond the immediate situation. This involves following projects across interrelated interactional events. For Mehan the project is the school's decision-making process about where to assign particular students. Objects are the children who become objectified in the bureaucratic work of designating them "learning disabled." For Suchman and Trigg, the artificial intelligence researchers' project is to find a solution to a theoretical problem in their field; the result is an emerging artificial intelligence program. Suchman and Trigg address the issue of how particular craftwork is both constrained by, and takes resources from, the intersection of several existing practices. They analyze connections among what they call the ancestral traditions of artificial intelligence – as it organizes its projects around "scenarios" (short, programmatic, story like proxies for the everyday-world problem the program is supposed to address), and the work of generating formalisms that can be turned into computer programs that will resolve the artificial intelligence problems that motivate the scenarios. "[T]he scenario serves as a coordinating device for project activities distributed over time and space" (1993: 151). The segment of work that they analyze "is located in a stream of activities whose concerns are both historically given and projected forward in time" (1993: 147). At each step in their analysis they consider how the work in which the researchers are engaged both mediates and is mediated by past and future steps in realizing the project. Suchman has recently suggested that concern with historical mediation has become a point of convergence between activity theorists and phenomenological analysts: The latter are beginning to recognize that immediate situations include historical artifacts, practices, and routines, and that historical practices and artifacts provide resources, interactionally, to be garnered and employed on next occasions (personal communication).

I have sketched two views of the context of activity and tried to indicate some of their implications for conceptualizing action and the mediated interconnections that partially produce its meaning. Both theoretical viewpoints expand the horizons of conventional analysis of situated activity, especially in temporal, historical terms. Rather than contrast them in terms of the original unit of analysis proposed earlier – persons in activity in the social world – it now seems more appropriate to sum them up, respectively, as exploring how it is that people live in *history*, and how it is that people *live* in history. Activity theory reflects the former, and with it the importance of the partially given character of an objectively structured world. Phenomenological views emphasize the latter and with it the partially cogenerated character of a meaningful world.

This seems an odd, felicitous, but still preliminary outcome to our attempts to come to grips with the "context" of activity. The emphasis on the historical mediation of activity in context may provide a clue as to how to proceed. The chapters stress the importance of interrelations among local practices; they give hints that local practices must inevitably take part in constituting each other, through their structural interconnections, their intertwined activities, their common participants, and more. The next step may be to reformulate the problem of context: Instead of asking, what is the constitutive relationship between persons acting and the contexts with which they act, the question becomes, What are the relationships among local practices that contextualize the ways people act together, both in and across contexts? The work represented in *Understanding Practice* succeeds in producing this new sense of the problem and, with it, an insistent and appealing recommendation to investigate those interconnections in a concentrated fashion.

Decontextualization as Local Practice

Usually, "contextualized learning" is not discussed alone, but as part of a duality of which "decontextualized learning" forms the other half. But the theories of context discussed in the previous section are intended to apply broadly to *all* social practice: They claim that there is no decontextualized social practice. Such a claim commits us to explaining what has often been taken to be "decontextualized knowledge" or "decontextualized learning" *as* contextualized social practices. This may not be a simple task: to discuss decontextualization it is first necessary to establish just what is meant, *conventionally*, by the term context. For there has as yet been no discussion of its most common dualistic conception, as a static, residual, surrounding "container" for social interaction. Given the formalist character of this view it should not be surprising that the head is often also conceived to be a container, in this case, for knowledge, while more general knowledge is the container of more particular knowledge, and language is an inert container for the transmission of meaning. Reminded by a flurry of defining gestures during the conference, Latour pointed out that when most people talk about context, they sketch in the air a shell about the size and shape of a pumpkin. Nor should this come as a surprise:

> [I]n all common-sense uses of the term, context refers to an empty slot, a container, into which other things are placed. It is the "con" that contains the "text," the bowl that contains the soup. As such, it shapes the contours of its contents; it has its effects only at the borders of the phenomenon under analysis ... The soup does not shape the bowl, and the bowl most certainly does not alter the substance of the soup. Text and context, soup and bowl ... can be analytically separated and studied on their own without doing violence to the complexity of their situation. A static sense of context delivers a stable world. (McDermott 1993: 282)

This sense of context (and with it common senses of decontextualization) is deeply held and embodied. It should remind us that a formalist view of context is a key conception in conventional theories of action, thinking, knowing, and learning, with significantly deep roots much more generally in a Euro-American worldview. The prevailing view of context furnishes the ground against which conventional views of decontextualization take on meaning. In fact, a detached view of context seems prerequisite for an analytic conception of decontextualization. In spite of its derivative character, however, we must not lose sight of the fact that decontextualization is the more salient and highly valued of this asymmetric pair. Until quite recently it has been more significant in the prevailing lexicon than context, especially where knowledge and learning are at issue.

To decontextualize knowledge is to form-alize (to contain it, pour it into more inclusive forms. To formalize is to contain more forms. It follows that abstraction from and generalization across "contexts" (qua soup bowls) are mechanisms that are supposed to produce decontextualized (general and thus valuable) knowledge. Along with this way of talking about decontextualization go several other claims. First, movement toward powerful (abstract, general) knowledge is construed as movement away from engagement in the world, so distance "frees" knowers from the particularities of time, place, and ongoing activity.[5] Second, language contains and can express literal meaning (Minick 1993: 349–50, discussing Rommetveit.) Rommetveit (1988) reminds us of the intuitive appeal of pervading pretheoretical notions such as, for instance (Goffman 1964: 303), "the common sense notion . . . that the word *in isolation* will have a general basic, or most down-to-earth meaning. Such presuppositions seem to form part of the myth of literal meaning in our highly literate societies." A third assumption accompanying claims for the possibility (and power) of decontextualization is that we live in an objective, monistic world. Minick elaborates this point:

Just as the myth of literal meaning posits a language that has meaning independent of local concerns, interests, and perspectives – independent of the formation of "temporary mutual commitments to shared perspectives" – the myth of the "monistic real world" posits a world that can be described and comprehended in isolation from such local concerns, perspectives, and commitments. (1993: 371)

Once the separate, inert, objective character of the world is assumed, along with the neutral, disinterested character of knowledge (because it brackets out local concerns), it is entirely consistent to think of institutions in the same terms. From this, assumptions are derived about the privileged character of schools and of therapeutic encounters as sites where knowledge is produced, where learning takes place, but where what is learned is independent of, and not affected by, the circumstances in which it is produced. Further, it is assumed that what is learned is of a general nature and powerful because it is *not* embedded in the particularities of specific practices. These assumptions are brought into question simultaneously once learning is conceived as situated practice.

McDermott, Minick, and other authors in *Understanding Practice* would surely agree that the pair of terms, context and decontextualization, has been borrowed unreflectively from the culture more generally, rather than derived analytically or theoretically. They would also argue that the dualistic division and categorization of experience that privileges "decontextualization" does not offer an adequate explanation of thought or action. Nonetheless, this pervasive perspective leads a robust existence *in practice*, in the contemporary world. Euro-American culture instantiates it, and in many ways is predicated upon it.

---

[5] The sixth essay, on Everyday Life with respect to learning, offers a critical exploration of this claim and its ramifications.

Beliefs, institutions, and a great deal of action operate in its name. A theoretical account of (de)contextualization as situated practice should account for how such formalist views of the world are sustained in practice (cf. Dreier 1993: chapter 4 for his account of psychotherapeutic practices). Accordingly, authors in *Understanding Practice* have raised the following question. How are conventional conceptions of context and decontextualization, and the myth of an objective, disinterested, asocial world, *made* part of our social practices, in situated ways? And how do conventions (beliefs and practices) that enact contextual dualism shape other social practices? I have come to see both these questions and ethnographic explorations of this issue as among the most novel and interesting contributions of the book.

Minick provides an example of a situated practice that inculcates belief in a monistic world and in literal meaning. Teachers' use of what he calls "representational speech" reflects the belief that complete, explicit, unambiguous representation in language should be sufficient to convey meaning. This is, of course, one way to subscribe to the myth of literal meaning. It has a crucial corollary: that if complete representation of meaning in language is possible, then the student, the receiver of explicit communication, need attend to nothing except its "literal" meaning. Minick argues that "the introduction of representational forms of speech to primary school children is . . . a study of their introduction to social and mental activities that take place in this 'mythical' monistic real world" (1993: 371).

Minick uncovers situated, cultural political mechanisms that produce "decontextualized" representational interactions.[6] One of these is the switching from common sense interpretations to representational directives: He describes a grade-school teacher leading children through a lesson, saying "Did I say raise your hand when you finished or did I say put your pencil down?" when the original sense of her instructions had been "Let me know when you're done." There is conflict between situational sense and representational directives; this creates uncertainty for children and anxiety about what is the right thing to do; it creates grounds for blame from the teacher and dependency of children on the teacher because only the teacher can resolve the ambiguity-through-decontextualization she has created along with conflict between situational and "desituated" meaning.

There are numerous ways, then, in which the specific social practices involved in interactions around literal meaning are means by which teachers maintain control of classrooms and move pupils through activities in an efficient and mechanistic fashion. (These practices themselves are, of course, situated in other relations that make control of children and their activities a

---

[6] Critical psychology's critique of "interpretive thinking" makes a similar argument (Dreier 1993: 110).

customary, even required, aspect of teachers' everyday lives.) One of the ironies of this is that the very act of attempting to turn language into the only site of meaning creates at one and the same time ambiguities of meaning and a basis for controlling learners. It reduces what is being communicated to operations (in activity theory terms), with predictable results. There is a second irony as well: It was emphasized earlier that improvisation, ambiguity, and open-endedness are essential aspects of activity. Teachers' attempts to disambiguate directives to children are no exception. Attempts to decontextualize – to achieve self-contained precision and thereby both generality and literalness of meaning – create ambiguity in the process of stripping away meaning. Thus, teachers' decontextualizing practices have (unintended) effects, which change practices and shrivel the meaning of learning for all concerned.

Representational speech is not, of course, limited to the classroom. Mehan focuses on this and other mechanisms for turning myth into reality in practice: "When technical language is used and embedded in the institutional trappings of the formal proceedings of a meeting, the grounds for negotiating meaning are removed from under the conversation" (1993: 259). Under such circumstances, institutionally grounded representations predominate (e.g., psychiatrists' representations prevail over patients' and, as Kvale demonstrates, examination committees' prevail over students'). The effect of technical language (its technologism is not accidental) is to bracket and delegitimize the situated understanding of other participants, including parents and teachers. Further, this particular "universalizing language, as invoked in settings such as meetings to decide on the classroom placements of children with learning difficulties," decontextualizes the (absent) child by reducing her or him (beforehand and elsewhere) to a collection of discrete variables. Mehan argues that this technical, psychologistic, scientistic language is a common source of power and authority in many contemporary settings. Patterns of removal and alignment across socially constructed boundaries (classroom, testing the child, discussing the child's placement) are material aspects of decontextualization processes (1993: 264).

Although there are many other ways of demonstrating the absurdity of claims that educative institutions such as school and therapeutic relations are privileged "noncontexts" for "context-free" learning, the examples here of specific, situated practices of decontextualization are surely among the most dramatic. Further, they offer clues as to lines of historical work within which to locate future analyses of the situated practices of craftwork and the nature of learning identity formation described throughout *Understanding Practice*.

There are yet other mechanisms for giving material existence to the myth of monistic realism: Dreier describes two such processes, one of them "desubjectification." Reasons for action are constitutive of human agency, but clients' subjective rationality only appears from an external perspective – the therapist's interpretation. The therapist couches the subjective rationality of his own actions from the external perspective of his client's needs (purporting to have no needs or interests of his own). The consequence is the desubjectification of therapist–client relations (1993: 105–6).

He goes on to describe processes of "deinstitutionalization," which also help to privilege therapy as "the building of an anywhere and nowhere" (1993: 107). As Suchman and Trigg describe them, the careers of artificial intelligence researchers follow a path of decontextualization (and recontextualization) through increasingly specialized communities – positioned mediations that distance the everyday practice of artificial intelligence research from some of its claimed constituencies, and insinuate it into closer connections with others. "In the course of their work, researchers selectively reproduce, make relevant, extend, and transform problems and solutions *given by their membership in progressively more specialized technical communities*, each with its own assumptions, commitments, and identifying technologies" (1993: 147, emphasis mine). This work, Dreier's, and that of other authors here as well, offer clues as to the relations between specialization and professionalization and specific social practices of decontextualization.

The studies under discussion take situated activity to be far more complex and contentful than formal, conventional notions of context could contain. They locate learning throughout the relations of persons in activity in the world. From this point of view decontextualization and appeals to it are active, interested denials of contextual interconnections (i.e., they are processes of erasure, collusion, and domination). Most broadly, "decontextualization" is a key process in the production of the culture of monistic realism, the historically located societal formation in which, as Mehan observes, there is consensus around psychological, technological, and institutional means for objectifying persons and legitimizing "generalization."

Conclusion

As the conference drew to a close, we tried to sum up our common endeavor. Three guidelines emerged for organizing the introduction to our work. The conference participants preferred not to emphasize learning because the traditionally narrow genre of research conjured up by the term might get in the way of readers' interest in our work. They hoped I would convey the spirit of the commitment we forged in the time we spent together, to the value of the *differences* among our theoretical positions. These differences offered multiple possibilities for interrogating social experience and this was a central intention of *Understanding Practice*. And we all hoped to produce chapters reflecting movement forward, motivated as little as possible by opposition to other views, which surely had driven us too much in the past. We intended to produce positive accounts of our changing understanding of how to investigate social practice.

I did not comply very well with any of these guidelines, and each one deserves comment. First, I indeed gave singular attention to questions of learning. The chapters clearly warranted it: they provided the most positive possible answer to fears that learning is a desiccated topic. The authors produced fascinating analyses of learning as situated practice. In doing so they opened out the scope of studies of learning, erasing old barriers between learning and participation in ongoing social practice, and locating failure to learn squarely in the latter.

Second, there is a remarkable variety of theoretical positions represented in the book. I initially intended to recount these differences more thoroughly, but found myself drawn to other issues instead, and have tried to demonstrate that a coherent account of understanding in social practice is to be found even among the diverse analyses of these chapters. Together they demonstrate that learning and not learning, and contextualization and decontextualization, are socially situated and socially produced. To the extent that my argument for this coherence is convincing, however, it obscures our intention to focus on the significance of the disjunctions among our positions. *Understanding Practice* would repay reading in two ways: for its strong common argument and for the resources of diversity it offers as well.

Finally, we were trying to explore new approaches without miring ourselves in the burdens of defending the value of doing so, and we tried to go beyond mere critique of dominant theories. There are reasons to question the feasibility of this goal. If our relations with currently dominant theoretical positions are difficult to escape, the problem may be one of rethinking *how* to struggle with such hegemonic theoretical practices. It seems useful to stop treating mainstream theoretical positions simply as unmediated alternatives to our own and start looking at them as historical manifestations of the sociocultural formation in which we are participants, and to which we have concrete connections of various kinds (cf. Chaiklin 1992; Kvale 1992).

There are not many precedents for doing this. Prevailing theory concerning learning, thinking, and knowing is for the most part ahistorical and acontextual in its understanding of itself. Further, so little has been done to denaturalize and historicize its analytic categories and questions that the assumptions and concepts of mainstream theories (though not the jargon) are difficult to distinguish from folk beliefs and practices. This should serve notice that the everyday, situated practices that the authors set out to describe may be significantly intertwined with the vernacular theory we were trying to transcend. We are left with the task of historical analysis and explanation of how rationalist, individualist, empiricist conceptions of learning, knowing, and the social world are kept alive and well in the culture at large.

Understanding Practice does not offer such an analysis of Euro-American culture. Some of the studies analyze detailed aspects of specific changing social practices. Others assume that what they have to say about Euro-American culture is incidental, a means through which to explore conceptions of socially situated activity. In neither case do I detect a keen sense that the crucial "move" in these projects is to lay bets on what constitutes the most important cultural underpinnings of the world in which we live, so as to study those in particular.

In the previous section, however, I argued that these studies examine sociocultural processes of participation, production, myth and sense making, inculcation and (de)legitimation, in situated processes that *are* central to Euro-American practices and worldview. Furthermore, I argued that the central cultural significance of understanding practices that have been analyzed in these chapters is not accidental. The question is, how did the authors come to investigate processual mechanisms by which mainstream, hegemonic, theoretical practices help to constitute the society wide underpinnings of belief and action about thought, knowing, learning, and the world?

It may be that the answer lies in our inability to escape from "saying no" to older theoretical practices: Existing theoretical perspectives contribute in a serious way to the sustenance of the existing social formation; to take them on, to turn mainstream theories into objects of analysis and critique, while accounting for their crucial role in organizing and justifying numerous Euro-American social practices, is to take on the culture more broadly. In short, there may be advantages as well as drawbacks to our unsuccessful struggles to stop grappling with old paradigms.

This suggests a program for the developing practice of studying situated activity and learning. It might begin with a conception of learning as an aspect of culturally, historically situated activity. It would focus on the content of and the ways people participate in changing social practices singled out for study *because* they appear to lie at the heart of the production and reproduction – and transformation and change – of the sociocultural order. The studies in *Understanding Practice* furnish strong beginnings for such a project.

3   Ethnographies of Apprenticeship

* * * * *

If "The Problem of Context" tries to situate social practice theory in a broader landscape of theoretical alternatives, the present chapter tries to do the same thing with respect to ethnographic research on apprenticeship. There are only very brief ethnographic examples in *Situated Learning* (1991). Eventually I realized we had never asked what anthropologists and sociologists who studied craft practices were engaged in doing if their main concern did not happen to be apprenticeship as a matter of learning. What did they mean when they referred to "apprenticeship?" Did it attract their attention as an example of situated learning? Of learning at all? This essay poses these questions in a review of the scattered and heterogeneous body of anthropological/sociological studies of craft/apprenticeship produced between 1975 and 1995.

Most ethnographers of craft apprenticeship in this period did not seem particularly interested in *how* apprentices learned a craft. But many of them did something else that I found interesting. They made vivid descriptions of the messily enmeshed social, economic, educational facets of everyday life around and in ongoing craft practices. They painted pictures of circumstances in which apprentices, learning, might plausibly be viewed as actively part of social being/ doing in the world and hence part of social relations more generally. I was also interested in the boundaries of the anthropologists' and sociologists' interests. One of these boundaries often turned out to be an uncritical division between all those messy social processes – and learning. Indeed, they often theorized learning in conventional rather than critical theoretical terms.

Though some of the studies discussed here occasionally cited my early papers on apprenticeship, they were all published before *Situated Learning*.

* * * * *

Lave and Wenger (1991) drew on a small number of ethnographic studies of apprenticeship that seemed particularly useful for working out an analytic

This chapter was written in 1995–1996. It has not been previously published. By the time it was written it was clear that a number of important new studies were emerging. Klaus Nielsen and I are working on a review of studies of craft/apprenticeship from 1995 to the present.

approach to situated learning as legitimate peripheral participation in communities of practice. I emerged from that project curious, however, about the much larger corpus of ethnographic studies of apprenticeship available at the time. I thought such studies might illuminate learning as part of given, complicated practices of daily life. Learning in practice. Great idea. Indeed, these ethnographies of apprenticeship almost all took a broad view of what it means to study apprenticeship and in this they offered a welcome contrast to my focus on apprenticeship-as-learning. The first part of this chapter examines how ethnographers deal with the articulation of educational, economic, and other social arrangements. The second part asks how ethnographic studies of apprenticeship embody and theorize "learning."

A number of the anthropological (and sociological) studies have focused on apprenticeship in West Africa where craft specializations learned through apprenticeship are dense, widespread, and have a long history.[1] They include Goody (1982) – cloth weavers and dyers in Ghana; Deafenbaugh (1989) – Hausa weavers in Nigeria; Dilley (1989) – Tukolor weavers in Senegal; Lancy (1980) – Kpelle blacksmiths in Liberia; McLaughlin (1979) – wayside mechanics in Ghana; McNaughton (1988) – Mande blacksmiths in Guinea and Mali; Pokrant (1983) – craft producers in Kano, Nigeria; Peil (1970) – tailors in Accra, Ghana; and Verdon (1979) – based on Terence Smutylo's (1973) data on artisan workshops in Accra.

Two ethnographers have produced extensive bodies of work on apprenticeship in West Africa. Esther Goody and her associates have worked for many years on an agenda of interrelated issues that incorporates and reflects historical and political-economic entailments of apprenticeship. The second project offers a different kind of history with different entailments and consequences than Goody's. Art historian Patrick McNaughton has worked extensively in West Africa on the apprenticeship of Mande blacksmiths in Guinea and Mali whose productive lives extend far beyond the forges where they work iron.

The Social Arrangements of Apprenticeship

Daboya Weavers

Esther Goody engaged in long-term ethnographic exploration of craft production, apprenticeship and child fostering among Daboya weavers in Gonja, northern Ghana. She makes a sustained, multi-faceted attempt to work out relations between educational and other, especially economic, social

---

[1] This stands in stark contrast to East Africa where local craft traditions seemed to be absent, and in fact were supplied by East Indians during the colonial period e.g., Kenneth King, *The African Artisan* (1977).

arrangements. This has taken her into the history of industrial production (especially transformations of cloth production) (1989), into changing family relations (1969); into Northern Ghanaian social organization and craft production (1980); and into forms of child rearing and especially child fostering (1982) which (interesting in their own right) seem suggestively related to apprenticeship.

Weaving is the main source of livelihood in the Bakarambasipe section of Daboya. Goody (1982) describes in dense detail social-historical differentiation between sub-regions of Gonja including weaving practices and their embedding in a tumultuous history of shifting empires and changing trade relations. She describes the social organization of the community of Daboya, its Muslims, commoners and representatives of the ruling Ngbanya group, the complex organization of its residential sections, and the kin and household relations within the weaving section of Daboya on which her study concentrates. She describes how these affect the organization of weaving in its relations with other interdependent practices (dyeing, purchasing raw materials for weaving, and distributing the finished products), the organization of weaving practices themselves, and the way apprenticeship comes about in stages so as to gradually draw little boys into the more extensive involvement typical of older apprentices, or "bobbin boys." This in turn becomes the main occupation of young men who are "dependent weavers" until, as they marry, they become independent weavers on their own looms, gradually taking on supervision of weavers and apprentices at several looms as their children begin to grow into the practice while they themselves become elder weavers with authority over those beneath them in the system and control over the assets of the kin group (Goody 1982: 77). In describing these "seven ages" of the weaver she makes amply clear the relations of boys' maturation to their changing social positions in the community and their changing participation in production. Both her broad program of Gonja history, political-economy, and social organization, and the account she gives of the life trajectory of weavers growing up, into, and through the craft emphasize that the apprenticeship process is inseparable from the social arrangements of their lives more broadly.

Goody's argument is especially interesting when she insists that the organization of craft production is influenced by the way in which people come to learn it as well as the other way around: In discussing the long history of adaptation and change in the weaving craft she tells about a master weaver from Daboya, interested in improving the industry, who asked her help in exploring innovations in loom technology. She took him to visit the weaving unit of the University of Science and Technology in Kumasi. There, he rejected two feasible devices, a new type of loom and a warping frame. She explored his reasons.

The rejection of the loom was immediate and complete. It was very expensive by Daboya standards, and must have seemed too complex to be made locally. While a master weaver might have been able to afford one loom, he would not have been able to buy additional ones for each of the youths and young men weaving for him. Abudulae certainly could not have paid for ten. A shift to the European broad loom would thus have meant no longer making use of the weaving labour of dependent weavers and bobbin boys, because there would not be enough looms for them. This loom would have promoted weaving, at least at first, from the semi-skilled to the skilled category. But if the master weaver was himself using the new loom, he would no longer be free to manage the processing of thread, warping and dyeing for the remaining traditional looms [which is apprentices' work]. This was not a decision based on relative technical merit, but on relations of production.

The more reluctant rejection of the warping frame is somewhat different. Warping enters the skill sequence at an earlier point, and particularly concerns the utilization of bobbin boys. The calculations of how many spindles of thread to wind onto the frame at one time, and the number of complete sets, winding from top to bottom, would have to be made by the master weaver. Older bobbin boys could probably manage . . . [But] no longer could boys of the awkward age between 5 and 10 be brought into help intermittently with the totally unskilled job . . . And the younger bobbin boys would be without their main work. To have adopted the warping frame would have meant shifting the balance of unskilled and semi-skilled tasks in favour of the latter, with a sharp drop in work suitable for older boys. Although efficiency in terms of the time required to prepare a warp would certainly increase efficiency as measured by the utilization of labour at different levels of skill would decline.

One solution could be to let the boys play until a later age than at present, and wait to train them until they could manage the more complex procedure. However, the present balance of unskilled, semi-skilled and skilled tasks provides a progression which allows boys from an early age to make a real contribution to the weaving process. Their participation is carefully managed so as to engage their interest while leaving them considerable freedom until they are old enough to have the patience to develop skills that they can take pride in. A major task in kin-based enterprise is motivating the next generation to participate effectively. (1982: 83)

The organization of weaving production in Daboya is integrally connected with the means for drawing new participants into and through it as well as the other way around. She pursues this two-way relationship (below), examining how they affect one another through the articulation of production and labor in market relations.

Goody is not alone in exploring the mutual entailments of educational and economic arrangements. Verdon (1979), an associate of Goody's, gives a telling critique of economists' attempts to assimilate craft workshops to firms and masters to entrepreneurs. The relation of apprenticeship and production is at the heart of his argument: Craft workshops should not be assimilated to development economists' notions of "firms" nor masters to "bosses" or "entrepreneurs." Masters cannot respond to changes in market conditions, he argues, because apprentices are not employees working for a wage. They are "applied learners." Their masters are responsible for their welfare regardless of whether there is business or not. Further, these relations involve masters in producing their own eventual competition. Here are two good reasons for the intergenerational conflict and tension inherent in relations between masters and apprentices.

Dilley (1989) also expresses critical concern, based on his ethnographic work, about narrowly economistic "readings" of craft production, again because of the integral part played by apprenticeship:

By placing these issues within a solely socio-economic discussion of craft industries, it is as though certain authors presuppose a logically-prior free labor market upon which act the institutions of kinship organization, craft knowledge, craft monopolies, apprenticeship, etc. in their functional role in the economy and the division of labor ... [But] being a craftsman is more than just a means of securing a livelihood: It is a means also of defining one's moral constitution and social position. Where an economist sees a labor market in which individuals would *want* to participate in craft industries for economic reasons, were they free to do so, and sees "imperfections" in the market as a result of social institutions, I see a social division of labor that supplies cultural meanings to its members through the experience of craft lore during the course of apprenticeship. (1989: 182)

He argues that we should attend to apprenticeship as, "the transmission of a body of lore that encapsulates the social meanings and cultural explanations of the weavers' social identity and conceptions of their craft" (1989: 183).

There are not many studies that begin with apprenticeship as a hybrid economic-educational phenomenon as a basis for a critique of reductive economism. There are even fewer that draw on ethnographic accounts of apprenticeship to resituate analyses of *educational* practice. The asymmetry that makes it harder to parse economic processes in educational terms than to read education in economic terms is another symptom of analytic problems I am trying to address. But at least we can say that it would be difficult to walk away from the ethnographies of apprenticeship without a sense that historical processes of political-economic transformation, production processes, and family relations are intimately bound up in everyday relations of learning and vice versa.

Market Articulation of Craft Production

Goody brings her studies of craft and apprenticeship together with her interest in child fostering practices in what she emphasizes is a tentative, speculative history of the transformation of domestic into capitalist market-driven production in West Africa, critically involving changing ways of learning that in turn contribute to changing divisions of labor (Goody 1989). She begins by reframing in market-economy terms both craft production and apprenticeship, arguing that the key relations linking them are made in the transformation of domestic production into production for the market, during periods in which labor has not yet been transformed into a commodity and is not yet regulated through the market as wage labor. She then asks (in the familiar argot of "skill transmission"): "In societies with domestic mode of production where skill is transmitted by children working together with adult producers, [and] where changes in economy [toward a market economy] lead to increasingly differentiated division of labor, how do occupational skills get transmitted?" (Goody 1989: 233). She also asks how apprenticeship has affected commodity production, on the one hand, and ways of learning, on the other

First, she argues that when differentiation of products for the market increases, under circumstances in which more homogeneous domestic production has previously been the order of the day, production still goes on in families but with two new wrinkles: sons (she says) may not be able to learn *en famille* the kinds of production skills they wish to live by, and fathers, trying to produce more in order to participate in capitalist markets so as to be able to purchase subsistence needs, have greater needs for steadier supplies of labor than expanding and contracting in-house relations can supply.[2] Apprenticeship is an answer to both dilemmas.

She speculates that apprenticeship may be one stage in a process leading to wage labor under growing capitalist market institutions and forces (1989: 245). This process evolves from family-based production involving only a gendered division of labor in which girls learn from mothers and boys from fathers. Domestic production processes are common to all households before the proliferation of the division of labor. (The "exuberant proliferation of occupations in West Africa during the present century" is certainly a major inspiration for this piece [1989: 243].) Fostering of children is an intermediate step, she suggests between rearing of children in their natal households and sending children to other families in search of specific occupational skills. Fostering children to designated kin in West Africa while still mainly a response to pre-market diversification involves a number of purposes and variants (Goody 1969, 1980). It cements relations and fulfills obligations between kin, including ritual obligations. It is often explained as good for the child because parents are too fond and indulgent of children, who will learn better when they respect those in charge of them and are treated in exacting ways. It is thought to be

---

[2] Studies of apprenticeship are with few exceptions about boys/men, and this without raising issues of gender. Almost without exception anthropologists and sociologists studying apprenticeship have focused on men's work. Kondo (1990) is the only exception I know of, by 1990, who takes on issues of gender in relation with apprenticeship. However, Hudita Mustafa's (1998) dissertation focuses on gender with respect to tailors' apprentices in Senegal.

good for children to learn the ways of another family.[3] Both these themes crop
up in discussions of apprenticeship (including my own e.g., Lave 2011).
Indeed, a stereotyped entry in essentially every description of apprenticeship
includes a statement as to whether children are apprenticed to kin or nonkin. In
many instances, certainly in Goody's material, the latter is the case.

These notions about the significance of "non-kin" relations figure in her
analysis of how apprenticeship affects commodity production and learning.
She suggests that when strangers come into new work situations, they cannot
be expected to know anything about the household's way of working. This
leads to long periods of initial participation doing errands and chores, only
gradually leading to participation in production work, while an apprentice
absorbs the work culture of the family. There is, Goody says, much to be
learned that cannot be taught, which may help to account for why there is very
little teaching in apprenticeship (though it does not help explain why there is so
much teaching elsewhere). From the master's point of view, having nonkin
coming to work has two effects on production: Household practices become
open to revision because laborers have no stakes in traditional methods or
ongoing kin relations, and it leads to the "rationalization of labor," to greater
labor discipline and efficiency. Further, she suggests, masters may be led to
reflect on the segments of work tasks, faced with the naiveté of newcomer
apprentices, and these reflections might translate eventually into new occupational specialisms based on divisions along the lines of old patterns of work
segmentation in a given form of production. Apprenticeship relations are
claimed to have a serious impact on the proliferation of occupational specialization in this way.

Goody underlines conflicts of interest she feels are basic to apprentice–
master relations: resentment of control and fear of exploitation on the part of
apprentices, suspicion that apprentices are malingering and the potential
recognition by masters that they are creating their own competition by taking
apprentices. And on this she bases one more point about the shifting of
production relations from father and son to master and apprentices (as a non-
kin relation): that in a domestic mode of production the interests and fates of
father and son are aligned and connected over time. In craft workshops the
ultimate economic interest of apprentices and masters compete and conflict.
Best that apprentices who have become masters move on rather than
staying on.

Goody's brief speculative history argues that capitalist markets have
penetrated and transformed West African economic organization (a good

---

[3] Kondo's description of *uchi* relations in Japan, relations also discussed by Singleton (1989)
provide an especially good description of the cultural implications and educational effects of
moving as an apprentice into a strange household.

point – craft and apprenticeship in West Africa in the late 1970s was surely not some pristinely "pre-capitalist" form of production and education), transforming production from a domestic mode through what she sees as a transitional, apprentice/workshop mode into what eventually will become wage labor. The production of labor moves from family to apprentice workshops, and presumably again in the longer run to capitalist-owned and managed settings of wage employment. These are interesting ideas worth pursuing. All the while the division of labor is assumed to be increasingly differentiated and labor increasingly rationalized.

Goody's "speculative history" is a kind of common sense account, and something very like it defines the agenda and boundaries of the vast majority of apprenticeship ethnographies: it is a tale of social evolution, from some primitive gendered division of labor to complex occupational differentiation. It is economistic and individualistic. It generates ages and stages assumed in most academic investigations of learning, child development (and studies of apprenticeship). The next history, McNaughton's (1988), disturbs this account. It raises questions about culture, politics and historical relations among things and persons that are articulated quite differently. It dwells on the complexity of social arrangements of which apprenticeship is a part. At the same time, it cuts through and throws into question the basis in too-Western categories of culture and economy most interpretations of apprenticeship in West Africa.

The Articulations of Mande Blacksmithing

Changes from a gendered division of labor and domestic mode of production to occupational specialization and merchant and then industrial capitalism is not the whole story of apprenticeship and craft production in West Africa. McNaughton (1988) writes about blacksmithing in the Mande diaspora in Guinea, Mali, and beyond (which includes, though quite marginally, the Vai on the Liberian border with Sierra Leone). He describes the lives and work of Mande blacksmiths from something much closer to a Mande historical perspective than a Eurocentric economic-historical view.

McNaughton describes the work of blacksmiths, in their endogamous clans of specialized professionals called *nyamakala*, which include bards and leather workers as well. Blacksmithing, the smelting and working of iron, has been going on in West Africa for several hundred years at least, though blacksmiths no longer engage in smelting.

[O]nly children born to families that belong to these professional clans can take up the trades their parents practice. It is first of all a matter of corporate identity and monopoly. A tremendous body of technical expertise is associated with each trade, and it must be learned over many years of apprenticeship that traditionally begin before the novice turns ten. (1988: 3)

McNaughton examines two puzzling relations that crucially define black-smiths' endeavors and place in the world. These go beyond the notion of "occupation" on which most analyses of apprenticeship rest. One has to do with the relations of the blacksmiths to the rest of Mande society. They are variously reviled, feared, live apart as near outcasts, and are crucial advisors and mediators in major political affairs both locally and more broadly. The other puzzle has to do with what else the blacksmiths do: They are black-smiths, making and repairing household and farm implements on a day-to-day basis, true. But they are also community sorcerers, healers, sculptors, performers of circumcision, and often heads of initiation societies. "Their services are so pervasive in Mande society and so embedded in the Mande world view that they literally infuse the culture with much of its character" (1988: 5).

Pursuing both puzzles McNaughton argues that it is not the production of commodities, but the social control of power in special ways in which bards, blacksmiths and leather workers are engaged. "[B]lacksmiths are deeply involved in the articulation of Mande social and spiritual space" (1988: 40), conceptions which he lays out in fascinating detail:

At sorcery's base lies a phenomenon that generates its own fair share of ambivalence and disquiet among the Mande. It is perceived as the world's basic energy, the energy that animates the universe. It is the force the Mande call *nyama*, which I refer to as special energy or occult power, and which most Westerners would consider supernat-ural. The Mande, in contrast, are inclinded [sic] to see it as both natural and mystical, and as a source of moral reciprocity. (1988: 15)

In ranging through the bush, and working in iron, blacksmiths must have the power to bring the world's energy or power safely under control. Sorcery and healing, which "are the focal points of the blacksmiths' credentials as mediators ... interface in a system of knowledge and articulation that shapes reality through the activation of nature's resources and the energy called *nyama*" (1988: 41).

[I]n all of their roles they attempt to create or maintain harmony and balance for their communities. People wholeheartedly depend upon them to do just that. They are believed capable of bringing rain to maintain the balance needed for farming product-ivity, and their tools encourage that balance by facilitating economy in farming and enlarging the scope in which it can be carried out. In divination they seek to maintain balance in their clients' future activities, or to reestablish it after a calamity by wisely seeking causes and appropriate courses of action. As doctors they maintain the harmony of healthy bodies when they offer the fruits of their *daliluw* knowledge to every member of their community. In circumcision smiths alter the physical state of young persons, forcing them into the realm of adulthood and ending their days of irresponsibility. At the same time they protect the newly circumcised from the dangers of that transitional state. (1988: 71–2)

McNaughton asks whether they are "really" blacksmiths who happen also to practice sorcery (some of them), and sculpture. Are they possibly "really" sorcerers for whom blacksmithing is a means to various, often occult, ends? Or are they entrepreneur traders who have learned over the years to tackle whatever needed doing. Rejecting each of these, he proposes that all of the practices in which blacksmiths are engaged, by his analysis and Mande ideology as well, are based on commonalities. The blacksmiths are masters of manufacture whether of utilitarian farming tools or as herbalists, sorcerers, soothsayers, or circumcisers.

[I]n a realm that ignores material and balances spiritual and social elements, black-smiths are masters at making, verifying, and helping to enforce arrangements among people. Their counsel is sought in important family and community matters. Their wisdom is sought when people compose new social or political alliances or break society's rules ... All of these acts have many things in common, and we can divide them into two categories. The first is one of prerequisites, what a person must possess to carry out the acts. The second involves the effects of these acts on Mande individuals and societies. (1988: 149–50)

The first includes knowledge, power and skill, physical, social and supernatural at the same time.[4] And as for the second:

In a variety of ways, then, each of these acts or the products they engender serves to aggrandize, refine, and reform, or to finish, bring to fruition, and make whole ... They shape or reshape objects, people, and situations by manipulating physical forms and their underlying structures of energy.

... the Mande perceive a fundamental unity in all these acts ... As we have seen, these smiths are almost automatically subjected to lengthy and complicated training periods. They are perceived as inheriting enormous volumes of *nyama*, as well as several kinds of secret knowledge [secret both because it is dangerous, and because] "its difficulty of acquisition makes it more valuable for people who have troubled to acquire it." (1988: 150) The technology used in their smithing is complicated and often augmented with spiritual elements, while their readiness to collect more *dalilu* knowledge has given them the reputation of being prodigious sorcerers. Their reputations afford them social and political clout, by submerging them in an atmosphere of competence in dangerous undertakings. (1988: 151)

The blacksmiths specialize not in blacksmithing but in the wielding and controlling of power. And what they specialize in, the articulation of

---

[4] With respect to the first puzzle, he concludes that the ambiguity of the blacksmiths' position in Mande society resides in the fear and envy of their enormous powers, which they are assumed to be able to use for ill as well as good. A broader analysis of Mande political relations would also show a polarization of political power between the blacksmiths and those charged with the governing powers the blacksmiths are forbidden, but for which they are vital mediators. The contradictions in such a system are intense and it is hard to imagine that ambivalence and ambiguity about the wielding of power could be any less so.

fundamental, multi-faceted, and dangerous manifestations of power, ranges far
beyond any "specialized occupation."

A history of changing kinds of production and apprenticeship would have to
start in the Mande case with the articulation of relations of power, natural,
social and supernatural, as these produce not segments in production
processes – the stages in producing trousers or weaving cloth, or working iron
into hoes – but as they articulate different ways of engaging with power
(healing, sorcery, blacksmithing, sculpting) and separate the different powers
of blacksmiths, bards, leather workers, and political office-holders.

We could ask how the cosmological-social-political mediations of the
"blacksmiths" rather than economic articulation of such relations might
change, perhaps splinter, fragment and diminish, or become compartmental-
ized, in the face of Western economic, political, and cultural penetration.
This should point up the limiting character of Western assumptions about
the nature of occupational specialization, craft niches in a market-run
division of products, labor, production and markets underlying most anthropological attempts to make sense of apprenticeship. It would be useful to
know why they are employed and what they are there to explain. These
should become relations to be explained, rather than explanatory devices in
their own right.

What Is "Apprenticeship"?

Among other reasons for dwelling on Goody's account of West African
apprenticeship under advancing capitalism and McNaughton's account of deep
historical West African roots of contemporary apprenticeship, the contrasts
between them should help to underline the complex historical character of
what is treated too often as an abstract category – for the most part apprenticeship has been addressed as if it were a tradition without a history. Goody and
McNaughton explore educational concerns that are part of the economic,
family, and political organization of life and labor for weavers and black-
smith/sorcerer/sculptors. McNaughton shows how deeply interrelated are the
powers to control power, long training, political reputation, and practical
activities of many sorts. Goody focused on the effects of Daboya apprenticeship, technology, kin, and family ties on economic practice and vice versa. She
too underlines the interconnected, given-together quality of relations of social
economic, political, and educational aspects of social life. The complex practices described in these ethnographies belie characterizations of apprenticeship
as simple mechanical reproduction of craft production processes. They raise
questions about the social constitution of persons and practices in historical
and political-economic terms for which social practice theory offers analytic
resources.

Indeed, it might be argued that accounts of craft practices with apprenticeship embedded in them capture everyday life and learning in a single social field. But it is not that simple – there is an abrupt disjunction here: When the force of these texts is descriptive, not apparently dependent on relations beyond those encompassed within the ethnographic purview, they describe social practice in relational terms. When the force of the text falls into a more abstract theoretical register we are back in familiar dualist dilemmas. For instance, in his classical account Meyer Fortes gives a rich and analytic description of Tallensi education. After the fact it is fit into a frame revealing this as a "primitive" versus some putative "civilized" educational arrangement. The meanings in Fortes' work depending on whether both sides of the polar opposition are in view at the same time (Meyer Fortes 1949). Studies of craft apprenticeship as context-embedded everyday practice easily become the concrete, uncreative, limited pole of a binary politics of educational distinction in theoretical terms that divide "formal" education from "informal" education. For that matter, given that economic issues are more salient in these ethnographies than in most accounts of learning, they are also caught up in disjunctions between circumscribed one-sided descriptions of "informal *economy*" and the binary politics of formal/informal economy distinctions, which play out much like their educational counterparts. In short, the theoretical conception of *apprenticeship* in these studies is not so much transformed by descriptions of its part in complexly interwoven practices, as crammed schizophrenically into a conventional theoretical template. This requires further discussion.

We can begin by asking how ethnographers identify instances of apprenticeship. Often the word apprenticeship is preceded by the word "craft." I have found Raymond Williams (1976) discussion in *Keywords* of historical distinction-making among uses of terms like artisan, art, craft, industry, and science vividly helpful in suggesting how "apprenticeship" carries along a long historical burden (Lave 2011: 23–5).

Some quite odd entities have been called crafts, sometimes I think, because they appear to be learned through something like "apprenticeship," rather than the other way around. This seems to be the case whether judgments are being made by anthropologists or by local practitioners. Indeed, it appears that everything and the kitchen sink can be claimed to be a craft learned through apprenticeship, ranging from shamanism (Dow 1989), to railroad union work (Gamst 1989) and high steel construction (Haas 1989), to West African blacksmithing (McNaughton 1988). Tailors in Liberia naming crafts include blacksmithing and weaving, but also taxi driving. Midwifery in Yucatan (Jordan 1989), bartending in the United States (Beach 1993), and intricate traditional sweet-making in Japan (Kondo 1992) are learned through apprenticeship. Becoming a zen priest in Japan (Johnson 1988) and becoming a political candidate (Graves 1989) or a doctor (Becker 1961) is taken to be a matter of apprenticeship as well.[5] This raises questions, addressed later, about professions as sites of apprenticeship. These are remarkably different enterprises, with remarkably different products and trajectories.

Goody and her associates have argued for the principle that apprentice-like training of workers goes on in many kinds of productive organizations – in a domestic division of labor, in crafts, or in more functionally differentiated occupational specialisms (Goody 1982). This argument rests on distinctions among divisions of labor it should be noted (rather than, say, relations of production, cultures of class consumption, or cosmological relations). But this argument challenges conventional limits on apprenticeship of the sort that by most economic analyses separate classes and kinds of production and corresponding means of inducting labor into them.

If there is no exclusive link anchoring apprenticeship in craft production and no obvious limits to what may be designated a "craft," what else provides a basis of agreement that leads observers to call something "apprenticeship"? There certainly seems to be one – the producers of ethnographic accounts seem comfortably sure that they know apprenticeship when they see it: Many would agree with Coy's conclusion that: "Apprenticeship is an endeavor that displays more similarity cross-culturally and historically than any of us originally realized" (1989: xv). Ethnographies of blacksmithing, weaving, potting, or tailoring are often about products, ways of producing them and ways of learning to produce them labeled "crafts" by Euro-centric references to the guilds of pre-capitalist Europe, I suspect. Here is a sample of introductory comments about apprenticeship from various ethnographers in Coy's edited volume on *Apprenticeship* (1989).

In a larger sense, apprenticeship is a social pattern of enculturation or cultural transmission; a model of intensely directed education in the skills, role and ideology of a professional craftsman. It draws its potency as an educational form from pre-industrial patterns of vocational initiation, though it is sometimes adapted to employment training in modern corporate organization and industry. It is a highly personalized set of social and educational relationships that defines the roles of teacher and learner, sharply segregated from the relations of kinship. (Singleton 1989: 13)

---

[5] There is an account of *English Town Crafts: A survey of Their development from Early Times to the Present Day* published in 1949, with among other things a list of British crafts at that time. It includes (but I have been quite selective):

> stained glass makers, masons, bell-founders, cabinet makers, clock-makers, carpet makers, silversmiths, glassblowers, potters, musical instrument makers, weavers and clothiers, drapers, producers of horsehair, hatters, skinners, tanners, cordwainers, bookbinders, parchment-makers, paper-makers, printers and engravers, coach builders, shipwrights, boat builders, chain makers, fletchers, gunsmiths, racket-makers, the makers of cricket bats and balls, footballs, billiard tables. (Wymer 1949)

Apprenticeship, in its broadest sense, has been defined as the process or period of learning a trade, art, or calling by practical experience under skilled workers (Webster's Dictionary). (Buechler 1989: 32)

Apprenticeship is a complex and multi-faceted concept. It clearly involves education, social relations, and economics, and it suggests an ideology of life and work associated with a specialized role. Apprenticeship involves at least two persons and probably many more than two. The two principals are a person possessing specialized skills and a person who wishes to acquire and develop those skills for him/herself. Apprenticeship thus consists of a social relationship. And inasmuch as the specialized skills sought by the apprentice are often, perhaps always, valuable, apprenticeship has an economic dimension" (Coy 1989: 1).

In this paper, *apprentice* means any neophyte beginning and learning an occupation either with or without a formal program of apprenticeship and the specific label of "apprentice." (Gamst 1989: 65).

Goody, comments in her capacity as reviewer and synthesizer of a number of these studies:

Like most of the contributions to this collection, my substantive papers on apprenticeship were written without specifically examining how it should be defined. Several different definitions are in fact used in these papers, and this did force me to confront the question: What is apprenticeship? I think all would agree with the broadest of these; "an apprentice is someone who doesn't know, learning from someone who does." (Goody 1989: 234)

The conclusions of the Vai and Gola apprenticeship analysis stand in conflict with this pronouncement (Lave 2011). Goody (along with many others) reduces apprenticeship to an individual relationship between unequally knowledgeable persons, to a teacher and a learner, to familiar dualist assumptions. These definitional efforts also excise apprenticeship from its historical social relations, separating persons learning from active engagement in their ongoing lives. The divided recourse to "individual learning" and mostly appeals to pseudo-feudal "historical precedents," suggests a subject/world separation also characteristic of the binary theory of formal and informal education.

Apprenticeship Is Not …

These scholars do not include all kinds of induction into participation in adult labors under the rubric "apprenticeship." Practices of negative definition appear frequently in identifying instances of apprenticeship. The determined distinction between "formal" education and "the rest" asserts that above all apprenticeship is not schooling. Anthropologists further distinguish their investigations of apprenticeship from the reproduction of social and cultural practices from one generation to the next including early family socialization.

(Perhaps this is why everyone feels compelled to stipulate that boys are apprenticed to masters who are "not-kin.") It is not about all times of life: It is not about children, it is not about adults, it is about moving into "adult society," into grown up life-work – occupations. Apprenticeship is not about the everyday sites or subjects that "everybody" learns, because it is part of specialized occupations, and it is not happening where everybody does the same thing, e.g., in "pre-market" subsistence farming. (Think of Fortes' account of Tallensi education.) This brings us to another set of distinctions in which apprenticeship is embedded: apprenticeship may not be schooling, but it is not "socialization" either.

Apprenticeship seemed to me to be brought under the reified rubric of "education" to the degree to which it is "rescued" from being only an uninflected part of everyday life. The distinction is carved out between what everyone shares – the stuff of cultural transmission and the reproduction of society generally – and "education," that is, processes of teaching and learning that compare, rank, and form superior knowers who leave behind the ordinary. Further, apprenticeship is more easily reified as the way in to some not-everyday locus of activity – a specialized occupation, specialized and not part of the ordinary world of subsistence farming, domestic production, or social-ization. In my experience, doubt about the educational force of apprenticeship increases (for those who subscribe to formal distinctions between "kinds" of education) with emphasis on apprenticeship as integral, ordinary, and situated in the practice of which it is part. The more ordinary and unexceptional it is, the more it is assumed to be "not real" learning but, from the perspective of the formal/informal theory, "merely socialization."

How does apprenticeship get affirmed as different from socialization in the apprenticeship ethnographies? Goody continues straight on from defining apprenticeship as a matter of one who does not know learning from one who does, by posing a question:

[I]t struck me as odd, given this conception, that none of these accounts is about children learning from parents. For most of human history virtually all learning has been of this kind ... Thus we need to ask what it is that makes us implicitly set aside this paradigmatic case of learning when considering apprenticeship without comment or explanation. And if we all agree that apprenticeship is about learning from an expert, what is special about apprentice learning, and why is it special? (1989: 234)[6]

---

[6] The discussion that follows concentrates on a socialization–apprenticeship division. But it is important that Goody also asks what separates apprenticeship from learning from an expert. This is one more division that helps define apprenticeship studies by circumscribing them in concep-tual terms: a distinction of social class at base, between professional expert and master, mental and manual labor; knowledge and skill. Both craft and profession are included in notions of distinctive adult occupational specialization but at the same time they are rigorously

Socialization in families is something that must happen to all small children; followed by kinds of learning supposed to transform children through schooling/or apprenticeship in specialized preparation for differentiated adult occupations (Parsons [1956], of course, offered a classic example). The evolutionary character (from non- to in-formal to formal) of this enterprise lies in claims that the progression moves from some putative undifferentiated everyday state, e.g., of families that produce children, education, and subsistence in one undifferentiated process, to greater and greater differentiation among them. Claims that apprenticeship is a matter of specialized, not general knowledge and skill derive not only from the notion that it is embedded in occupations that are by definition specialized, but because, as well, apprenticeship is distinguished from generalized socialization as "specialized" education.

Examples can easily be found, as Goody and Graves discuss "adult socialization":

> Discussions of socialization tend to centre on the years of infancy and early childhood, and to concern the character of early emotional and 'caretaking' relationships and the learning of impulse control. Not only are those areas of special interest to the psychologist, but clearly, with the learning of language and the basic cultural repertoire of custom, gesture, and idiom, this period is a vital one for the formation of adult character in a given society. If, however, we are concerned with the technical skills and role structure of this same society, we must give more emphasis to the context of learning in later childhood and adolescence. [thus the importance of fostering and apprenticeship]. (Goody 1969: 51)

> Attention to socialization has a long history in the social sciences, although the serious recognition of adult socialization is fairly recent. The Freudian influence apparently so directed our attention to the childhood and early adolescent years, that we assumed that adult socialization was merely an unfolding of processes begun in childhood. Consequently, we neglected the fact of adult socialization. (Graves 1989: 53)

---

distinguished: apprenticeship is always a matter of acquiring technical skills – read "manual, material, hands-on facility."
   Buechler (1989), offers a sort of negative instance:

> In both the neo-classical and Marxist views the skilled component is doomed to shrink progressively, taken over, perhaps, by a small number of specialists whose role is important, particularly in the initial setting up of a factory. From this perspective, apprenticeship is essentially an anachronism to be replaced by general education for basic literacy, mathematical skills, enculturation into basic work routines, and in addition, a short period of narrow on-the-job training for the mass of workers and longer periods of formal institutional education for the specialists. (In Coy: 32)

The division that equates mental-labor learning with schooling, and manual skill with craft production, even defined as "tacit" knowledge, in the certainty that "they" cannot talk about what they do, is another of the boundaries that prescribes the subject matter for studies of apprenticeship.

A standard outline for a treatise on something confidently identified as apprenticeship should now make better sense:[7] it must deal with the social evolutionary question of how differentiated is apprenticeship from family social-ization and domestic life: this generates discussions of payments for entry, rituals of exit, forms of recruitment, and the relations of kinship between master and apprentice (or not). Such a scenario responds to a question about how much apprenticeship is differentiated from the moral, general relations of socialization (Is the master *in loco parentis*? Does apprenticeship involve character build-ing?), and how differentiated it is from school. This generally has pejorative connotations because the question is asked from a schoolish perspective focused on teaching, which masters might not do well enough, and on concerns that what is to be learned is a matter of techniques for producing objects rather than "abstract" knowledge. It assumes apprenticeship is to learn a specialized form of production, so describes that production process; and that apprentices move "up" as they get older, so pegging changing skills to changing ages or life stages.

On the other hand, if nothing else, in an evolutionary argument apprentice-ship cannot be fully disentangled from either the everyday ordinary backdrop of family or of work. This very "primitivism" provides an opportunity, how-ever awkwardly taken up, to take learning-in-everyday life as the object of study. These assumptions, I have tried to show, deeply affect what is and is not said in discussions of apprenticeship, and reasons for taking an interest in it in the first place.

Under these circumstances, with negative definitions supplying boundaries, Goody's is a good question as to why we never talk about the socialization of children in families as a matter of "apprenticeship," for there is nothing about "apprenticeship" – described as someone who wants to know learning from someone who already knows – that would draw a line between it and child-rearing.

Perhaps the more urgent problem lies in characterizing *any* relationship of which learning is a part in these direly dualistic terms. Taken-for-granted images of one full and one empty party in ethnographic studies of apprentice-ship (consider again Goody's broad definition of apprentices, novices, and children as "one who doesn't know learning from one who does"), separates in polar terms "those who know" or those who have the authority to inculcate, from "those who don't" – inculcatees (in the language of Bourdieu and Passeron [1990]). It leads to easy equations of masters to teachers and

---

[7] Singleton tries his hand at summing up a "culture of apprenticeship" that "describes a common base for craft apprenticeship in a variety of settings and crafts. Some of the commonalities include the emphasis on craft discipline, concerns for character-building, avoidance of kinfolk as masters, and the exchange of labor for education in a craft. 'Stealing the master's secrets' seems to be a widely shared explicit theme of apprenticeship" (in Coy 1989: 29).

apprentices to pupils. (I have argued against this in my ethnography of tailoring in Liberia [2011].) The economic–education synthesis examples at the beginning of this chapter also do this. If you can only know or not know, it empties the middle where we all dwell, in the midst of apprenticeship, a matter of partially knowing, where partial knowing is differently connected as it is made in and through other situations. Such a dichotomy makes no allowance for what I take to be the actual, ubiquitous state of affairs: that no one ever entirely falls into one category or the other; that the complexity and multiplicity of what is brought to bear in any given situation where learning is in process is fundamental to that process in the first place. Learning must be characteristic of "those who know" as well as of "those who don't."[8]

Anthropologists of Apprenticeship, on Learning

A major strength of ethnographies of apprenticeship is their commitment to the interconnections of economic and educational arrangements captured in a semi-seamless way, as they are given together in practice. The connection between particular economic and educational practices and learning as part of that practice loosens and disappears when the discussion turns to talk about "learning."[9]

In *Situated Learning* we characterized learning in ways intended to emphasize the relational character of participants' engagement in practice and the practice as in part composed of its participants, as "legitimate peripheral participation in communities of practice." We discussed misconceptions about

---

[8] The dichotomy [between learner/teacher, empty/full, is deeply ingrained in notions that learning is an effect of knowledge *transmission*, which in turn reflects an uncritical concern with the reproduction of social order. (Reciprocally, the latter leads to the claim that what is being reproduced is "adult society.") The argument goes something like this: What is there to reproduce? That which is already known. Why is learning a matter of filling up an empty vessel? Because those who have filled up *are* the adult society. Children, in such a view, are the underdone, incomplete versions of their parents (or apprentices of their masters). Assumptions like these lead to stage theories of skill acquisition, and to novice–expert theories of learning as linear steps from beginning to "end." There are several points in this perennial but vulnerable argument where it may be broken up. One anthropological means has been to call into question that questionable relation of children to adults as only unformed and incomplete. In Christina Toren's (1993) ethnographic studies in Fiji she shows in detail how Fijian children's day-to-day participation in ongoing community life involves them in distinctive relations, activities, and values that are found nowhere in adult life except as made, and made part, of adult life through childhood relations.

[9] The anthropologists whose work is discussed in this chapter do not all share the same theoretical perspective, e.g., Cooper takes a Marxist perspective, Kondo a post-structuralist one, and Bartusiak a phenomenological view. But with the possible exception of Johnson (1989) (or cultural assumptions of Zen Buddhism?) when addressing issues concerning learning, their differences seem to disappear into the "general wisdom" on the subject, perhaps because of the disciplinary hegemony that displaces "learning" to the astonishingly monolithic professional domain of (educational) psychology.

apprenticeship common in studies thereof,[10] and the striking differences in technologies, recruitment, master–apprentice relations, and the organization of learning activity in different specific settings (1991: chapter 3). We drew on different studies to illustrate different facets of our argument. These included Jordan's research on midwifery in Yucatan (1989), my work on Vai and Gola tailors, Hutchins' research on US Navy Quartermasters (1993), Marshall's research on butchers' apprentices in the United States (1972) and Cain's research on Alcoholics Anonymous (1991).

Both Lave and Wenger (1991) and Goody (1989) assumed that ethnographic studies of apprenticeship are focused on learning. I now think that this is not the case. In fact, they are predominantly discussions of *education* as the transmission and reproduction of culture. That is, they presuppose that learning is brought about by, and unproblematically duplicates, the transmission of knowledge or culture. "I went to Daboya to learn about the *teaching* of weaving, as an example of *institutionalized 'informal' education*" Goody explains (1982: 50 emphasis mine). In these studies there are myriad references to apprenticeship as training, to learning in the passive terms of adaptation or acquisition of things to be learned. There are characteristic slips within sentences that set out to address learning but dissolve into instruction, e.g., Kondo "*Learning* through observation (. . . literally seeing and learning) was, and often still is, the primary mode of *instruction*" (1990: 238). Or Beuchler, "We shall argue for a more contextual approach in which ways of *acquiring* technical and related skills are examined in conjunction with alternative modes of *transmission* under particular conditions. We hope that such an approach will lead to more sophisticated models of *learning*" (in Coy 1989: 31).

Michael Coy introduces the concept thus:

[Apprenticeship] training has a readily discernible character. It is personal, hands-on, and experiential. Apprenticeship training is utilized where there is more to performing the role at hand than reading a description of its content can communicate. Apprenticeships seem to be associated with specializations that contain some element that cannot be communicated, but can only be experienced. (1989: 1–2)

---

[10] These assumptions included: (1) Claims that apprenticeship only occurs with feudal craft production. We joined Goody (*From Craft to Industry* (1982)) in arguing that apprenticeship is found with a diversity of modes of production. (2) Master–apprentice relations are diagnostic of apprenticeship. We argued that masters were important for legitimizing apprentices' presence and only partial participation; as concrete exemplars of what the apprentices are there to become; as *in loco parentis*; but not as the direct or literal transmitter of skill or knowledge. (3) Learning in apprenticeship "offers opportunities for nothing more complex than reproducing task performances in routinized ways." In the present essay this is identified as a key political article of faith in theories of learning, and therefore in need of investigation at several different levels. (4) Apprenticeship has some standard or typical degree of organization. Clearly it varies from only after-the-fact recognition to formal contractual arrangements; from years of preparation for a lifetime of craft production, to a few months of preparation for a temporary occupation.

Goody, as we have seen, proposed that apprenticeship boils down to "a role which is indigenously defined as someone who doesn't know, learning from someone who does" (1989: 255 the author's italics omitted), and "apprenticeship–in the sense of working with and learning from an expert outside the natal family" (Coy 1989: 239) "learning through practice, which is the essence of apprenticeship" (Coy 1989: 254).

Here is a brief list of problems with conceptions of learning in the ethnographies of apprenticeship. First, I am struck by the pristine division between those who know and those who do not, a simplification that enables transmission theories to prevail.[11] Second, the ways in which studies of apprenticeship distinguish what masters do from what teachers do in schools points up the school-based perspective from which it could conceivably make sense to observe that masters are "not-teachers." Nor do such distinctions speak to the issue of whether *learning* is properly thought of in terms of transmission.[12] "Learning from" is a way to reposition "learning" as an effect of transmission. Next, we just saw how apprenticeship often comes to be conceptualized in developmental stages, pegged to age or generalized stages of maturation, or to "levels" of difficulty of what is to be learned, or to correspondences between them.[13] Whether constituted in spurious terms or not, we must ask what they are stages "of." Not learning, I think. Rather, what is being described in "stages" are in fact arrangements by authoritative others *for* learning, not stages *of* learning. There are two additional points: Learning is conceived as an individual matter, as discussions focus on an apprentice working with a master. And finally, technical skills are to be learned through mechanisms of

---

[11] The Japanese sweets makers' concept of the development of an apprentice (Kondo 1990) in some respects echoes the empty/full metaphor of simple bipolar notions of teaching/learning. The ideal is one portion for one person; and that an apprentice or journeyman has as yet only a part of a portion. At the same time there is another image: that of the young as rough and hard, and maturation involving a kind of scouring down, or rounding off, of the rough edges. Maturity, then, requires suffering and hard work to "polish" the person, the person's skill, etc.

[12] Masters are often assumed to be slackers as teachers. At best they are assumed to be teachers, though not in the same sense as teachers in schools. John Singleton (1989: 26) on a master not being equivalent to a teacher: "When an apprentice presumes to ask the master a question, he will be asked why he has not been watching the potter at work, where the answer would be obvious ... A master is simply not expected to teach craft skills in didactic instruction. It is as improper to ask that he do so, as it is considered ineffective in transmitting the craft skills. Teaching, or instruction, is the provision of a context for long observation and persistent rote practice of basic skills. Standards for such participant/observation are more arduous than those generally employed by cultural anthropologists in their ethnographic field research."

Cooper (1989) attributes the "insufficiency" of teaching to the effects of increasing proletarianization of labor in Hong Kong workshops.

[13] This seems to be based on salient dimensions for ordering pupils' lives in schools. This is not to say that age and/or the relative difficulty of work tasks are not relevant in any given case; but care is needed in specifying the basis for ordering descriptions of apprenticeship in this way.

demonstration, observation, mimesis, trial and error, and repetition. Coy describes learning in reduced terms as "ways of knowing" and "learning to see," both of which pertain to hands-on production skills. Learning mechanisms appear to be closely tied to "skill transmission."

Goody is one of the ethnographers of apprenticeship who tries to explore corresponding conceptions of "learning" in the field of cognitive psychology.[14] She focuses on schema theory and the acquisition of schematic mental representations of concepts through interaction in a (Vygotsky prompted) "zone of proximal development." Again, we encounter a discussion of how transmission occurs rather than learning:

> This [zpd] refers to the "space" between what a child can do when working jointly with an experienced adult, and what he can do on his own. Normal everyday learning involves the child doing things with more experienced people – adults or older children – who "set the agenda" – line up goals and means–and carry out most of the activity ... The term *scaffolding* has been used by Brunner [sic] and his colleagues to refer to the process by which those who are already expert, structure an activity so that novices can participate. (1989: 235–6, italics the author's)

Goody observes that cognitive theory fits conventional approaches to the study of apprenticeship quite well. Most of the apprenticeship research discussed here is characterized by an easy association of apprenticeship with a naturalized cognitive view of learning. Together they inhabit the same (theoretical) world view. Early in my work on apprenticeship I certainly agreed. But I have become increasingly critical: *Cognition in Practice* was a sustained attempt to grapple critically with the dualist assumptions of cognitive theory that begin with divisions of mind and body, subject and world, and assume social life is a matter of social reproduction (cf. Lave 1988). Such assumptions stand in contrast and conflict with those of social practice theory, which now seems to me a preferable perspective.

Apprenticeship as a First-Person Project

It might seem by now that if apprenticeship studies are only about teaching, instruction, and transmission, we should simply despair of encountering "learning" in complex given-in-practice terms in the literature on apprenticeship. But anthropologists of apprenticeship do have something to say about learning, as opposed to transmission/inculcation – when they talk about taking up apprenticeships themselves. Somehow the most vivid accounts of changing embodied knowledge come from anthropologists telling what it was like to be

---

[14] For a major theoretical/ethnographic appraisal of the implications of craft practice for cognitive theory see Charles Keller and Janet Keller, *Cognition and Tool Use: The Blacksmith at Work* (1996).

an apprentice when they tried it themselves. Several anthropologists have written, at Coy's urging, about apprenticing themselves as part of their fieldwork. His intention was to assess apprenticeship as a field method. Having tried it, Johnson, Cooper, Coy, Dilley, and others also have something to say about participating as learners (as does Kondo from the point of view of masters and part-timers with whom she worked in the sweets factory in Tokyo). They talk of being a target of suspicion by others over a period of months initially, periods of boredom, of painful and repetitive body-shaping work (hundreds of table legs, thousands of sake cups [Bartusiak 1975; Singleton 1998]) requiring sustained concentration over a long period of time; feelings of anxiety and self-doubt, and occasional moments of recognition that they have actually changed in the process (e.g., Cooper 1989: 145), often by contrast to others even less competent. Cooper tells a wonderful story:

[M]y boss, under pressure to keep me productively occupied, and not wishing to assign me any work too far beyond my limited capabilities, gave me a piece to work on that had already been begun by someone else. It was really poorly done, and for a while I wondered who was responsible. Slowly, a deja vu took shape; the piece was really familiar. I had started it some three months before. I was shocked. It was all I could do to make the piece look presentable, but by that time I was much better equipped to do so. I was greatly encouraged by the advance of my skill. (Cooper 1989: 145)

Coy comments that "The results of being made a 'real' apprentice are at times comical, frightening, intensely anxious" (Coy 1989: xiv); Cooper that "my anguish was less physical than mental as I struggled with (excuse the expression) carving out a niche for myself in the factory by gaining my fellow workers' respect" (Cooper 1989: 140). Johnson's teacher, a priest at the Tenryu-ji temple of the Rinzai sect of Japanese Zen Buddhism, reminds him of the conflicting feelings and intentions of a beginner at meditation:

The new posture is difficult, and you want to give up. You want to get up and go somewhere else, or do anything else except the one thing you are doing. Your mind wanders. It is difficult to control yourself, to do what you want. You must discipline your will. There are obstacles inside you, and you initially will not want to do what you want to do. "This is important," he cautions me. "You must study more about intention in Zen. This will help you better understand." (Johnson in Coy 1989: 222–3)[15]

We do not hear reports of *masters'* ongoing engagements in learning, but there are very occasional masters' reports of their feelings about their work. These do not sound at all like those of the struggling apprentices. Instead the

[15] All these reports are from or about beginners. These anthropologists do worry about the distorting effects of their "apprenticeship method" of fieldwork on the results of their research. But they do not mention the possible distortions arising from the fact that none of them became a master practitioner. (What would Charles Keller, anthropologist and working blacksmith, say?).

stern, silent artisan, critical of others and contemptuous of outsiders, expresses confidence, pride, identification with his craft and affection for it (Bartusiak 1975: 85–9; Kondo 1990: 229).

Bartusiak, talking about master cabinet makers:[16]

They take great pride in working with their hands in order to directly produce a whole product. They feel pride of accomplishment in both the physical manifestation of what they have done and in the skill with which they have done it. [she describes the challenge of producing a set of drawers that fit perfectly.] Connoisseurs, cabinetmakers, their *shokunin* colleagues and dealers seek out this feature and have a regard for the care and dexterity that goes into perfect drawers that surpasses mere admiration. It is a sensitive awareness and esteem for the skill of the maker and the devotion that he has shown to his work to produce a superb product. . .Pride in a difficult job well done and the esteem of those that can readily understand and appreciate it, is a significant feature of Ojiisan's and Yukio's attitude toward their labors. It also reinforces their identification as *shokunin*. This pride and identification is also manifested in other ways. For instance, Ojiisan and Yukio are, understandably, severe critics both of their own work and that of others. (Bartusiak 1975: 85–7)

. . .This pride in their status molds Ojiisan's and Yukio's attitudes toward others who are not *shokunin*. It is not that they have no respect for other occupations but feel that their own is superior. They have a slightly disdainful attitude toward carpenters and the like, whom they consider to be engaged in relatively unskilled labor. Moreover they are rather contemptuous of salary men. They feel the salary man is tightly bound to a corporate structure where he has no ability to enjoy any personal freedom, and more unfortunately, can obtain no gratification from his labors. (Bartusiak 1975: 88–9)

Kondo, after describing the temper tantrums of the boss, the grumbling resentment of the sweet makers, and the conflicting assessments of each other's actions in the sweet-making shop, switches gears abruptly when she describes hearing from a master craftsperson how he feels about his work. She begins: "I had been working in *wagashi* for only a week or so, and Ohara-san was, quite frankly, a daunting presence. He embodied a stereotype my informants often invoked: the stern, silent, severe artisan. In the factory, he would work for hours without a word, occasionally stalking about to glower at his subordinates as he inspected their creations." One day she asks him about his work:

I was astonished, in the course of our conversation, to see how animated he could be. The gaunt, stiff countenance now assumed a variety of expressions: frowns as he described the hardships of his childhood and his apprenticeship; an air of pride and confidence as he spoke of his craft; a softness, even, as he poetically described the delicate, aesthetic emotions he expressed in his art . . . Long afterwards . . . I began to recall . . . conversations with other artisans, who often spoke in tones of affection and respect for their craft, even for the tools and the materials they used. (Kondo 1990: 229)

---

[16] She conveys a wonderful feel for everyday life/work in the cabinet makers' workshop/home. Her's is not a conventional account of apprenticeship/learning.

These fleeting glimpses of apprenticeship firsthand, leave me wishing for more and feeling cautious about making the following observations: These accounts take one step toward a social understanding of changing participation in everyday practice by taking learners to be more than knowledge acquirers, task masters, or merely skillful knowledge vessels. The accounts by anthropologists-turned-apprentice of their apprenticeships are not disquisitions on tasks, technical skills, or their acquisition. They are principally focused on sustained dilemmas, identity-stakes, fears of being inadequate to the job, and their desires for fellow-workers' respect. They also focus on ways in which what the apprentice is doing is fateful for the apprentice's feelings about him/ herself as he/she is engaged in a process of life transformation. Perhaps those who report their own experiences as apprentices are trying to convey a sense of the relations of identity creation that are inherent in any sustained apprenticeship. A further – important – point is that the feelings reported by apprentices in the process are not conceivably internalized copies of masters' feelings about their own work, or presumably the feelings of masters about their apprentices', transmitted by masters and acquired by watching and imitating masters. They seem more understandable in terms of reaction and resistance to social arrangements for what anthropologists might describe less convincingly as the "transmission" of the "schemata," "representations," or "skills" of the craft. In fact, they involve a painfully-distinguished sense of where the apprentice stands –differently – from masters of the craft. In short, when in this literature the moment arises in which there are possibilities for confronting differences in the relations of apprentices' and masters' engagement with each other and various parts of their craft – when the anthropologists describe a little of what happened to them in their everyday lives – it is worth noting that those experiences are not relayed to us in the terms of transmission or the usual mechanisms of learning. The focus is on the precarious process of producing the craft and its producers, rather than in-principle debate about whether/how today's apprentice will become a copy of yesterday's master.

Social Skill, Identity, and Secrets

The apprenticeship ethnographies almost never limit apprenticeship to technical skill narrowly defined, as we would expect when apprenticeship is approached with assumptions that it represents "informal education." More interestingly, they contain contradictory strands with respect to learning identities. Their accounts of secret knowledge, secret societies and the stealing of secrets from masters, embedded in *descriptions* of apprenticeship contribute to analyses of learning in practice (e.g., McNaughton [1988], quoted earlier).

Discussions of identity are fairly common in ethnographic accounts of apprenticeship. Sometimes they are loosely implied in labeling masters by their crafts, or in saying "he's becoming a master weaver," or a professional craftsman. Sometimes artisanal identities are themselves the subject: Dilley suggests (quoted early in the chapter): "Being a craftsman is more than just a means of securing a livelihood: It is a means also of defining one's moral constitution and social position" (1989: 182). His aim is to consider "a different facet of apprenticeship than in more usual economic or vocational training terms: "that of apprenticeship and the transmission of a body of lore that encapsulates the social meanings and cultural explanations of the weavers' social identity and conceptions of their craft." (1989: 183). The chapter in which the master's feelings are described in Kondo's book is called "The Aesthetics and Politics of Artisanal Identities."

Academic notions of "identity" are no doubt over-used and under-specified, but the point of interest here is the opposite: it is unusual to find conceptions of identity appearing in and around efforts to theorize about or carry out studies of learning. Indeed, it is rather unlikely that issues of identity (other than social labels presumed already in place), arise in studies of school learning (novices/ experts?) or children's learning (even when this takes off from the metaphor-ical use of "apprenticeship" in ways akin to those suggested by Goody in discussing "the zone of proximal development").[17]

One ubiquitous characteristic of ethnographies of apprenticeship is that they contrast skill *and* something else: identity is one of those things, but if not that, lore, or general codes of behavior, or roles; something social, or cultural, or a matter of character, or (unfortunate distinction), just whatever gets learned that is not economically important (like the empty secrets Coy talks about).

(Emphasis in quotes below, mine.)

COOPER:	Apprenticeship has as its function "to instruct not only in technical skills *but also* in the appropriate deportment, shared assumptions, behaviors and values (i.e., culture) of one's future fellow workers. (1989: 137)
COY:	*Two specific kinds* of insights came out of the apprenticeship experience: those relating to technology, *and* those relating to the smiths' social relations. (1989: 121)
HAAS:	... initiation into the group involves tests that will assure the development of a trustworthy competence. The evaluations are typically based on *two criteria* – the explicit mastery of skills and techniques particular to the work, *and* the adoption of a related set of implicit qualities that the initiate is expected to display as an aspiring member." (1989: 89)

---

[17] E.g., in Rogoff's (1990) *Apprenticeship in Thinking: Cognitive Development in Social Context* "identity" does not appear to be relevant in discussing small children's engagement with adults in learning. Eckert's *Jocks and Burnouts* (1989) is a rich exception to this point.

GRAVES: . . . changes from one stage to another. . .involve changes in technical
                 knowledge. But *more than that*, the stages represent changes in
                 relationships between the apprentice and others who participate in
                 the training. (1989: 54)
SINGLETON: Mastery of the technical craft skills are a goal of the educational
                 process, *but* the apprentice should *also* absorb the professional
                 values of the craftsman. (1989: 29)

In each case the social or "esoteric" aspects of craft practice are classified separately from the utilitarian/material world, carefully designating what belongs to each. Indeed, the social/technical split is scrupulously maintained as it is woven through discussions of apprentices who learn occupational skills, and who also learn how to behave, or learn valued but "economically useless" lore. Such a division is prejudicial to the project of understanding learning in apprenticeship as social practice.

There are two ways in which the ethnographic studies conceptualize learning identities. I will discuss them in turn, in order to then consider how they have different implications for theorizing learning. All this is intricately interconnected with a peculiar topic that crops up in these studies as hardly anywhere else. For sandwiched in between an economics of craft production and labor preparation on the one hand, and, though rarely, a psychology of learning on the other, apprenticeship also gets embedded in discussions of craft secrets, secrecy, and that theme noted as typical of apprenticeship studies by Singleton – the stealing of craft secrets by apprentices (1989: 24).

The fascination that craft secrecy seems to hold for anthropologists is reflected in the variety of explanations they offer for it. Kondo suggests that Japanese apprentice sweet makers were "supposed to . . . learn through stealing, learn on the sly, for one could not necessarily count on formalized instruction" (1990: 238), her way of accounting for the "lack" of sufficient instruction, a school-based perspective. These range from sociologists' suggestions that secrecy/stealing of secrets is about impression management by novices or attempts to control "backstage" by experts (e.g., Haas 1989), to economists who propose that it is a gate-keeping mechanism for monopolizing critical knowledge and hence controlling the size, profit, and survival of communities of producers (e.g., Clark Kerr 1964). Anthropologists talk more about notions that esoteric power requires careful transmission, and only to those who are prepared (e.g., McNaughton 1988).

One line of argument about guarded secrets assimilates apprenticeship to an initiation that happens to have economic aspects and consequences, equates guilds or groups of craftspersons with secret societies, and sees apprenticeship as a matter of transforming identity and gaining membership in an exclusive and homogeneous "brotherhood." Close parallels are drawn between initiation into adulthood and apprenticeship into a craft. While the control of specialized knowledge ("secrets"), access to apprenticeships, and access to tools are viewed as gate-keeping mechanisms for creating identity within the craft and excluding "outsiders":

part of education is into craft secrets, of quite varied kinds ... Taken together, the secrets of the craft might seem profound and intricate or trivial and relatively meaningless. It is not the content of craft secrets that is so important as that there are "secrets" at all. What is implied to those outside the craft is that there is specialized knowledge that is controlled by those within the craft ... "privileged knowledge ... What this privileged knowledge provides for practitioners goes beyond practical aspects of production and creates a sense of identity, a notion of distinctiveness, a community and membership in it ... The capacity of a craft community to control the secrets of its work has an enormous bearing on the distinctiveness and survival of the craft. (Coy 1989: 3)

Discussion of secret knowledge, acquired through "initiation" into membership in an exclusive special group, grows out of and/or produces a unitary notion of identity as membership in a homogeneous closed community. This is a role-theory notion of identity – the whole person is assumed to be shaped or constrained or coerced into occupying a preexisting slot as a sharing member of a closed and exclusive group.

The complex and conflicting interests and predicaments reflected in the anthropologists' accounts of their own apprenticeships are not captured in the view of identity that arises when secrecy is explained in this fashion. And yet: If some place emphasis on acquiring access to secrets as an increasing sign of membership, there are other discussions of craft secrecy in which secret knowledge "belongs" exclusively to masters and must be stolen by apprentices. Such accounts suggest a process of opposition, conflict, tension, hierarchy, and reluctant admission of apprentices to "the club," if such exists. Stealing secrets from masters is not the only way in which conflicting interests are characterized in this research. On the whole, anthropologists who take such a view do not have trouble talking about conflictual aspects of apprenticeship. This might not be so surprising in ethnographic work that takes conflict and the open-endedness of social life for granted. Kondo suggests that master sweet makers use stories about how much they endured and how hard apprenticeship was, how unreasonable their masters, in part as a means of marking and justifying their position at the top of a social hierarchy of which their listeners, apprentices and part-time workers, fall below. Herzfeld's study of craft and apprenticeship in Crete takes mutual suspicion and mistrust as fundamental to relationships between masters and apprentices (Herzfeld 2004).

Other ethnographic studies also recognize that deep tensions and conflicts inflect relations of apprenticeship: Goody (1989), quoted in this chapter, emphasized relations of conflict and distrust between masters and apprentices, not just as a quirk of life in Daboya but in structural terms. Coy sums up this basic character of conflicting interests:

Apprenticeship is at one time the means of perpetuating the craft and the means of destroying its power. It is in this context that specialists' social relations become an essential aspect of the apprentice's education. Apprentices are necessary if these skills are to be perpetuated in the next generation, and at the same time they are the most serious threat to the control of specialized knowledge by the craft. (Coy 1989: 4)

Johnson (also quoted earlier) points to the conflictual intentions pulling an apprentice in different directions – someone who "doesn't want to do what he wants to do."

What should be evident from the above examples is that most accounts of apprenticeship take conflictual relations for granted – *except when talking about learning*, where transmission models prevail. Kondo's work provides a good example. In an argument that takes conflict and multiplicity for granted, her assumptions about learning are directly in line with those described here. Kondo tells us of

pedagogies of the workplace. Like other forms of pedagogy linked to processes of self-realization, artisans' training sometimes began with ... tasks having no apparent relation to their chosen trade. Even when the artisans began to take a more active part in learning appropriate artisanal techniques, there might be little explicit verbal instruction from the master. Learning through observation (*minarai*, literally seeing and learning) was, and often still is, the primary mode of instruction. In more vivid terms, they were supposed to *nusunde oboeru*, learn through stealing, learn on the sly, for one could not necessarily count on formalized instruction. (Kondo 1990: 237–8)

Uncoupling Learning from Teaching

A view of trade secrets and master identities shared over generations does not move away from transmission theories of "learning" merely by virtue of including a notion of identity in the process, or for that matter by including social arrangements for learning. It is quite possible to simply add "identity" to the agenda of things to be transmitted and slip social arrangements into the slot reserved for masters and other transmission instruments. On the other hand, "stealing secrets from masters" does seem to imply recognition of differences between masters and apprentices, conflicts of interest, contradictions, and tensions shaping these relations. This draws into question notions of learning as following simply from craft (identity) transmission. This has the potential to rupture the duplicative peace entailed in views that learning is the reproduced result of transmission.

The ethnographic studies of apprenticeship provide occasional opportunities to question the top-down perspective on learning as merely a result of transmission, and this also ruffles a simple reproductive understanding of learning. Anthropologists point out that apprenticeship studies offer opportunities to address questions about how learning might happen separately from teaching.

But does that imply an understanding of learning in terms other than those of transmission? For Goody probably not:

I would see the special contribution of apprenticeship here as the way it forces us to separate learning from teaching. Precisely because apprenticeship is embedded in activities which are ends in themselves, separate from teaching, it gives us a window on how skills and knowledge are *transmitted through practice*. (Goody 1988: 255; italics mine)

Does evidence against the coincidence of masters' and apprentices' points of view, interests, and ways of doing things break the passive, reproductive character of common views on learning? Yes and no. Herzfeld argues that insubordination is inculcated while being denied by masters in Rethemnos, opening possibilities for more than mere replication of existing practice, which leads to learning how to learn to do things differently.

Care is required: There is a kind of paradox that reminds us of the multiple time frames and analytic levels of social practice: is it not possible to transmit subversive, combative competitive identities reliably, homogeneously, from one generation to another, and without noticeably transforming craft practice? The answer requires that we consider processes of learning in both short and longer terms, and accept the ambiguities that participating in practice is both content and process of producing skill, identity, and what have you. Whether reproduction of practice or changing practice is the intent or effect of various participants, it may well take one to produce the other (and of course vice versa).

I have focused on the significance of master–apprentice conflict as a lever with which to disrupt "learning" as merely the reproductive reception of "transmission." It is a very crude instrument. It is not a good idea to use it to *reduce* notions of complex identity to conflictual facets of identity or assimilate identity to conflictual relations or to one-on-one relations of "the one who knows" and "the one who doesn't."

Conclusions: Ethnographic Openings and Theoretical Closings

Political stances mold, and political implications follow from, assumptions about change and social division. Binary politics with respect to learning embody both. Take them one at a time: Anthropologists engaged in research on apprenticeship do not appear to be concerned about the implications of their work either for challenging or (counter-intuitively) confirming claims that apprenticeship is merely an authoritative means for *reproducing* a craft (Cooper may be an exception here). But in spite of commitments to the theory of formal versus informal education, which makes creativity the exclusive prerogative of a schooled elite, researchers on apprenticeship do raise questions as to whether apprenticeship produces creative/innovative approaches to craft. Interestingly, studies of apprenticeship display a broad range of perspectives concerning innovation in craft production as a part of apprenticeship or master craftsmanship. It is simply an assumed aspect of the art of Mande blacksmiths (McNaughton 1988), for weavers in Sierra Leone (Dilley 1989), and among the Vai and Gola tailors in Monrovia (Holsoe 1984). Japanese apprenticeships emphasize the reproduction of classical models – but also the latter as a means to become able to engage in creative artistry (e.g., Japanese potters described in Singleton 1998). Sometimes there appears to be no relevant stance with respect to innovation (cf. Jordan 1989). It is interesting that high value is placed on "creativity" by anthropologists (e.g., Defeanbaugh [1989] in development economics parlance touting Hausa weaving "innovation" as a prerequisite for economic survival) at the same time as they conceive of apprenticeship in terms of social reproduction via transmission. In spite of widespread ideological commitment to the conservative, continuity-preserving character of apprenticeship as "informal education," these ethnographic accounts do not support notions that apprenticeship is a matter of social reproduction. For purposes of rethinking conceptions of learning this is serious news, but none of the ethnographic accounts takes it up as the basis for a critique of the binary politics that inform theories of learning.

Apprenticeship studies incorporate assumptions that to learn is to move away from some everyday, "ordinary," common basis of social existence, in this way drawing a line between apprenticeship and "general" socialization. These studies do more to support than to challenge the "anti-ordinary" politics of (school-centered) learning theories. Points about this premise have been raised throughout the chapter: The comparison of Goody's research on Daboya weavers and McNaughton's on Mande blacksmiths offers a critique of the naturalized character of "occupations" and of the relation of this notion to assumptions about their specialized character. Specialization is basic to a binary politics of "learning" as a process of moving away from the everyday (Chapter 6 this volume). Arguments (from an apprenticeship-focused stance) about the differences between apprenticeship and early childhood socialization have close relatives in arguments about relations between schooling and apprenticeship, thus the pejorative dismissal of apprenticeship with respect to schooling for its "lack of separation (specialization)" from family relations or socialization processes.

So how can a world divided into elite (more specialized and un-ordinary) and inferior (less specialized, more ordinary) treat professional inculcation as a matter of apprenticeship? I noted (as has Kvale and others) that it is increasingly common to speak of apprenticeship as the basis of education into elite occupational specializations – professions. Goody asks, "What's so particular to apprenticeship about 'learning from an expert?'" The Dreyfus brothers lay out a theory of tacit, apprentice-like training as linear steps to valued endpoints in the knowledge of experts (Dreyfus and Dreyfus 1986). Coy, quoted earlier, distinguished between education where communication "is enough" or where experience is required, and I'll quote him again:

[Apprenticeship] training has a readily discernible character. It is personal, hands-on, and experiential. Apprenticeship training is utilized where there is more to performing the role at hand than reading a description of its content can communicate. Apprenticeships seem to be associated with specializations that contain some element that cannot be communicated, but can only be experienced. (1989: 1–2)

Professions scarcely figured in the discussion about apprenticeship but (perhaps because of the very limited assumptions about processes of learning available to us) we characterize movement into any specialized occupation (including a craft), as movement away from some more ordinary "everyday" state of affairs, toward something less common rather than something that is simply different. The word "specialized" ceases to look like a casual choice of terms; it is a definite, politically-charged claim about relative value and power. "Special" in the sense of "privileged" gets confounded with the specialist and the specialized, and taken out of the "ordinary" complexities of social existence not so designated. Whether craft or profession is under discussion there seems to be a single understanding of trajectories of learning (movement away from the common, ordinary and everyday toward the exclusively special). (Chapter 6 returns to this issue.) When Goody asks "what's special about apprenticeship if it merely involves learning from an expert?" her implicit answer may well be, "Nothing." This is an unexpected irony, after all the social-political-cultural-historical distinction-making documented in this chapter. It is clear evidence of how easily we bracket off questions about learning from its situated production.

Turning to apprenticeship studies themselves: In what sense have the studies of apprenticeship invited exploration of learning as a matter of everyday social practice? If in ethnographic studies of apprenticeship anthropologists had analyzed their own theoretical perspectives, they might have arrived at concerns about the implications of such theory in general, with its propensities for producing and justifying mythical social hierarchies in ways that have (had) inimical social consequences. But with the few exceptions discussed as they arose earlier in the chapter, ethnographers of apprenticeship have not seriously criticized the theory of learning on which their work depends. However, some of their converging emphases, perspectives, analytic questions, and findings together do flag intriguing discrepancies between theoretical prescription and apprenticeship practices, disturbing different facets of that perspective to varying degrees.

My nominees for most interesting discrepancies within ethnographic descriptions of apprenticeship include: (1) Ethnographies of apprenticeship offer discrepant views about "identity," sometimes in the same account: one about the transmission of shared roles and common membership, the other about long struggles involving conflicting interests, points of view, and feelings between apprentices and masters, and through the course of apprenticeship. (2) To argue, as several do, that close descriptions of apprenticeship require a separation of learning from teaching is promising (until it gets reframed as proposing different modes of transmission, rather than granting an independent life to notions of learning). Both of these address critically the issue of education as social reproduction or historical practice. (3) There are startling differences between first person accounts of apprenticeship and third person accounts of what and how "the apprentice" learns. (4) Another disjunction is to be found when descriptions of complex social (economic, political, historical, cultural) arrangements for learning stand in tension with conventional theoretical claims that assign *a priori* binary opposed agendas re learning, or different "modes of education" to higher and lower classes, genders, races, generations and contexts. (5) Long-term transformations of identities seem important to discussions of apprenticeship, sounding more like the transformational projects of social practice than the minutes' worth of mental exercise characteristic of psychological theories of learning. (6) As it has been shown that school-centered perspectives shape intrusively the agendas, values, expectations, and categories of analysis for studies of apprenticeship, surely anthropologists could worry about this particular variety of ethnocentrism, one that takes Western class-cultural institutions and their academic, theoretical apparatuses as the orienting, canonical source of assumptions about what apprenticeship should (fail to) be like.

This exercise in detecting conflicting possibilities is not just any "wish" list, of course, but reflects my account of apprenticeship among Vai and Gola tailors (2011) and anticipates the social practice-based account of everyday life and learning that has followed in the years since. I view both my flawed research on Vai and Gola tailors' apprenticeship and the ethnographic studies under discussion in this chapter as demonstrations of the value of ethnographic research, not because anyone gets it right in the first place (were that even possible) but because the ethnographic accounts confront us with ongoing practice in persistent, potentially instructive ways. They are bracing invitations to a searching critical look at theoretical assumptions and the conclusions that inform them.

4   Teaching as Learning, in Practice

* * * * *

Teaching as Learning in Practice began life as the Sylvia Scribner Award lecture of Division C: Learning and Instruction of the American Educational Research Association at their Annual Meeting, April 1995 in San Francisco. It was published in *Mind, Culture, Activity* (Volume 3 (3): 149–64) in 1996. For an audience of education researchers it seemed useful to address the way in which social practice theory offers a way to analyze learning in/as practice in quite different historical periods and educational practices. So, the chapter begins with ethnographic examples of apprenticeship that inquire into learning as part of (and made possible by) ongoing participation in becoming master tailors in Liberia, and law practitioners in nineteenth-century Egypt (Mitchell 1988 [1991]). The chapter ends with a third example – US high school students' changing participation in an American high school.

It is common for researchers whose professional identities are located in school practice (and theory) to insist that school is so different from craft apprenticeship that ethnographic research on apprenticeship could not possibly be relevant to understanding what goes on in school teaching (and learning).[1] This chapter develops theoretical and empirical arguments to confront common assumptions that learning in a school is fundamentally different from learning everywhere else, not by arguing that apprenticeship is (or is not) "really" like schooling but by arguing that decontextualized characterizations of learning are an inadequate basis for addressing the question.

This chapter is all about learners learning rather than learners being taught. Because, as it tries to show, the latter is neither necessary or sufficient to produce the first. Thus, the discussion of social practice theory in the middle of the chapter focuses particularly on questions about how participants, in their relations with each other, engage in dividing, separating, relating and interrelating what they are learning as they move across the different contexts in which they are producing their changing identities. That learners are thus engaged has implications for what it means to be a high school teacher. Learners' collective conduct across their everyday contexts are conditions that govern the possibility for teaching in high

---

[1] Such arguments often make abstract claims that decontextualize learners and knowledge – extracting them from everyday life. (See Chapter 2.)

schools in the United States. To contribute in (skillful, effective) ways to learning must often require teachers to learn how to engage the collective identity-making (and other) relations of their students in their practices as learners learning.

I aspire to do to conventional theoretical/ideological accounts of "education" what Marx did to Adam Smith and Ricardo's accounts of political economy. That is, to analyze educational history, institutional forms, processes, and practices from the point of view of those who labor to learn, rather than from bureaucratic, bourgeois liberal/neoliberal perspectives, for which learners are objects not actors (cf. Danziger 1994; Packer 2001; Sims 2017). In this spirit, Ray McDermott and I experimented with re-reading (and rewriting – literally) the alienation of contemporary learning through Marx's essay on Estranged Labor from the *Economic and Philosophical Manuscripts of 1844* (Lave and McDermott 2002; Marx 2009 [1844]). To adopt Marx's strategy with respect to classical political economy, good advice is to be found in his theory of praxis, for which the Theses on Feuerbach is a touchstone. The intentions of this chapter are those of e.g., Thesis 3.

The materialist doctrine that men are products of circumstances and upbringing, and that, therefore, changed men are products of other circumstances and changed upbringing, forgets that it is men who change circumstances and that the educator must himself be educated. Hence, this doctrine is bound to divide society into two parts, one of which is superior to society … The coincidence of the changing of circumstances and of human activity can be conceived and rationally understood only as revolutionising practice. (Marx 1998[1845]: 572–3)[2]

* * * * *

Why pursue a social rather than a more familiar psychological theory of learning? To the extent that being human is a relational matter, generated in living, historically, in social formations whose participants engage with each other as a condition and precondition for their existence, theories that conceive of learning as a special and particular kind of mental process impoverish and misrecognize it. My colleagues and I have been trying to convey our understanding of this claim for some years (e.g., Lave 1988; Lave and Wenger 1991; Chaiklin and Lave 1993). I will try to develop the argument a little further here.

There is another reason for pursuing a theoretical perspective on the social nature of learning. Theories that reduce learning to individual mental capacity/ activity in the last instance blame marginalized people for being marginal. Common theories of learning begin and end with individuals (though these days they often nod at "the social" or "the environment" in between). Such theories are focused on individual differences, with notions of better and

---

[2] "The eleven theses on Feuerbach jotted down by Marx in 1845 when he was only twenty-seven … [were] published with some revisions only after his death as an appendix to Engels' *Ludwig Feuerbach* …" (Bernstein 1971: 13).

worse, more and less learning, and with comparison of these things across groups of individuals. Psychological theories of learning prescribe ideals and paths to excellence and identify the kinds of individuals (by no means all) who should arrive; the absence of movement away from some putatively common starting point becomes grounds for labeling others *sub*-normal. The logic that makes success exceptional but characterizes lack of success as not normal will not do. It reflects and contributes to a politics by which disinherited and disenfranchised individuals, whether taken one at a time or in masses, are identified as the un- or dis-abled, and thereby made responsible for their "plight" (see McDermott 2001). It seems imperative to explore ways of understanding learning that do not naturalize and underwrite divisions of social inequality. A reconsideration of learning as a social, collective, rather than individual, psychological phenomenon offers the only way beyond the current state of affairs that I can envision at the present time.

This re-envisioning is by no means simple. It requires reconsideration at many levels of alternative assumptions that might support a social understanding of learning from the ground up. Such an enterprise would not be possible today if there had not been changes in conceptions of the field of education in recent decades. This view of the field of education is laid out by Holland and Eisenhart (1990: especially chapter 3): that we have moved in the last quarter century from implicit to explicit theory, increasing our ability to reflect critically on our own research practice. It seems crucial to me, as it does to them, to base the academic field of education on explicit accounts of its different theoretical perspectives.

The region of social theory that seems richest in clues for how to conceive of learning in social terms, in my view, is an historical, dialectical theory of practice. Such a perspective takes learning to be an aspect of participation in socially situated practices. My understanding of the theoretical implications of learning as social practice could not have developed outside my research on Vai and Gola tailors' apprenticeship in Liberia. Research on apprenticeship in West Africa casts learning in a different light. The characteristics of apprenticeship among the Liberian tailors did not match claims about the nature of informal education, and hence the theory underlying those claims needed to be re-examined.

Further, apprenticeship studies offered an especially clear window on issues about learning. But even supposing this claim is correct, how could apprenticeship studies be relevant to learning in school settings? The argument we developed (Lave and Wenger 1991) is that learning is an aspect of changing participation in changing "communities of practice" everywhere. Wherever people engage for substantial periods of time, day by day, in doing things in which their ongoing activities are interdependent, learning is part of their changing participation in changing practices. This characterization fits schools as well as tailor shops. From this perspective there are not distinguishable "modes" of learning. Because however educational enterprises differ, learning is a facet of the communities of practice of which they are composed.

It may seem paradoxical to turn to studies of apprenticeship in developing a perspective on teaching, when apprenticeships deploy many resources for effective learning, but in most cases teaching is not the defining or most salient of these, and rather often it appears to shape learning little or not at all. Yet an argument has emerged from the apprenticeship research about the character of teaching. To begin, I shall illustrate what it means to characterize learning as a facet of social practice through two examples of apprenticeship, distant from late twentieth-century public schooling in the United States. One is the apprenticeship of Vai and Gola tailors in Liberia, the other the learning of law practitioners in mosque schools in nineteenth-century Egypt. Together they help to demonstrate what it means to view "learning" as social practice, and the social practice of learning as the fundamental social phenomenon in relation with which practices of teaching are constituted. This in turn leads to a series of issues about what teaching is, from the perspective of learners learning.

Research on Apprenticeship

In the early 1970s, as I was beginning research on apprenticeship, Scribner and Cole (1973) articulated the common theoretical assumptions of both the psychology of learning and the anthropology of education in a justly famous article in *Science*, summing up a two-sided formal/informal education model, in which schooling was synonymous with the formal side, while apprenticeship clearly fell into the informal. Formal education was supposed to involve "out-of-context" learning in which instruction organizes learning activities; learners build understanding through abstraction and generalization, which produces less context-bound, more general understanding, and results in broad learning transfer to times and places elsewhere and later. In informal education learning was supposed to be embedded in everyday activities, taking place through demonstration, observation, and mimesis. The product was supposed to be a literal, context-bound understanding, one not conducive to general learning transfer.

There is a set of contrasts here concerning how schooling effects were supposed to come about, and how these effects were *not* supposed to emerge in other educational enterprises, such as apprenticeship. Researchers were not talking about two different but equally good ways to learn. Rather, they assigned positive value to the formal side, negative value to the informal – the same basic assumptions as cognitive theories of learning. It should look familiar.

Between 1973 and 1978 I pursued my concerns about common characterizations of "informal education" in field research in Liberia, exploring the
apprenticeship of Vai and Gola tailors in a poor and marginal location at the
periphery of the business district of the city of Monrovia. There were
250 masters and apprentices in the Tailors' Alley. They made mostly ready-
to-wear trousers, a pair or two at a time, working at foot-treadle sewing
machines, and using the profits of one day's sales to buy the materials to make
the next few pairs of trousers. Many of the masters took a new apprentice every
few years, so that co-apprentices would be differently situated with respect to
the ways in which they could participate in the ongoing life of the shop. (None
of the masters were wealthy enough to take two apprentices at the same time,
for they would then occupy similar positions in the division of labor rather than
complementary ones.) I spent many hours in tailor shops watching life proceed, getting to know the tailors and apprentices, the ups and downs of daily
life and local gossip, while trying to figure out what apprenticeship was
all about.

Like the authors of the *Science* article, and on the basis of the Liberian
research, I have since argued against many of the major assumptions in
the comparative model of education: We have challenged assumptions that
decontextualization is the hallmark of good learning, and have questioned
the abstract and general character of what constitutes "powerful" knowing.
Learning transfer is an extraordinarily narrow and barren account of how
knowledgeable persons make their way among the multiply interrelated settings of their lives. Distinctions between the rational knowledge content
attributed to school "curriculum" and the broad moral (but narrow skill) focus
assumed for "informal education" ignore the skills and moral content of
schooling and the knowledgeability that is part of all educational practices.
From a perspective based on apprenticeship I have also argued against the
assumption that teaching, understood to be "intentional transmission," is
necessarily prior to, or a precondition for, learning, or that the apparent
absence of teaching calls processes of learning into question.

A major aspect of the research on tailors focused on another claim characteristic of dualistic theories of learning. Such theories assume that possibilities
for creative activity and the production of new "knowledge" are limited to
certain kinds of education. One kind of learning is supposed to underwrite such
"capabilities" while the other supposedly does not. Apprenticeship is often
assumed to merely reproduce existing practices. So I was interested in the issue
of whether mechanical reproduction of skill at, for instance, making trousers,
would be the only outcome of years of apprenticeship. I began to inquire into
just what was being learned by the apprentices, and found that the apprentices
were learning several complex "lessons" at once. They were learning relations
among the major social identities and divisions in Liberian society which they

were in the business of dressing. They were learning to make a life, to make a living, to make clothes, to grow old and mature enough to become master tailors, and to see the truth of the respect due to a master of their trade. It seems trivially true that they were never doing only one of these things at a time. This recommended serious skepticism about the assumption that the "informally" educated should not be able to produce knowledge but only reproduce existing practice.[3] Further, skepticism on this issue basically undermines the other claims of dualist models of education and learning.

Let us turn now to the other example. It concerns learning in nineteenth-century mosque schools in Egypt. Political theorist Timothy Mitchell writes, in *Colonising Egypt* (1988 [1991]), about the historical relations between the Western obsession with representation as the mode of knowing, and colonial empire-building by Europeans in the Middle East. He extends Foucauldian arguments about knowledge/power relations as he links empire-building and representational practices in Europe from the eighteenth century to the present. He describes the pejorative contrast made by European visitors and colonial officers in Egypt, between notions of "European" order and "Egyptian" disorder as perhaps the most significant ideological tactic for deriding existing educational practices in Egypt. Indeed the colonial government quickly set about replacing the mosque schools with a system of Lancaster schools. The colonialists' dual educational theory was consistent with that just described for the late twentieth century.

Mitchell offers an alternative view of educational processes in the mosque:

Al-Azhar, the name of a particular mosque but also the general name for a group of mosques and lodgings gathered in the older part of Cairo, was not a school for law, but the oldest and most important center in the Islamic world of law as a profession. As with other crafts and professions, one of the continuous and pervasive activities of those involved was the learning and teaching of its skills. *Learning was a part of the practice of law, and it was from this practice, rather than from any set of codes or structures, that it took its sequence and its form.* [my italics.]

The process of learning always began with the study of the *Quran*, the original text of the law (indeed the only original text, the only text which could not be read in some sense as the interpretation or modification of an earlier writing). The student then moved on to the *hadith*, the collections of sayings attributed to the Prophet Muhammad which interpret and extend Quaranic doctrine, and then on again to the major commentaries upon the Quran and to the other subjects dealing with its interpretation, such as the art of its recitation and the study of variant readings. From there one moved on to the studies related to the reading of the *hadith*, such as the biographies of the transmitters,

[3] It might seem (barely) plausible to talk about learning by imitation or the mechanistic reproduction of existing practice if "informal education" were equated with narrowly specific tasks, e.g., to sew seams straight, or make "standard" pairs of trousers. But this is absurd once it is clear that learning to make trousers is part of vastly more complex and extended relations, times, places, and meanings.

then to the principles of theology (*usul al-din*), then to the principles of legal interpretation (*usul al-fiqh*), then to the divergent interpretations among the different schools of
law, and so on according to a sequence given in the reading and interpretation of the
law, *which was the nature of the art being studied* [my italics]. Though the choice of
secondary texts might vary, there was no need of a syllabus or curriculum. The order of
learning disclosed itself, by the logic of interpretation, in the order of the texts.

In the same way, there was no need for a daily timetable. The ordinary sequence of
the day's lessons mirrored on a smaller scale the same textual order. The first lessons
would be given immediately after dawn prayers, by those teaching the *Quran*. These
were followed by lessons in *hadith*, followed by Quranic interpretation, and so on,
working outwards eventually to the study of mysticism, left to the period after evening
prayer. The order of teaching, in other words, even the order of the day, was inseparable
from the necessary relation between texts and commentaries that constituted legal
practice. Practice was not something organised within the indifferent order of the
timetable; it unfolded in its meaningful sequence.

The sequence of learning was also the sequence of scholarship. A scholar at al-
Azhar, we are told, would prepare a legal opinion, a lesson, or a disputation, by
placing all the books which discussed the question he wanted to elucidate on a low
table in front of him, arranging them in sequences radiating from the middle: 'at the
center is the original text (*matn*), then the commentary (*sharh*) on this text, then the
gloss on the commentary (*hashiya*) and finally the explication of the gloss (*takrir*).
The books often repeated this arrangement themselves. . .: a text might be accompan-
ied by a commentary written between the lines, or even inserted between the words
themselves, with a further gloss upon the commentary written in the margin, surrounding the text on all sides, just as the circles of commentaries on the table
surrounded the central text.

There were other respects in which *the patterns of learning were repeated in the
forms of legal practice.* The lessons in which the works of law were read took place
with the participants seated in a circle, each participant's place in relation to the teacher
determined by his or her command of the text being studied. Again the process of
mastering the art was what gave learning its order. The circle of participants, in fact,
was the common form of all the aspects of the legal profession carried on within the
mosque. It was variously used to hear cases and issue opinions, to dispute questions of
law, to deliver addresses, and to dictate and discuss the texts. *The activity of learning, in
other words, was simply one aspect within the daily practice of the law.* (1988 [1991]:
82–4 italics mine)

In short, the substantive relations among kinds of texts and interpretive
practices were reflected in the sequence in which texts were studied, the
arrangement of apprentices and scholars with respect to each other while
studying or practicing law, the order of lessons on these texts throughout the
day, legal scholarship, and legal practice. They were all part of the ongoing
practice (of which learning was a part) so that the apprentices learned about the
texts, scholarship, the round of daily life of masters, and the practice of law
while engaged in life each day at the mosque. And the masters likewise.
Mitchell has captured in his analysis of the mosque schools the integral
character of learning in the practice and he shows us just how various

dimensions of life are saturated with the significant patterns of law practice, so that it was part of many aspects of social life for its participants. This work, which goes against the grain of common readings of educational practice both then and now, offers a delicate and insightful perspective on learning as social practice.

It is not entirely without problems. Mitchell's interpretation involves an uncritical acceptance of the idea that the masters who are practitioners of law are also teachers of apprentices, while his own account of their daily practices calls this division into question. Indeed, this work raises questions about what teaching *is*, from the perspective of learning. In Liberia it appeared that masters were most importantly embodied exemplars of what apprentices were becoming. The law practitioners fit this description also. And as Mitchell describes them, it is not difficult to imagine them as changing learners themselves as their engagement in the many day-to-day activities in the mosque changed through time. Also, an apprentice law practitioner was not alone with a master, rather both were participants in larger, varied, constellations of participants. Much of what is attributed to "teaching" by Western interpreters of these settings is almost certainly crucially made in relations among near peers. We do not know enough about how these relations generate, recontextualize, interrupt, conflict with and enrich the multiply-sited cultural patterning of the practice in question.[4]

Before turning the discussion further to processes of teaching, I want to underline similarities between learning processes in tailor shops in Liberia and in the mosque school. In becoming acquainted with the sequence of garments they were learning to make, tailors' apprentices were learning as well the sequence and relations of informal and marginal to formal and socially important clothing, social categories, and occasions. The shifting practice of tailoring across the lifetime, the daily round of life as a master, and the practice of learning to tailor were all similarly patterned but differently lived aspects of life in the tailor shops. Presumably such "textured landscapes of possibility" (Lave and Wenger 1991) are common to all effective learning practices, breaking down distinctions between learning and doing, between social identity and knowledge, between education and occupation, between form and content. And at the same time they suggest that intricately patterned relations between practices, space, time, bodies, social relationships, life courses – ubiquitous facets of ongoing communities of practice – are both the content

---

[4] The significance of multiple settings of activity in constituting learning identities seems increasingly crucial to research on social practice. Dreier (e.g., 1994) has generated a theoretical framework for such research and a rich example in his analysis of the process of family psychotherapy as constituted in both therapeutic and domestic settings. Osterlund (1996) offers another example, concerning newcomers becoming salespersons, which requires them to mediate between their own company and the companies to which they sell products and services.

and the principle of effectiveness of learning. These examples offer grounds for arguing that multiply, richly structured processes of learning look very different from the impoverished simple, non-creative task learning more conventionally attributed to apprenticeship.

It is now possible to take a long view of the research on tailors' apprenticeship, and to see fairly clearly how it transformed my understanding of learning in three major respects. First of all, I admired the Vai and Gola tailors' apprenticeship, while (according to the values embedded in the formal/ informal model) I should reserve my admiration for schooling. This opened the value-laden meaning of each part of the model to a new perspective and the possibility of new conclusions. Why was the tailors' apprenticeship an appealing kind of educational practice? I happened upon a case of enormously effective education, benign (and inexpensive). The result, for very poor people who might be expected to experience their lives and themselves as miserable in all senses of that word, was a strong sense of their worth and self-respect. They were without a doubt poor, *and* able, respected and self-respecting, with a "take" on the world that had a considerable penetration of the real conditions of their lives. Eighty-five percent or more of those who started as tailors' apprentices finished, and continued their practice, as tailors. In short, in contrast to the negative value conventionally placed on apprenticeship in contrast with school learning, the research on the tailors shifted my perspective to one that took apprenticeship to be a complex phenomenon worthy of respect. This shift in view did not lead to an argument that school should be replaced by apprenticeship or that apprenticeship should displace teachers from classrooms. Neither US school practices nor Liberian apprenticeship can be copied into other times and places, for they are historically, socially situated practices, deeply interconnected with other practices beyond their immediate purview. Rather, it led to the view that better understanding of learning in apprenticeship settings might be a resource for better understanding how learning transpires in other historical circumstances, including US schools today.

Second, research on apprenticeship transformed my understanding of just *who* the central actors are in theories of socialization, cultural transmission, or learning. From the point of view of the dualist formal/informal model, indeed cognitive theory in general, culture becomes shared via cultural *transmission*. It is the transmitter's point of view that is implicitly privileged. By contrast, one central point of the apprenticeship research is that learning is the more basic concept, and that teaching (transmission) is something else. Teaching certainly is an object for analytical inquiry, but not an explanation for learning. Indeed, whole apparatuses of explanation for learning appear to be merely cultural artifacts about teaching – in need of explanation – when learning is taken to be the basic concept. Our understanding of both learning and teaching are thus problematic, inviting new analysis, which in turn requires novel analytic units and new questions.

The third transformation growing out of the research on West African tailors' apprenticeship concerns the situated character of activity in the daily practices of people's lives. The tailors' apprenticeship as a whole was an elegant illustration for this. Yet there is nothing even revisionist about recognizing the situated character of participation in apprenticeship. After all, the concrete, "context-embedded," immediate confinement of learning in educational forms such as apprenticeship is basic in claims of dualist theories of learning.

Such theories insist on the importance of distance, perspective, and disengagement from immediately relevant practical concerns in order for powerful, knowledge-producing learning to occur (and assume that other educational experiences such as apprenticeship cannot produce it). But there was another facet of the research on Vai and Gola tailors that made possible a break with the dualistic view of context-embedding. In order to develop a critique of cross-cultural research on learning transfer, I invented a dozen "learning transfer" experiments in an attempt to test widespread assumptions that schooling provides a unique kind of mental training. Math seemed to be a reasonable subject for these experiments, for transforming quantities was part of both Liberian schooling and tailoring practices. After much analysis of experimental protocols describing the problem-solving activity of the tailors, it became clear that whether the tailors had been to school or not, they engaged with math in tailor shops very differently than in the experiments. This led to another round of ethnographic fieldwork in the tailor shops to try to characterize everyday math. The differences were striking, leading to the conclusion that the tailors' math practices – that were supposed to be quintessential "formal," "abstract," "decontextualized" kinds of knowledge from the point of view of the formal/informal model – were socially situated, and had a contextually embedded character. This in turn led to the conclusion that it was not just the informal side of life that was composed of intricately context-embedded and situated activity: there is nothing else.

Further, if there is no other kind of activity except situated activity, then there is no kind of learning that can be distinguished theoretically by its "decontextualization," as rhetoric pertaining to schooling and school practices so often insists. This has two implications at least: Decontextualization practices are socially, politically, situated (See Chapter 2), and they are part of didactic practice in school classrooms (Minick 1993). It seems sensible then to explore examples of apprenticeship. Because they do not mystify and deny the situated character of learning they may offer less obscured sites for the understanding and theorizing of learning than do schools. For the latter institutionalize, and are predicated on, widespread beliefs about learning that are called into question by views of learning as situated activity. It suggests that new research questions are in order, about how learning in practice is characteristic of schooling.

The research on the tailors did not result immediately or even very soon in an alternative to the theory for which it offered a critique. It did impel a search for ways to conceptualize learning differently, encouraged by those three interconnected transformations that resulted from the project (1) a complex-ification of the polar values assumed to reflect differing educational power for schooling and "other" forms of education; (2) a reversal in perspective so that the vital focus of research on learning shifted from transmitters, teachers or care givers, to learners; and (3) a view of learning as socially situated activity. This work could not replace existing theories, but it provided incentives to ask new questions about learning.

From Apprenticeship to Social Practice Theory

Those new questions included, among others: What are theories of learning "about?" What is a theory of learning? What would happen if we stopped reifying learning and began to think of learning as something historically specific? I took up questions like these in a series of seminars – a reading group at the Institute for Research on Learning at a certain productive moment in its history, a seminar with Paul Duguid at the University of California, Berkeley on the educational implications of early British cultural studies, a seminar on Subjectivity and Social Practice with critical psychologist Ole Dreier from Copenhagen University, and a seminar on Everyday Life and Learning with Martin Packer. As colleagues and students, we explored these issues over a half dozen years or more (1989–1995).

First, we asked ourselves, what are theories of learning *about*? I suspect the most common assumption is that they are about individuals' psychological processes. But in a way, though worth critical examination, that is beside the point. What seemed far more startling was the incredibly narrow, completely pervasive history of philosophical and later psychological treatments of "learn-ing" as wholly an epistemological problem – it was all about knowing, acquiring knowledge, beliefs, skills, changing the mind, moving from intu-itions to rules, or the reverse, and that was all. Just as the history of philosophy is sometimes characterized as an abstract individualist, "third person singular" project, so is the project of theorizing about "education," knowledge, culture, and their production and reproduction.

Second, we began to wonder about theories of learning themselves. Martin Packer and I decided to explore the social theoretical underpinnings of theories of learning and everyday life, since clearly they were intertwined and also displayed interesting differences (Lave and Packer 2008 [2011]). Martin raised a surprising and acute question. He wanted to know what *is* a theory of learning. I could point to some, but had no idea what one was; he already had an answer in mind. At minimum, he proposed, a theory of learning consists of three kinds of stipulations: a *telos* for the changes implied in notions of learning; the basic relation assumed to exist between subject and social world; and mechanisms by which learning is supposed to take place.

(1) *Telos*: that is, a direction of movement or change expected through learning.
(2) *Subject–world relation*: a general specification of relations between subjects and the social world (not necessarily to be construed as learners and things to-be-learned).
(3) *Learning mechanisms*: ways by which learning comes about.

We found this a useful analytic tool – a set of questions for interrogating anything claiming to be an example, or for that matter a theory, of learning. It provided a way to organize our understanding around an inventory of things it seemed essential to know in every case. It gave us a kind of creative license to play with what learning might be about. Further, the notion of *telos* seemed useful in turning the focus away from a vista of educational goals set by societal, cultural authorities, which would make teaching the precondition for learning. It encourages instead a focus on the trajectories of learners as they change. "Learning mechanisms" also seem obviously relevant to understanding how learning comes about.[5] The centrality of assumptions about subject–world relations may seem less obvious. But different epistemologically-based theories depend on the variable answers to two questions: Where does reality lie (in the world or in the subject)? How can we come to know it (descriptively or analytically)? And if one adopts the perspective proposed here, the subject–world relation is central also, though conceived differently. The question is, "how is the objective world socially constituted, as human beings are socially produced, in practice?" Rejecting the analytic philosophical distinction between persons and things, this question presupposes that social becoming is fundamental to all other social processes (Bernstein 1971). Any way you look at it, subject–world relations are at the crux of differentiation of one theory of learning from another.

We can now turn back to the nineteenth-century mosque school for scholarly/law practice to consider how this way of conceiving of theories of learning could be addressed to specific educational practices. Conventional views on everyday learning would argue that those becoming law practitioners were

---

[5] More recently I have come to question the characterization of learning processes as "mechanisms," and to wonder about the reification of learning as always and only a unique process in and of itself. Nonetheless, as a means to compare existing theories of learning it has been useful.

marginalized learners, engaged in a disorderly process of rote reproduction of existing practice, as they memorized a limited corpus of written texts, in a haphazard way that would easily account for the narrow and merely reproductive character of what the would-be lawyers could learn. By contrast, the view derived from social practice theory is that Egyptian law apprentices were engaged in long-term projects as persons becoming lawyers known for their learned practice.

The *telos* of tailors' apprenticeship in Liberia and legal learning in Egypt was not learning to sew or learning texts. It was also not moving toward more abstract knowledge of the law or separation from everyday life into specialization of production skills or broad generalization of tailoring knowledge. Instead, the *telos* might be described as becoming a respected, practicing participant among other tailors and lawyers, becoming so imbued with the practice that masters become part of the everyday life of the Alley or the mosque for other participants as others in turn become part of their practice. This might even be a reasonable definition of what it means to construct "identities in practice." It seems that the tailors and law participants as subjects, and the world with which they were engaged, mutually constituted each other. That is, of course, the subject–world relation implied in a social, historically situated perspective on learning.

Rather than particular tools and techniques – mechanisms for learning as such – there are ways of becoming a participant, ways of participating, and ways in which participants and practices change. In any event, the learning of specific ways of participating differs in particular situated practices. The term "learning mechanism" diminishes in importance, in fact it may fall out altogether, as "mechanisms" disappear into practice.

The question of subject–world relations that we explored was what would happen if we took the collective social nature of our existence so seriously that we put it first. From that perspective crafting identities in practice becomes the fundamental project subjects engage in – it is a *social* process. Becoming more knowledgeably skilled is an aspect of participation in social practice. By such reasoning, who you are becoming shapes crucially and fundamentally what you "know." "What you know" may be better thought of as doing rather than having something – "knowing" rather than acquiring or accumulating knowledge or information. "Knowing" is a relation among communities of practice, participation in practice, and the generation of identities as part of becoming part of ongoing practice.[6]

---

[6] Eckert's analysis of the formation of jock and burnout identities in American high schools makes this point elegantly (Eckert 1989a, 1989b). She gives an especially interesting account of contrasting participation of jocks and burnouts in their various communities of practice that involve different processes of knowing in practice.

Teaching in Schools

At this point we can turn to a particular historical moment in which participants in certain communities of practice are separated into teachers and students: contemporary schools in the United States. In such settings teachers are ubiquitous. People who have attended school for years may well assume that teaching is necessary if learning is to occur. But teaching is neither necessary nor sufficient to produce learning. Further, the social-cultural categories that divide teachers from learners in schools mystify the crucial ways in which learning is fundamental to all participation and all participants in social practice.

The way we conceptualize teaching can be rethought within the perspective that takes learners, learning, as the fundamental phenomenon of which teaching may (or may not) be a part. Learning, when it is taken to be first and principally the identity-making life project of participants in communities of practice, has a crucial implication for the teaching in schools: The powerful, multiply structured processes of learners learning in school settings encompass and *subsume* what is generally assumed to be the *dominating* agenda of school classroom teaching. Classroom "instruction" in schools falls into that subsumed part. This implies that school teaching has as a condition of possibility other aspects of learners' learning projects. Whether and how classroom activities result in the incorporation of class activities into the life projects of students (and all others in schools) depends on the ways they are taken up in those life projects. This suggests a radically different proportionality for the role of classroom teaching in the learning that indubitably goes on in schools.

Teaching, by this analysis, is a cross-contextual, facilitative effort to make high quality educational resources truly available for communities of learners. Great teaching in schools is a process of facilitating the circulation of school knowledgeable skill into the changing identities of students. But there are challenges for teachers in high schools in the United States that are not problematic for Liberian master tailors or Egyptian lawyers. Earlier I pointed out that much of the effect of craft masters comes from the fact that they are concrete, embodied exemplars of what the apprentices are trying to become. Unlike craft masters, high school teachers engaged in their everyday practices are rarely immediate and compelling embodied exemplars of what US high school students are trying to become. Students are rarely legitimate, peripheral participants in the process of becoming teachers. Teachers are probably recognized as "great" when their identities are changing with respect to (other) learners through their interdependent activities, that is, when they are concrete, embodied *learners* for and with their students.

It is difficult to find research on learning that focuses on great learners learning, but it rarely focuses on great teachers teaching/learning either.

Research on learning is mostly research on "instruction," on depersonalized guidelines for the teaching of specific lesson-like things in school settings. The "teaching" that "learning research" is research *on* has little recognizable relationship to the creative, productive work that arouses admiration for great teachers. Yet it seems likely that most people who devote their lives to education do so in part because they have been deeply affected by one or more.

It may be worth inquiring how it is that most of us are able to remember great teachers, but do not have routine ways to talk about what great teaching is. And if we cannot even talk about it, it is surely difficult to build into research/practice on learning. Our poverty is a symptom of a general difficulty with much educational research. A close reading of research on how to improve learning shows that questions about learning are almost always met by investigations of teaching. This disastrous shortcut equates learning with teaching.[7] It reduces teaching to narrowly specific prescriptions for what should be transplanted into the heads of kids. It takes the teacher out of the teaching. It reduces teaching to curriculum, to strategies or recipes for organizing kids to know some target knowledge. It also takes learners learning out of the picture. The circumstances are very like those analyzed by critical psychologists (e.g., Dreier 1993) with respect to the difficulties encountered by practitioners of family therapy. Neither therapist nor client (read teachers and students) participate in their joint activity as clearly located subjects. Therapists take charge, via interpretation, of characterizing the subjectivity of the clients, and direct their own actions toward clients in terms of those interpretations. When it comes to their own participation, therapists reduce it to the view that they are acting on behalf of the clients, as if they had no situated reasons, interests, goals, or concerns of their own that enter into and affect what transpires.[8] The result is that it is not clear what it means for either kind of participant to engage in their joint activity, as each is characterized only through the other. A similar situation governs much research that purports to be about learning. It deprives us at one and the same time of clear analyses of learners as subjects – and of teachers as subjects as well.

I have several reasons, then, for proposing that we should address questions about teaching through research focused on learners learning. The requirement that we treat both learners and teachers as subjects in their own right recommends the importance of looking at each as a located participant, and at their relations with one another (rather than at some subject-less displacement of those relations into "instruction"). Further, if teachers teach in order to affect learning, the only way to discover whether they are having effects and, if so,

[7] This is not a new point: Klaus Holzkamp (1987) explored these issues some years ago. See also Chapter 3: 78.

[8] McNeill's (1986) description of teaching in US high schools can be read in this way.

what those are, is to explore whether and, if so, how there are changes in the participation of learners learning in their various communities of practice. If we intend to be thorough, and we presume teaching has some impact on learners, then such research would include the effects of teaching on teachers as learners as well. Together these comprise a short agenda for research on teaching.

But beyond this it seems useful to begin with learners, because they constitute the working conditions for teaching. Given teaching work as defined here, teachers need to know about the powerful identity-changing communities of practice of their students, for these are defining conditions of their work. It is a puzzle, however, as to where to find these communities of practice, and how to recognize them, if the teaching work found in, say, US high schools is subsumed in processes by which students' identities change. This is a very different "take" on teaching than one that characterizes teachers as leaders, in control, setting the agenda for students, in ways intended to take precedence over students' life projects.

It may be of value to look for effects in high schools similar to those described for the studies of the Vai and Gola apprenticeship and the learning and practice of law in mosque schools in nineteenth-century Egypt. Each was impressively effective in the production, sustenance, and transformation of participants' knowledgeable identities, because the order, meaning, and substance of these practices converged in so many registers – where and how people arranged their bodies and how these related to what different participants were and knew, the different but interconnected and interdependent daily round of activities of differently situated participants, the practice at its most substantive, learners' careers, and the careers of participants already in place.

In what central ways do bodies, trajectories, timetables, daily practices, and changing careers create registers of identity-changing activity among learners in American schools? One powerful multiply-sited, intersecting, identity-producing effect of school communities of practice is racialization. The generation of identities, knowledge and meaning in racial terms is so salient in the United States that racial meanings are generated both in the presence and in the absence of given ongoing activity. Other powerful effects of school communities of practice involve the production of social class divisions and gender and sexual identities. Racialization, gender-, social class-, and sexual orientation-making, are aspects of American adulthood that kids are deeply engaged in constituting among themselves. Like the tailors' apprentices in Liberia they are learning in practice the salient social divisions and identities of the social formation in which they live their lives.

One way to get at these learning practices in the ongoing communities of practice of American schooling is obliquely, through an examination of the experiences immigrant children undergo in the process of "Americanization" for which schools are held very much responsible.[9] These issues have been explored recently in a two-year ethnographic study of a high school near San Francisco that had recently experienced a large increase in immigrant children (Olsen 1995). Olsen's dissertation explored the processes of Americanization in which newcomers from around the world participate in various ways and to different degrees. She concluded that in complex and unintended ways Americanization, in practice, is a process of racialization of social relations and identities (and thus of "knowledge" as well).

Olsen points out that the issues about immigration and schooling presently convulsing public politics and schools alike in California, have shaped US high schools over at least the last two centuries. The notion of schooling as the major means to integrate/assimilate immigrant populations led first to the creation of common schools nearly two centuries ago and then to the introduction of tracking in comprehensive high schools a century later (Olsen 1995). So, the historical structuring of schools in many ways embodies practices of "Americanization." There are very few discussions of what, in practice, for immigrant kids in high schools, Americanization *consists*. There is, according to Olsen, an official position in the school she studied: Administrators and teachers were of the opinion that, like American society, the high school is multicultural and relatively harmonious, a place where students with different social origins freely intermingle. They felt that newcomers from outside the United States must first and foremost learn to speak English so that they would be able to join in American life. For teachers and administrators, Americanization is primarily a language (perhaps culture) issue. The school does its job by teaching English as a second language.

In general, with brave exceptions, the school administrators and almost all the teachers are silent to each other and to the students about racial segregation, racism, and sexism.[10] Asked to produce a social map of the school they divide students along three academic tracks. Teachers with more seniority receive desired higher-track teaching assignments. Their careers and their positioning in relation to one another reflect the ordering of time, space, social categories, and activity in those tracks in their daily locations, schedules, work assignments, and shared students. The classes students take are tracked, and the classes in different tracks are very different from each other.

In keeping with the perspective under discussion here, Olsen explored Americanization-in-practice through the perspectives most especially of

---

[9] Another powerful, oblique approach to processes of racialization is to be found in the research of Nadine Fernandez (2010). See also Fernandez (1996). Fernandez' study of interracial romantic relationships in socialist Cuba addresses the working out of racial identities in relations of class and gender.

[10] See the work of Holland et. al. on official silence about race/gender issues among grade school children in a recently desegregated school (Holland et al. 1979; Holland and Eisenhart 1990).

students. Among other things she asked groups of students, immigrant and non-immigrant, to make social maps of the school.[11] Their maps displayed no tracks – they did not register activities in classrooms at all. Their maps had no (immediate) congruence with the teachers' maps. Non-immigrant students started by noting where different groups of students "hang" (in their daily round of activities). The categories they describe are racial ones – a world filled exclusively with "black," "brown," "white," and "yellow" young women and men. Students described as painful and difficult the practices by which they separated themselves into racial groups and practiced daily coexistence. It took skill and coordination to bring this off. Immigrants appear on these maps not at all, or as a single category, undifferentiated by national or linguistic origins – just "immigrants."

Immigrant students also produced maps that located groups of students that "hang" together, most often in terms of the geography of students' national origins and languages and length of time in the United States. So, their "reading" (of what for non-immigrant Americans are diversities of race and ethnicity) is one of nationality, national language, and historical differences in the timing, circumstances, and meaning of leaving countries or continents at given historical moments and arriving in the United States likewise. Olsen documents the process by which immigrant children become participants, often tenuously, in the ongoing social life of the school, coming to "hang" with other students, with whom they share teachers, classes, and a track. For immigrant students, then, Americanization, or "assimilation," is first and foremost a process of racialization through the practices of their daily lives, whether in the official sites of tracked classrooms or in the social sites where they gather and socialize. It involves transforming their identities, in spite of deep perplexities over poor correspondences, from national to racialized ones.

This is an all-consuming job for children nearing adulthood, reason enough to explain why curricular "innovations" or teaching methods designed to improve teaching in classrooms often seem to have little impact and short lives. But contemporary examples exist in which the task of teachers has been reconceived as activity directed "into" the ongoing processes through which high school kids engage in changing identities, with startling results. One such example is to be found in work begun by Margaret Carlock a few years ago to generate a chemistry program aimed at non-wizard students in an East Bay

---

[11] The differences among teachers', "US-born" students,' and immigrants' views on the social diversity of the school are obviously important in constituting the school as an institution. It does not have a unitary meaning, purpose, or activities, and the meaning of "the school" for one set of participants is contested by others. This is a good illustration of the complexity and conflicting understandings that make up any "community of practice."

high school (personal communication).[12] This program ballooned in numbers of students, students who learned chemistry so well that, incidentally, they made record national test scores in record numbers, over a period of years. The problem as the teacher construed it was to figure out how to make it possible for students to participate intensively in chemistry as part of their collective identity-changing lives. This involved a complex process of transforming the chemistry lab space into one whose social organization was very much shaped by the students, with laboratory and class work collaboratively developed with students, breaking lines between teaching and learning as all learners became tutors; drawing students in through tutoring arrangements that created opportunities for them to engage with chemistry first for purposes of helping others and, through that, to deepen their engagement with chemistry as an object of study. In various ways she made students dependent on each other for much of what was to be learned. Together they created multiple settings for the community of chemistry learners as the ski club became the project of chemistry students and its outings the site of chemistry work. She suggests that one way to evaluate the results is by how much talk there is about chemistry among students in the cafeteria. Carlock's knowledge of chemistry and of how to make it available to students was a critical part of this effort. But instead of "teaching chemistry" she engaged in a different kind of "learning practice," making it possible for chemistry to become part of the hard work of learners who were becoming gendered, racialized, classed adults – in this case adults with an impressive interest in chemistry.

Conclusion

I began by arguing the importance of exploring a social rather than psychological theory of learning, motivated in part by a concern not to add blame for "failure to learn in school" to other burdens of marginality. It is not accidental that the path from this concern to a theoretical perspective that takes learning to be an aspect of social practice led through a close examination of marginalized cultural-historical formations, and through theoretical ideas at the periphery of the intellectual fields of social theory, anthropology, and education. Where better to engage in a process of demystifying the suppressed poles of the dualisms that justify contemporary denigrating practices? (Stallybrass and White 1986)

I set out, therefore, to describe what happens when a theoretical perspective loosely labeled "social practice theory" is employed as the basis for analysis of

---

[12] Margaret Carlock, was a PhD student in the Graduate School of Education at University of California, Berkeley and was writing her doctoral dissertation on her work teaching chemistry at the high school in the mid-1990s.

learning in very different settings. It began with an exploration of changing interpretations of one ethnographic example, that of the Vai and Gola tailors in Liberia. The second was an historical example generated for other purposes, and about another epoch. Both the Liberian and Egyptian examples focused on preparation of adult practitioners, as a process of interdependent learners learning, not as an effect of teaching. We then turned to other examples, in American high schools, to discuss both learning and the practice of teaching in the lives of students both outside and inside classrooms. School teaching is a special kind of learning practice that must become part of the identity-changing communities of children's practices if it is to have a relationship with their learning. As for the different ways in which social circumstances for learning are arranged: through these examples I have tried to show that common assumptions about supposed differences among modes of education and their outcomes are more apparent than real. By this argument it is counter-productive to compartmentalize the West from the rest, socialization from specialized education, so-called informal from formal educational endeavors, and classroom learning from everything else. Because learning, wherever it occurs, is an aspect of changing participation in changing practices.

This is not, however, a claim for a theory of universal learning mechanisms. Quite the opposite. There are enormous differences in what and how learners come to shape (and be shaped into) their identities with respect to different practices. Going back to the examples again, the garment inventory of the tailors, the relations of the different commentaries to the *Quran*, and the racialized "curriculum" of spaces and sequences of participation that divide and reassemble children, teachers, and administrators in the high school are substantive, situated, and historically specific. Researchers would have to explore each practice to understand what is being learned, and how.

At the same time, the conditions for the transformation of persons are the same whether the *telos* of learning is movement toward growing "up" from babyhood, or from adolescence, becoming a craftsperson or a philosopher, and/or becoming a marginal person in a world where participation in and thus learning divisions of race, ethnicity, social class, gender, and sexual orientation determine strongly who is consigned to the advantaged cores and disadvan-taged margins of society.

This perspective on learning has methodological implications, in the narrow sense. Ethnographic research is a good way to come to understand learning as part of practice. It is useful for trying to focus on the specifics of changing participation in changing practices, most especially on learners' changing conditions and ways of participating. At the same time it requires commitment to an inclusive focus on all participants equally, as each contributes to the making of differences of power, salience, influence, and value for themselves and other participants.

For educational researchers whose major identity is in research on schools, the approach taken here recommends research to identify locations in which, and the processes by which, the most potent identity-constituting learning conjunctures occur. It requires a refusal to take as given the hierarchical social divisions among participants, among activities and settings that seem "natural" to schools in order to pursue research designed to look for intense foci of identity-changing activity. For researchers whose major identity is in research on the teaching of high culture in school settings, the key questions revolve around how to make pedagogic situations (organized to produce deeper scholastic understanding) effectively available to the school-specific, identity-changing participation of kids together in their own lives. Those most concerned with relations between learning and teaching must untangle the confusions that mistakenly desubjectify learners' and teachers' positions, stakes, reasons, and ways of participating, and then inquire anew about those relations. And for researchers concerned most especially with the conditions and effects of public schooling practices of xenophobia, racism, sexism, and homophobia on what is learned in schools, the argument made here recommends research on understanding how schools *in particular ways*, ways not identical with the xenophobia, racism, sexism, and homophobia structuring other social institutions, make the learning of these divisions in practice ubiquitous. Any or all of these would be useful next steps in ongoing research on learning (and teaching) as social practice.

5   Production Schools

* * * * *

It was through collaboration with Danish colleagues and students that I had the opportunity to learn about the Kalundborg Production School. This essay is a brief account of a too brief encounter with a remarkable school-that-is-not-a-school for young people in Denmark who have dropped out or been expelled from state-sponsored schooling. This experience is referred to again in Chapter 7. The detail here anticipates the argument in that chapter. The school offers a remarkable case of contradictions in practice (just as the Weight Watchers of Chapter 1 also offer an example of that somewhat difficult idea, with their resolvable, but not solvable, conflicts over dieting). Those who founded the school were determined that working toward these futures should not box young people into dead-end jobs to which they have been consigned by their school biographies. At the same time, the everyday practices of participation at the Production School should not style "success" as a return to a formal educational trajectory. Nor should it make literate competence either necessary or impossible. The contradictions and struggles of the young people whose challenges and dilemmas reflect their imbrication in conflicts around class, nationality, and gender inequalities and exclusions (as well as with challenges like dyslexia), shaped practices within the Production School. The school's careful strategies around access, participation, and changing practice had as their ultimate everyday aim to support the students' development of a stronger grasp on their own future possibilities.

* * * * *

Since a half-year stay in Denmark (January–June 2000) I have not been able to get the Kalundborg Production School (KPS) out of my mind. I was struck by what a rich, serious, living example of transformative education – in the best sense of that word – was happening before my eyes. Further, it was taking place in conditions that were carefully, skillfully, humanely developed by Niels Jacobsen, the director, and those who work with him. I often describe

I wrote this essay as a contribution to a report intended to explain production schools to the Danish Ministry of Education: Niels Jakobsen et al. Fra undervisning til Laering – Produktionsskoleerfaringer (2001). My part was later republished in the Danish edition of *Situated Learning* (2003).

the school and talk about it in a variety of academic settings and would like to share my impressions, for it illustrates in powerful terms what learning is all about.

In a recent interview with a Danish colleague, a professor engaged in educational research, I asked him, "What do you know about production schools?" "Not much," he said. "Those are the places young people are sent to when they have failed at school and at vocational education. I know that school teachers don't want to teach there – they think it's the worst possible teaching assignment." Shortly the conversation turned to vocational schools. He told me that these are viewed as more desirable teaching posts – the vocational education system is aiming to have 50 or 60 percent of its teachers with advanced academic qualifications. It is also striving for increased classroom-based teaching. He was surprised by my interest in the powerful educational vision I saw embodied and worked out in the KPS. He was also surprised by my skepticism about the value of turning vocational schools increasingly in the direction of classroom teaching.

The School that Is Not a School

The KPS consists of a cluster of white buildings set well back from the road in open countryside outside the town of Kalundborg. Forty to sixty young people are enrolled at any one time, ranging in age from fifteen to twenty-five. They will spend on average twelve to eighteen months at the school, some longer. To convey some idea of how it felt to be there, let me start with the workshops in which young people spend much of their time working and learning. Later I will try to move out from these most obvious places to look for lessons and learning, seeking more vivid indications of learning-that-changes-persons'-relations with learning possibilities in their lives. To see how changing participation in the changing practices of the school takes place, we must criss-cross the school grounds and beyond with the young people, with the craftmasters and the school head, and with the products that also travel through and beyond the school. Learning possibilities unfold, and thus must be studied, across the multiple contexts through which they contribute to the life of the school.

Walking into the metal shop is overwhelming: it looks (and sounds) chaotic. It is full of machines, tools, raw materials, and partly finished and completed products (e.g., various graveyard gardening and cleanup tools; barbecue grills with rain roofs). The craftmaster is engaged with young people doing many different jobs, all of them contributing to the products the school designs, makes, and sells. (The master craftspersons in the shops all have had careers as craft producers, not as schoolteachers. They bring to the school a strong commitment to, and a lived, critical knowledge of, the social value of their working lives.)

Conventional teaching is not the basis of learning here. The practical work of the craftmasters is to manage production in a shop where new "workers" arrive at different times throughout the year while others are preparing to leave, in such a way as to meet production goals and deadlines and produce transformative possibilities for the new producers of those products at the same time. When these priorities come into conflict, craftmasters look for ways to tip the balance in favor of the participants. This is a challenging task; one the craftmasters I watched seemed skillfully observant of and engaged in. In this one sense KPS is most definitely a "school." It provides a broadly applicable high standard for what serious teaching is always all about.

There is a big, ruled whiteboard on the wall in the metal shop with the name of every person who works there. Checkmarks on the board indicate certificates acquired by each participant so she or he can properly follow safety guidelines while working on various dangerous machines. It is kept up to date as a matter of collective health and safety, but it has multiple social effects. As the contents of the whiteboard change, it shows how the workshop and its participants are gradually changing, as it also provides clues to the observant novice about relations among kinds of equipment and kinds of skillful labor. Further, it is possible to figure out at a glance, as Niels Jacobsen pointed out, who might need, and who can be asked for, "neighbor instruction" on using particular machines.

Some of those working in the shop are doing very skillful complicated work on the machines, others less complex jobs. Together they are managing several different production lines that require coordinating uses of the same equipment, spaces, and participants. They do so in a way that feels relaxed and easy. The atmosphere is friendly, with talking and joking – sometimes shouted over the noisy machines – punctuating the concentrated productive labor going on in the shop. It immediately seems like a great place to work.

The print shop is quieter, but there is evidence of productive, creative hard work here too: quantities of paper of all kinds, finished newsletters printed and waiting to go out, layout tables, computers for formatting texts, and of course multiple jobs under way at the same time.

The wood shop, like the metal shop, is full of vigorous activity on different parts of several production lines. The shop master and a couple of young people are working over detailed drawings and specifications for making beautiful wooden screens with regular small square holes. How is it done? By clever collaborative design is the answer. In this work, which also involves workers changing places, trading woodworking tools, table saws, sanders, and drill presses, the same comfortable ease came across as in the metal shop.

There was one withdrawn, silent, sullen-looking young man working doggedly, but unconnected to the others, and very unhappily (it seemed to me) – the newest newcomer, expecting the worst. I was reminded of the histories of poverty and marginalization of immigrants to Denmark and the miserable experiences of failure and rebellion in academic and vocational school systems that had been the lot of virtually all the students at the school. I noticed extraordinary differences between those who had been around for a while and the newcomer (whose stance I saw echoed in a few other new students still alienated from the other students and their daily life at the school). Here was comparative evidence before my eyes for the transformative power of the production school.

In each workshop there are two kinds of production going on at all times. The main staple items being produced for sale have special qualities. Not only are they the "bread and butter" profit-earners for the shop, they are also products designed so that young people can take part in making them immediately on their arrival. Further, as they work at different phases of producing them over time, these particular products offer possibilities for developing increasingly knowledgeable skills while contributing from the very beginning to the general social welfare. Other products, more peripheral to the economy and daily practice of the shops, require more complicated manufacture. Coming to participate after a while in these production processes is easier after watching and occasionally assisting various old-timers at work. That economic contribution and changing personal skill have somewhat *different* trajectories in the shop is one important way in which the production school creates opportunities for self-transformative changes in confidence and worth.

There is a third kind of production activity in the shops, one-of-a-kind projects that take concentrated, collective planning and labor to produce. Many of the students worked with the wood shop master to restore an old windmill nearby; they recently built a stage for a local festival; and various of them worked together on a large sculpture whose production has become a source of hilarious stories of tribulations overcome. A drawing of the sculpture has become the logo for the school.

Each of the three ways of engaging in the production activity of a workshop contrasts with the other two and offers possibilities for young people to consider their differences. They have other kinds of opportunities to make connections, comparisons – analyses if you will – of KPS practice, as they sometimes take part in VET (Vocational Education and Training) courses, spend short periods working in local businesses, travel on school expeditions, and take part in exchange visits to other countries.

The greenhouses looked rather bare at the moment we stopped in, but they had been busy recently, selling spring bedding plants and houseplants to local florists. Workers in this area were cleaning up, counting up, discussing how their work had been going, making plans for their next weeks' work and their new projects. They took us to visit the garden across the school grounds near the playing field (along a path with outdoor lighting designed and made in the metal shop). Strawberries would soon be ripe, we saw, as they took us to inspect the rows of produce coming along nicely, and in large quantities.

The garden produce was an important contribution to shared daily lunches where all of the students, staff, and visitors eat together. These meals are prepared in the kitchen where yet another group of young people was learning cooking and catering. We ate the bread they made, the main dishes and dessert, and the extravagant, many-layered tower of vegetables in a special composed salad. We sang to the guitar accompaniment of one of the students. There was news, discussion, and planning before everyone went back to work. Carl Nissen, a long-term consultant to the school, pointed out to me that besides simply being places of opportunity, the production school built fellowship, responsibility, and acceptance among the participants.

In each shop the young people or the craftmaster showed us a small office area where small bookkeeping tasks need doing often and by all participants. Here student workers become peripheral participants in the logistics of running a workshop. Records of materials, expenses, and sales are kept on computers in some shops, by hand in others. However, computers are always used for filling out time sheets for wages and lunch sign-ups. Shop participants also update the notebook where the shop's projects, designs, and ways of doing things are written and kept together as a collective record of their efforts. Reading and calculating skills are not prerequisites for being allowed, indeed required, to take part – the bookkeeping is often done collaboratively. (Any worker in the shop would have a good grasp of the meaning of what needs entering in account books, computer, or production log, whether he or she acts as scribe or not: Life is *not* an arithmetic word problem, in which the numbers stand out but their meaning is a mystery to the problem-solver. On the contrary!)

The computer room is crowded with computers, manuals and participants working on projects. This place is different from the other shops: all those who pass through the school spend time learning to work on the computer. (Quite a few have acquired their international "PC driver's license," a test on widely used programs at an ordinary user level.) A computer master is present, and as usual young people with more facility are learning (among other things) just how far they have come, as they do their own computer work and incidentally help those who have a longer way to go. Reading and reckoning skills are not a prerequisite here either. Their computer-based learning programs come with options to choose between text and sound files. Close, very serious, attention is given here to defusing the issue of literacy as a critical sign of personal capacity (or lack thereof), or as a sign of previous, thus future, failure. (Another extraordinary sign of this concern: faced with EU funding regulations that required student-kept records of their progress, the KPS stopped business as usual to conduct a short course in photography so students would have the option of documenting their changing participation visually.)

Fundamental Dilemmas for Production School Education

It would be difficult to come this far in observing the school without seeing extraordinary evidence of legitimate peripheral participation among new-comers in their relations with old-timers, craftmasters, and former students in the shops and community. On those grounds alone it seems likely that learning is going on, learning that changes identities and thus changes the meaning and relations of knowledge and skill in the lives of learners.

But this is only part of the story. This school works under difficult condi-tions with, nevertheless, high expectations for the transformative possibilities of the young people. Consider some of the dilemmas to which the school is a living changing, complex response.

First, the head and craftmasters must make a successful school for young persons who have learned, in practice, to despise school and themselves as pupils. To change this state of affairs the staff cannot prescribe recipes from the top down, cannot in fact fall back on teachers, classrooms, lessons, and tests to organize daily life. What instead? New participants come into the school as paid workers engaged in producing products for sale – on which the future of the school in part depends. When "schooling" is not on the agenda as the only (or apparent) end of everyday practice, this radically changes the ways they enter into participation in local practice, and the meaning of participation with respect to learning.

The production school is working for the possibility that they can transform themselves from failing, marginal participants in social life, to confident producers of their own social possibilities and futures. This involves dilemmas for all concerned. How do you transform yourself in practice, starting from a position as an alienated, often damaged, person who has been taught that you are not competent to do so? From a different perspective, how is the school to take part in this process? What if the workshop alternatives to school classes, teachers, lessons, etc., appear to the student workers to be only condescending substitutes for "real" school? This would defeat the production school's purpose. It may be less a problem here than in academic or vocational schools: The KPS depends on participants' growing responsibility for (and pride in) producing their everyday life and financial resources for the school – together – to minimize readings of inferiority into the school's possibilities.

From the craftmasters' points of view, trying, in a multitude of careful ways, to facilitate young persons' labors to transform themselves – without trying to do it for them– is also difficult. For there are contradictions of class and culture here that can easily push educators into approaches that forsake transformative ambitions for young persons, in haste to "do" remediation, or "do" upward mobility, or, failing these, to fall back on "only doing" minimal wage labor qualifications *to* the students. Attempting to "do something to" others is all too likely to kill transformative possibilities otherwise present for participants.

Transformative Expectations that Succeed

Surprisingly – given the contradictory and difficult conditions of operation of the production school – expectations at KPS are exceedingly high for trans-formation rather than mere training of young people. Talking with masters, with Niels Jacobsen the school head, and with senior consultants on non-formal youth and adult education Carl Nissen and Lone Kaplan,[1] I saw clearly just how deeply the school is committed to a vision of real and deep education. This is about the transformation of relations of these young people *with(in)* *their growing knowledgeable skillfulness at work*, transforming their relations with others, with their future laboring lives, and with schooling in its various forms in Denmark. To do this is both part of, and partly produced by, changes in their relationships with themselves so that they can grasp confidently their own capacities to make good and productive lives.

The difficulty of realizing the school's goals, coupled with the extraordin-arily ambitious seriousness of purpose they reflect, together make the KPS an inspiring place.

It is inspiring because, more often than one would expect, it seems to work, in practice, day by day, to facilitate participants' changing possibilities for shaping their future lives. In this sense I would say that I *saw* it working in many ways. Students at the school also see it working and see that it has worked for others who have taken part in the KPS. How? A unique feature of the school is that students spend time in the company of KPS graduates who are themselves following a variety of employment and educational trajectories. Some of the graduates live on the KPS grounds in ecologically experimental apartments that everyone in the school helped to build, at the insistence *of the graduates.*

Nearly all students in the mid-1990s came to production schools because they were unemployed and lacked post-compulsory education. A 1997 report showed that only 15 percent were unemployed at the end. The KPS's efforts to follow its graduates into the next phase of their lives suggest that "as average transition results go among production schools our results are quite good." "Still," comments Niels Jacobsen, "we are not able to follow up on those results, not least because many participants leave the region for further

---

[1] Carl Nissen was senior consultant for folkeoplysning and ungdomsarbejde; He worked in the Youth Ministry of the Danish Government for many years. Lone Kaplan was the Consultant fra koordineringskontoret for EU's uddannelsesprogrammer.

education or better jobs." The KPS staff tell inspiring stories about some who have made radical transformations of their lives, confirming that genuine possibilities for so doing are to be found there.

Challenges to Production School Practices

Two connected challenges to the KPS and other such endeavors require comment here: How are the young people to get an expanding understanding of the work practices in which they are engaged, if not in a classroom through "theoretical instruction" on those practices? And how can production schools do better than just dig students deeper into overdetermined lives at the bottom of the economic ladder?

Unreflective and narrowly limited practices are occupational hazards for us all, of course, not somehow essentially and specifically characteristic of the learning of craft labor for wages. Learning through labor is often the target of criticism based on value-laden assumptions about severe and unbridgeable distinctions between mental and manual labor, theory and practice, pink and blue collar jobs versus white collar professions. But "inferior (read 'literal,' 'not theoretical') learning, through inferior forms of schooling" is not the explanation for these old historical-cultural distinctions in theoretical perspectives emerging collaboratively in the work of Danish colleagues (to name a few) Ole Dreier, Morton Nissen and Line Mørck, Uffe Ule Jenssen, Bente Elkjaer, Marianne Hedegaard, Seth Chaiklin, Steinar Kvale, Klaus Nielson, Carsten Osterlund, and Tove Borg. They have much to say about learning as participation in changing social practice, "wild learning" on the streets, the changing everyday world of clients of occupational therapy, practices of apprenticeship and relations between trade schools and jobs in the trades, the struggles of immigrants and educators to make schooling work for newcomers to Denmark, learning organizations, and learning to work in large corporate settings. They all resist the urge to scholasticize. They would not agree that institutionalized formalities – schooling, in classrooms – is the necessary, indeed the only way to provide possibilities for theory, or for reflection, or for liberation from narrow construals of labor and life. Nor do they assume that powerful learning is a process of meta-learning – acquiring abstract generalities about more particular knowledge, from theoretical instruction.

Let me put it another way. When we try to get a grip on a vision of "education" it is very easy to get confused: if you think the subject of education is knowledge, then to make it more powerful, wonderful, and inclusive, it follows that knowledge should get more general, that some knowledge should illuminate other knowledge. Perhaps that is why the idea of "theory" is so appealing. But the subject of education is not knowledge – it is persons. To make them more powerful, wonderful, and inclusive, we can only help create with them circumstances in which they can gradually transform their own needs, knowledgeability, and grasp of their future possibilities.

What constitutes the equivalent of "reflection," or "theory," if we take learning to be a matter of changing participation in changing practice? For an answer we attend carefully to how quite different but multiply interconnected participants participate differently across their multiple contexts of practice, and in so doing develop a variety of perspectives on, and stances with respect to, those practices. In the different, partial, conflicting, and changing ways that persons take part in social practice, lie possibilities for complex understandings and penetrations into the broader societal and cultural scaffolding of practice. Call it theoretical practice or theory in practice, realized as part of the knowledgeable identities (rather than knowledge as such), taken up as part of ongoing practice. This must be very important in "reading" cultural and personal meaning into everyday practice. This is what production schools are very, very good at providing.

Many societal practices – including school practices – make it difficult for many young people to take up more inclusive, more deeply contextual, understandings as part of their changing theoretical practice. Some of those practices forcefully convince participants that they are not entitled to legitimate access to possibilities to broaden their grasp. But this is a far different argument, with far different implications from one that insists that (learning to) labor with the hands provides no basis for reflection while (learning in classrooms to) labor (also with the hands!) in offices, concert halls, and scientific laboratories does.

How are we to understand such possibilities in the KPS? I will end here, with one all-too-brief glimpse of significant transformative possibilities for the students, in this case developed in response to another common production school dilemma. The basic mode of day-to-day life in the school happens through producing goods for sale. What the shop students make and sell must be commercially viable if those producing the goods are to be socially productive. Yet it is a tenet of production schools that they must not compete with local businesses. In response, a decade ago Niels Jacobsen, along with some of his co-workers and a few local business people, started a Product Development Club. The KPS has built an Exposition Hall where the business people meet, and where products from each business are on permanent and changing display. With the help of the workshops in the KPS and the students who work there, designs are emerging for new products, new methods for producing those products, and new product prototypes. The students in their workshops work with local businesses to modify and perfect them. If the new products sell well, the school recovers its expenses, and more. Consider the various ways in which participation in these new product projects opens up possible trajectories of employment and creative activities in local businesses in their future lives – ones that may depend on and draw on the relations beyond the school that are laid down as they work with those local businesses.

Conclusion

I have traced KPS student workers from shop to office, among different kinds of production work, from coordinated daily work to collective sociality, and on journeys out of the school and back again. It is possible to see their labor translated into products whose sales translate into resources for the daily operation of the school. Produce grown by some becomes the material with which others learn to cook, preparing the meals that the gardeners, cooks, and all the rest share. Literacy here is a practical necessity that can be accomplished collaboratively, but one can work on print, laying it out aesthetically and making thousands of copies for paying customers, again through labor that in completely unambiguous terms contributes to the common welfare.

I began by illustrating a few of the many ways in which the KPS provides rich possibilities for learning through legitimate peripheral participation in overlapping communities of practice. As we have gone along I have increasingly drawn attention to the significance for learners of the trajectories they move through as they take part in the multiple contexts of the KPS. My own understanding of learning is changing through collaboration with colleagues like Niels Jacobsen, Carl Nissen, Ole Dreier, and the others mentioned above: I have come to think that if we want to understand and influence learning possibilities we must attend carefully to the rich, conflicting, interconnected ways those designated "learners" and we other learners take part in life activities. These are the basis for expanding life-transforming possibilities that can only become inhabitable through hands-on everyday practice.

For the Near Future

Given the deep dilemmas in the lives of the students who come to the KPS, for which an effective solution surely involves a deeply educative everyday practice that cannot be a school, the students need time – a year, two years, sometimes more, to transform their lives. The KPS needs to keep right on doing what it is doing, in its own powerful, lively, and innovative ways, neither narrowly training young people nor formalizing training in classrooms.

As a concerned educational policy maker, I would look to those who have made the KPS an extraordinary educational practice for advice on how to emulate in other educational contexts the hard educational work they do so brilliantly. And I would give the KPS recognition and support for continuing on its chosen path.

6 Everyday Life
Logical Operator, Social Zone, or Social Practice

* * * * *

I have often invoked the term "everyday life" as a casual equivalent to "social practice" or "situated activity." The question here is, What work is this unanalyzed term doing? A similar question led to the exploration of different conceptions of context (and decontextualization) in Chapter 2. The present essay contrasts three theoretical accounts of everyday life and what they imply about related conceptions of learning. One common vision of everyday life makes it principally a foil – just the opposite of high cultural visions of philosophy or science. The second takes "everyday life" to be a matter of stereotypical social zones – home, laboratory, school – presumed to differ from one another by the different sorts of knowledges which furnish life activities there. (Chapter 1 discussed social zones representing different everyday knowledgeabilities of garage mechanics or housewives, and from which kids proceed to school and return after school.) These two approaches both conceive of learning as moving away from the ordinary and the everyday toward science, philosophy, the exceptional and the expert, and toward the realms of elite knowledge and high culture. These characterizations of everyday life interest me in part because they are both decontextualization practices that lead to abstract accounts of learning.

Steven Shapin and Pierre Bourdieu – historian of the development of early science and sociologist of class cultural differences in France respectively, offer insight into the cultural and political effects of banal characterizations of "the everyday" articulated in opposition to high cultural production (Bourdieu 1984; Shapin 1991). They, in effect, provide historically specific insight into subject–world relations and the historical/structural production of the *telos* of movement from ordinary to extraordinary learning (two of Packer's diagnostic criteria for theories of learning). They offer help with pinning down both *telos* and subject–world relations that is hard

---

This chapter had its beginning in a collaborative graduate seminar with Martin Packer over a period of two years in the early 1990s called Everyday Life and Learning. Martin's theoretical sophistication was central to the seminar, to the development of the argument here, and to Lave and Packer (2008). There was an earlier version or two (Lave 1999; Murphy and McCormick 2008). A brief version of the argument here was published as "Everyday life and learning" in Hall, Murphy, and Soler (2008). Many of these ideas were developed in Lave and Packer (2008) and in Klaus Nielsen et al. (2008), and in the Spanish translation of "Towards a social ontology of learning" (Lave and Packer 2011). I have rewritten the chapter extensively. This chapter represents work from the early 1990s to about 2010.

to find in most educational research. For conventional research on learning stays narrowly (and uncritically) centered on the third component of such theories: learning mechanisms (see chapter 4: 94); Lave and Packer 2008). Shapin's and Bourdieu's analyses, in contrast, are big road maps that explore the *telos* and subject–world relations of conventional theories about everyday life and learning. They give us clues as to why we conceive of learning mainly in terms of making tracks away from everyday life (toward realms of high cultural accomplishment).

The third account of everyday life and learning addresses the problematic claims of the first two. It proposes an account of learning as moving into and through engagements in everyday practice. That requires a concept of culture not as high culture, but culture in a small "c" – anthropological – sense. Instead of remaining attached to an undialectical severing of learning *from* everyday life, the point is to assume a conception of learning in everyday life.

* * * * *

Different broad theoretical frameworks open up, give salience to, compel, repel, and exclude different conceptions of "everyday life," "learning," and their relations. "Learning," in the lineage of positivist, empiricist social science represented by cognitive theory and its behaviorist ancestors, has generally been construed as an epistemological problem. In vernacular terms it has long been assigned (by dualist divisions between person and world) to some conceptual individual and mental realm as opposed to a social-material realm. Just as we would expect (given that we grew up going to school), learning is assumed in common sense terms to be about individuals' mental processes, leading to the acquisition of knowledge. This is typically framed as a result of knowledge transmission (teaching, inculcation, training) that leads to internalization of what is transmitted. After that it can be used by the knower, that is, transferred and applied to "*new problem solving situations.*" That is surely a remarkably curious characterization of everyday life, one that reduces the lives of its inhabitants to an endless series of problems to be solved. Anthropologist Tim Ingold points out similarly,

The notion [of competence] suggests a knowledgeability that is detached from action and from the contexts of actors' bodily engagement with the world, and that takes the form of interior rules or programmes capable of specifying, in advance, the appropriate behavioural response to any given situation. Competence, as Dreyfus and Dreyfus have pointed out (1986: 26–7), "underwrites the kind of process that, according to cognitive science, lies at the heart of *all* intelligent action, namely 'problem-solving.'" (2001: 134)

Such claims reduce the contexts of actors' bodily engagement with the world to a collection of problem-solving situations.[1]

---

[1] Enskillment, apprenticeship, learning, and development as matters of bodily engagement in the world, have been central concepts in various attempts (Ingold's and mine, among others) to elaborate theoretical ways of querying human engagement as part of everyday changing

It might seem that what is included in common sense meanings of "learning" and "social life" is neatly separated by a division between epistemological concerns with regard to learning, in individual terms, and the social nature of arrangements for doing things in the world. A history of philosophy, social theory, anthropology, and Western cultural practices might be taken up almost anywhere and furnish arguments, mostly in favor of the proposition that everyday life is *socially constituted*, while learning happens by operating in the head on *mental representations* of that world. Sociological approaches to organizations, institutions, and social relations mostly reflect this view, as more often than not they bracket off processes of learning, leaving what they assume to be mental, individual phenomena beyond their purview. This is not without drawbacks. Much sociological scholarship creates customary – problematic – patterns of silence about issues of learning. Or slips into a discussion of "education" or "teaching" while claiming to discuss learning, or perhaps most commonly gets along without acknowledging that there is one theoretical stance with respect to the constitution of institutions, groups, social movements and other collective phenomena, and another about assumptions about processes of learning.[2]

A closer look at these academic and more broadly distributed common sense ways of making classificatory sense of social life suggests a different argument, however: There is a preoccupation (when theorizing about learning) with a conception of *social life* conceived in epistemological terms every bit as strongly as conceptions of learning. Subject and world are assumed to belong together on the epistemological side of the analytic divide (think of social life reduced to "problem-solving situations"). From this perspective, lines are drawn and distinctions made between subject and world, more specifically, between subjects learning and everyday life, in terms that reduce social life to knowledge (knowledges, information), its different kinds and places, its distribution, compartmentalization, acquisition, exchange, production, truth value, politics, and power.

practices. At the same time they represent strategic efforts to confront disembodied theories of mind, learning, thinking, and knowledge; recognizing the necessity of ongoing critiques of classical cognitive theory; other variants of common sense cognitivism; and their Neo-Darwinian roots.

Ingold and I have both produced critical diagnoses of cognitive theory (for a particularly fine example, see Ingold (2001) "From the transmission of representations to the education of attention"). But our theoretical roots are distinctly different. Ingold describes his work as based in phenomenological, ecological and practice-theoretical perspectives – J. J. Gibson, Heidegger, Wittgenstein – while my roots are in historical, dialectical theory of praxis. Our paths diverge, then, when positively engaged in ethnographic-theoretical projects (see the section "The Question of Decentering" in Chapter 7).

[2] Remember Packer's succinct description of theories of learning as a subject-world relation, a *telos*, and mechanisms for learning (Chapter 4). I am beginning here with the subject/world relation and will go on to conceptions of *telos* later.

Such theories of learning at their core require, and always imply, conceptions of the subject/world relation and a *telos*. We cannot get at these key commitments of different theories of learning if we insist on addressing learning as a discrete activity or discrete object of isolated theoretical interest – or by focusing exclusively on "the world" by itself either. Yet these are the strategies typical of Western learning research.

How does one go about unpacking assumptions about the subject/world *relation*, especially if that relation is typically claimed to entail a categorical separation between subject and world. We can begin with, say, "learning in everyday life" and ask what is assumed or implied about subject/world relations when the question is not how is individual learning supposed to happen, but rather how is learning in relation to everyday life supposed to happen? This is a two-part question because dialectically it needs to be asked in both directions. So, it must *also be* asked, "how is everyday life theorized with respect to learning?"

Everyday Life (with Respect to Learning)

Do scholars really go around thinking of "everyday life" in epistemological terms – as matters of characteristic, commonly assumed kinds and qualities of knowledge and conditions for "problem solving"? After all, "the everyday" in common parlance is widely taken to be one of those "natural" terms for a thing without a compelling history. It does have an interesting cluster of common meanings: life experience that is mundane, prosaic, humdrum, boring; that which reoccurs, the routine, the unchanging, a matter of social reproduction (but not creativity), the ordinary and expected, the inescapable round of daily existence. It is sometimes equated with culture, the customary, the commonplace; sometimes with the fabric of belief, value, and lived experience, the domestic, the everywhere of our lives that is nowhere in particular. If anything, these meanings sustain a vague and open sense of the term. The problem with appealing to a concept of "the everyday" in rethinking "learning" could turn out to be this very lack of specific meaning in a field of endeavor in which its pivotal role should entail a more searching acquaintance.

But in fact the problem is just the opposite: The typical Western conception of *learning as knowledge acquisition* (that separates it categorically from the everyday world) underlies common assumptions about *everyday life*. The "everyday" arguably has more broadly shared but more narrowly constrained meanings than we might expect. Some years ago the Critical Theory Program at the University of California, Davis sponsored a conference entitled "The Problematics of Daily Life in the Human Sciences."

The titles of the talks by literary, anthropological, and historical critical theorists were consistent with the meaning cluster above. Speakers began in similar ways, however, with a disclaimer. None of them felt that they had any idea what a conference on the everyday might be about. Then they went on to discuss a surprisingly closely related set of issues. All of them claimed dissatisfaction with some well-known ways of conceiving of the everyday. All of them took the matter at hand to be a question of how and what people *know* under "ordinary" circumstances. "Everyday life" appeared to stand in as a reference to certain sorts of knowledge in certain sorts of contexts.

This essay first explores two ways of theorizing everyday life with respect to learning that are part of conventional (including academic) theorizing about learning. Both depend on epistemological characterizations of everyday life with respect to learning. The work of Henri Lefebvre and Michel de Certeau can help to illustrate this point.[3] Lefebvre has written critically on numerous occasions about theorists and philosophers who are prone to distinguish what they do from "everyday life." they treat philosophy as a genre of knowledge in opposition to an abstract, epistemological "everyday," a dualistic contrast between what the philosopher produces and the residual other, everyday knowledge, which, as the *object* of reflection, is "not philosophical."

A second common strategy for characterizing everyday life, involves an apparently social view in which different zones of social life (the domestic, or private, or otherwise residual spaces, or persons, or practices) are distinguished from one another by their varied sorts of knowledges (e.g., housewives in their kitchens (Hallpike 1979; chapter 1). De Certeau points out common epistemological distinctions among a conventional compendium of life's typical social locations and circumstances. He describes ways in which "everyday life" is typically understood as (what I would call) differently inhabited knowledge-spaces in a world divided between the ordinary and the special or privileged.

Indeed, whether the everyday is drawn into service as a hypothetical contrasting sort of knowledge – as what I have called a "logical operator," or whether the everyday is conceived of as a bunch of zones of different typical knowledgeabilities, both imply that there are other aspects of life

---

[3] Partly this essay is intended as a challenge to socio-historical scholars who think their work is in no way dependent on an implicit theory of learning, since arguably every theoretical/empirical problematic makes assumptions about subject–world relations, theorizes (critically or not) teleology; and expresses ways in which iterative processes, reproducing practices, traveling knowledgeabilities, etc., are produced.

that are not everyday. How are such conceptual accounts produced and sustained? They are surely vastly over-determined. But Steven Shapin's (1996) historical account of early scientists mulling over the proper place to locate and ways to organize their work offers one window on the embedding of this styling of everyday life in pervasive common sense understandings. Pierre Bourdieu's (1984) sociological analysis of class cultural differentiation in France offers another. Bourdieu calls attention to the specific social location of the producers of dualist epistemological theories; to the reduction of learning to the acquisition of high cultural "knowledge" and distinction; and to the inability of these theories to address the social production of everyday life and learning in their relations.

Social practice theory, however, offers a different theoretical lens through which to consider everyday life by assuming that it is the very fabric of social existence. That raises questions about related assumptions about "learning" as part of that fabric. In a dualist theory of everyday life learning assumes a teleological character. But not all conceptions of learning are understood as processes of moving away from the ordinary and everyday toward high cultural ends. A dialectical account of everyday life and learning-in-practice characterizes both of them in historical processual terms. This theoretical stance is neither dualist nor cast in epistemological terms. It assumes that one cannot divide person from world, and further that as a relation, persons-in-ongoing-changing practice are participants in, and producers of, social historical processes including learning.

Table 1 sums up the contrasting theoretical accounts of everyday life (with respect to learning).

Table 1

The Everyday as Logical Operator[a]	The Everyday as Social Zone	The Everyday as Social Practice
A residual category vis a vis philosophy, high culture, science, that is, in some sense merely a logical operator.	As banal, a form of existence with particular times, places and characteristics – e.g., as categories of private, domestic spaces.	As the fabric of social existence and the landscape of possibility for changing participation in changing practice.

[a] I have adopted the term "logical operator" from Favret-Saada's (1980) analysis of witchcraft in the Bocage in France.

"The witch," she argues, is not a person, but a concept that enables the complex relations involved in episodes of suffering, annunciation, unwitching, etc. to unfold. It also reminds me of Caroline Islands navigation practices as well (Hutchins 1993; Gladwin 2009).

The Everyday as Residual Pole, Merely a Logical Operator against Which to Define the "Not Ordinary"

Lefebvre's wide-ranging, (wildly ranging too) critique of everyday life takes, as one small theme, alienated distinctions between philosophy, art, and everyday life. These distinctions are both ideological and lived in a world in which "the everyday" is in need of deep transformation.[4] His descriptions furnish examples of how the everyday is thus treated as merely a logical operator, an abstract foil or residue. He points out common hierarchical distinctions between philosophy and the "non-philosophical everyday." He points out that everyday "reality" is not only commonly invoked as merely the opposite of philosophical "truth." It encompasses a view of modernity as high culture that turns the everyday into low culture. (Lefebvre sums up the commonplace ambivalence of the philosophical toward the non-philosophical, "vacillating between scorn and admiration.") Thus, at one point in his analysis he speaks critically of the interdependent realities of the quotidian and the modern: "while the quotidian is that which is humble, solid, taken for granted, its parts in regular recurrence, undated, and (apparently) insignificant . . . the modern is that which is novel, brilliant, paradoxical, technical, worldly and (apparently) daring and transitory" (1968 [1991]: 24). These oppositions are clearly a hierarchical matter of the valued and devalued, powerful and powerless, cultural production and "merely" reproduction, that draw dramatic attention to historical/ideological lines between philosophical thought and the "thinking" of everyday life. Such a philosophy/nonphilosophical axis sustains the view that questions about everyday life are first of all about knowledges, where they reside, and their comparative value and effects.

Groups, Practices, and Locations: The Everyday as Ordinary, Residual Knowledge Zone

If the previous example distinguishes "the everyday" from philosophy and high culture as if the difference were one of kinds of knowledge/culture, the view of everyday life as epistemological zone, still in dualistic terms, characterizes parts of social life, e.g., home, school, office, the kitchen, the laboratory, factory floor, and the management suite in terms of differences of knowledge, its value and its production (cf. Thomas 1994). Salient social locations are typified in terms of different kinds of knowledge and knowledgeability and so social groups, practices, and locations are familiarly furnished in such terms.

---

[4] Lefebvre's oeuvre and critique of the everyday spans several volumes of work including *Critique de la vie quotidian* in three volumes (1947 [1991], 1962 [2002], 1971 [2008]) and *Everyday Life in the Modern World* (1968).

The Practice of Everyday Life (de Certeau 1984) makes a particular argument against common dualist conceptions of the everyday.[5] His project is:

a continuing investigation of the ways in which users – commonly assumed to be passive and guided by established rules – operate ... This goal will be achieved if everyday practices, "ways of operating" or doing things, no longer appear as merely the obscure background of social activity, and if a body of theoretical questions, methods, categories, and perspectives, by penetrating this obscurity, make it possible to articulate them. (1984: xi)

In developing his "categories and perspectives" he divides social life into two spatial, temporal zones characterized by differences in power that shape and inflect the contrasting *epistemological* characteristics that are central to defining them. In doing so he insists on the active and creative character of everyday intellectual action: "as persistent as it is subtle, tireless, ready for every opportunity, scattered over the terrain of the dominant order and foreign to the rules laid down and imposed by a rationality founded on established rights and property" (1984: 38). He argues that there are both strategies and tactics in the world, the latter the recourse of the weak. Everyday tactics are a kind of production, but a derivative, secondary production, with distinctive characteristics of its own. The procedures are narrowly defined: the "tactics" of everyday life (in opposition to the "strategies" of the powerful), he argues, have no spatial terrain of their "own." De Certeau wants to "bring to light the clandestine forms taken by the dispersed, tactical, and makeshift creativity of groups or individuals already caught in the nets of "discipline." Pushed to their ideal limits, these procedures and ruses of consumers compose the network of an antidiscipline" (1984: xiv-xv). Everyday tactics bet on a clever utilization of time. Everyday action implies a different mentality.

For de Certeau a conception of everyday life composed of particular kinds of social zones, producing knowledgeability and procedures in the world is always political – not simply a thing in itself. He distinguishes between (everyday) tactics and the proper spaces where the (specialized) strategies of the scientist, philosopher, and expert unfold. Weakness is reflected in the absence of power to claim spaces and draw boundaries as "properly" those of strategies imposable on others. So tactics can only appropriate "foreign" or perhaps better "alien" territory for the moment. "Lacking its own place, lacking a view of the whole, limited by the blindness (which may lead to perspicacity) resulting from combat at close quarters, limited by the

---

[5] There is also a trace here of a critique of "logical operator" stylings of everyday life and ordinary persons, e.g.: "the ordinary man ... is both the nightmare or philosophical dream of humanist irony and an apparent referentiality (a common history) that make credible a writing that turns 'everyone' into the teller of his ridiculous misfortune ... an Other who is no longer God or the Muse, but the anonymous" (1984: 2).

possibilities of the moment, a tactic is determined by the absence of power just as a strategy is organized by the postulation of power" (1984: 38).

De Certeau's analysis distinguishes between (a proper) science and (residual) culture, between strategy and tactics, and (critically) between the "artificial languages" of a science he deplores versus a popular ratio-cination or "unself-conscious thought."[6] He develops a critical view of specialized science in proper, defined spaces, the purview of the scientist, philosopher, and expert. Science exists within an undefined residual sea of everyday "culture." Science "constitute[s] the whole as its remainder ... what we call culture ... scientific dominant islands ... against a background of practical 'resistances' and symbolizations that cannot be reduced to thought" (1984: 6).

De Certeau's characterizations of everyday life are not those of a theory of practice so much as a theory of action.[7] The procedural definitions he employs turn practices into actions of talking, walking, reading, cooking, these mainly in linguistic mode, a mode that takes as its subject a fatal "the": the walker, the reader or the cook – in the third person singular.[8]

Both the "everyday" as logical operator, distinguishing kinds of knowledge and the "everyday" as the product of an epistemological differentiation of zones of social life lay bare a deep distinction between the ordinary and the exceptional and their locations, however these may be conceived. The poles of such a divide are evidently asymmetrical. Sometimes the low/everyday is a residual category, just that which is not high culture, while the latter indicates idealized endpoints of learning. Sometimes the "everyday" is assumed to be the banal locus of activity of kinds that supposedly produce a limited and private knowledge (particular, context-bound, unselfconscious, tacit, silent). In both cases learning – "acquiring knowledge" – involves movement away from everyday life toward something else: from ignorance to knowledge, from empty to full, from child to adult, from novice to expert.

Such asymmetric polar distinctions between the everyday (with respect to learning) and its prized "others" result in assumptions that "learning" is singular and one-directional in scope and purpose. Engaging in learning implies

---

[6] Concepts of strategy and tactics were important in Lefebvre's complex theory/method; De Certeau explored their analytic potential in his own way in his analysis of consumer culture.

[7] Michel Trebitsch, in the preface to Lefebvre's second volume of *Critique of Everyday Life* "The works of Henri Lefebvre on everyday life were 'a fundamental source' for de Certeau ... Unquestionably, the two part company on numerous points – notably, the historical apprehension of daily life, which is relocated by the philosopher in a history of modernity, whereas the historian confines himself to a 'phenomenology of social micro-behaviour pitched at the level of the *long durée*'" (1962: xxiv).

[8] De Certeau makes his anti-individualist intent clear in the very first sentence of the first chapter (1984: 1). But at moments when "practice" gets reduced to "action," it is surely difficult to avoid "the individual" as the unit of analysis. This issue will return in Chapter 7, with respect to Ingold's characterization of learning as "the education of attention."

movement away from ordinary knowledge when "the everyday" is conceived as a logical operator, and as moving into segregated zones for producing knowledge, and away from everyday locations, in social zone conceptions of everyday life. Processes of learning can only be, then, movement away from everyday life and at the same time movement toward more, or higher, cultural knowledge or movement into specialized social zones. These are surely negative, and odd, representations of learning with respect to everyday life.

"Authentic" Intellectual Agents, Ease and Necessity, and *Telos*

These peculiar representations are nonetheless deeply engraved in historical sensibilities, class, and cultural relations. We can get a brief sense of how these sensibilities and relations have been produced and sustained over centuries in a historical study of early efforts to decide where and how to locate and engage in the practices of science (Shapin 1991). Another source of insight lies in Bourdieu's sociological analysis of distinction-making as a matter of French class culture (1984). He offers insight into class–cultural relations that inhabit conceptions of learning with respect to everyday life. Each explores deeply practiced beliefs about how everyday life is infused with (negative) epistemological significance while the learned *withdraw* from everyday life. Both Shapin and Bourdieu address the cultural production that separates high cultural knowledge from everyday life.

Shapin describes the strong presence of these separations and social hierarchizations in Christianity, Greek thought, and early science. He insists on the historical depth of very general beliefs about the direction, or movement, indeed, the *telos* of the extraordinary knower presently inscribed in conventional assumptions about learning. "Certain understandings and stipulations about the place of knowledge have ... scarcely changed from their Greek and Roman origins, and indeed, remain fundamentally unchanged today ... In our culture we do not have to listen hard to hear the hermit's voice" (1991: 208). Further: "[W]e inherit the historical legacy of so much testimony that the producers of our most valued knowledge are not in society. At the point of securing their knowledge, they are said to be outside the society to which they mundanely belong. And when they are being most authentically intellectual agents, they are said to be most purely alone" (Shapin 1991: 192).[9] He

---

[9] For a contemporary example of logical operator distinctions between the ordinary and the expert from the point of view of the expert, see Traweek (1988). As one of her physicist informants explained, "culture is like a Poisson distribution. You have to understand that scientists are drawn from out here in the tail of the distribution where cultures have very little impact." Because other people have culture, but we're physicists – we don't have culture" (1988: 42).

catalogues a long list of religious prophets, artists, poets, writers, painters composers, and philosophers struggling in or sitting on an assortment of hilltops, wildernesses, cells, garrets, logs in forests, islands and pond-sides, both literary inventions and real. He quotes popular poetic views such as the lines of Wordsworth on Newton: "Voyaging through strange seas of thought, alone." He observes that Descartes prefaced his *Discourse on Method* with a picture of chilling aloneness ... Descartes decided that his renewal of philosophic method depended on separating himself from society, resolving "to remove myself from all places where any acquaintance were possible, and to retire to a country such as this [Holland] ... where ... I can live as solitary and retired as in deserts the most remote" (quoting Descartes, in Shapin 1991: 194). He describes separation-solitude-withdrawal in terms of "retirement," and it applies equally to "scientific discovery" and "moral enlightenment" (Shapin 1991: 202, 206), Further, the solitary philosopher, like the religious isolate, might be seen as separated from the corruptions and contaminations of social life," from "publics" or "civic society" of various kinds, or mundane life (1991, 206). In Lefebvre's critical terms, these are ways of living with intent to pursue truth unsullied by reality.[10]

The nature of that "solitude," as one guise for the separation of (everyday) social life from sites of knowledge discovery or enlightenment, requires careful thought – it can only be a symbolic (or ideological) solitude as Shapin points out. In concrete social terms it requires withdrawing *into* certain kinds of – notably privileged – social and institutional settings (the company of gentlemen or the brotherhood of monks) and often pointedly announces withdrawal *from* specific contaminants (e.g., the company of women and the hurly burly of "ordinary" life. For seventeenth-century scientists in England it implied refuge from participation in a dangerous political scene as well). This is also only made possible by the scientists' access to wealth and position, and by the labor of others. "No solitude without servitude," is the way sociologist of science Leigh Star once summed it up.[11]

[10] Lefebvre in the first volume of *Critique of Everyday Life* also has something to say about "solitude." "... the study of everyday life would dispel several literary and philosophical myths whose spuriousness is one decadent tendency among many. For example, the myth of *human solitude*. ... It is the most 'private' individuals – intellectuals, individualists, separated by abstraction and bourgeois scholasticism from any relationship or social life – who have invented solitude" (1991: 198–9).

[11] De Certeau might well concur with Shapin's analysis of the historical tradition of solitary science, and withdrawal from the everyday as a condition of elite knowledge. Wherever scientists or other powerful persons retreat, he argues, they have the power to make, name, and delimit the boundaries of proper spaces; it is not that they withdraw into a non-place, a neutral space, nor an abstract epistemological domain. Withdrawal would be in de Certeau's terms a powerful move to claim proper space, e.g., laboratories, universities, monasteries, and even schools.

Shapin does not say a whole lot about "what" the scientists felt the need to withdraw *from*, though class prejudice and misogyny both seem heavily implicated in their arrangements. But even without elaboration, withdrawal – indeed the making of such distinctions – seems to be a fundamental elitist gesture of conventional practices, including withdrawing into "neutral objectivity," away from dominated, common and crude, persons, activities, locations, collectivities, and ways of knowing. In sum, Shapin argues, separation from the ordinary and everyday is seen as a prerequisite for engaging in science. But he also paints a picture of early science emerging through and from a politics of social privilege.

The distinctions that define "the everyday" for Bourdieu are epistemological, most especially, the relation that for him lies at the heart of culture, acts of classification, and the making of cultural categories. His analysis of classification – culturally arbitrary, its imposition a matter of symbolic violence – runs throughout his work. Along with the constitutive political character of cultural distinction making he insists on the social, structural conditions in relation with which, he argues, day-by-day internalized dispositions are laid down. So it is not knowledge alone that reproduces knowledge. He argues that everyday life in France operates in differentiated class-cultural terms, on the basis of an ideology that would fit very well with a notion of "the everyday" as a matter of social zones. Bourdieu elaborates an argument, resonating with Shapin's, that separation from everyday "necessity" is part of what defines social privilege and the appreciation and production of high culture. By his analysis different, class-specific, relations with art and culture are based in an ideology of everyday social locations widely separated from zones of rarefied privilege, and profoundly divided from autonomous or semi-autonomous fields of high cultural production.

He elects as an obvious candidate for high cultural endpoint, artists' and connoisseurs' command of "the pure aesthetic gaze" in pursuit of the conditions of production of French cultural understanding (and practice). It is notable that its acquisition depends deeply on various kinds of separation from "the everyday."

The aesthetic disposition, a generalized capacity to neutralize ordinary urgencies and to bracket off practical ends, a durable inclination and aptitude for practice without a practical function, can only be constituted within an experience of the world freed from urgency and through the practice of activities which are an end in themselves, such as scholastic exercises or the contemplation of works of art. In other words, *it presupposes the distance from the world ... which is the basis of the bourgeois experience of the world.* (1984: 64; italics mine)

Bourdieu pursued this line of argument in his analysis of what he calls "the axis of ease and necessity" in *Distinction*. The cultural valuation of wealth and prosperity as freedom *from* necessity (as separation from the concerns of "ordinary" folks who must act according to their economic necessities) is characteristic of claims about cultural production in the schoolish-academic terms that infuse and shape the broad cultural constitution of high culture.[12] They make distance from necessity the keystone of privilege and the deeply embedded characteristic of high-cultural endeavors, including the production of knowledge and the identification of culture-heroic destinies or destinations (or the directional beacons of academic assumptions about learning). This involves movement away from the ordinary in two senses, from lower social class positions, and from economic functional urgencies.

> Economic power is first and foremost the power to keep economic necessity at arm's length ... This affirmation of power over a dominated necessity always implies a claim to a legitimate superiority over those who, because they cannot assert the same contempt for contingencies in gratuitous luxury and conspicuous consumption, remain dominated by ordinary interests and urgencies ... The tastes of freedom can only assert themselves as such in relation to the tastes of necessity, which are thereby brought to the level of the aesthetic and so defined as vulgar. This claim to aristocracy is less likely to be contested than any other, because the relation of the "pure" "disinterested" disposition to the conditions which make it possible ... has every chance of passing unnoticed. The most 'classifying' privilege thus has the privilege of appearing to be the most natural one. (1984: 55–6)

He argues that the manner of using symbolic goods (whether artistic or intellectual) "especially those regarded as the attributes of excellence, constitutes one of the key markers of 'class' and also the ideal weapon in strategies of distinction, that is, as Proust put it, 'the infinitely varied art of marking distances'" (1984: 66).

I conclude along with Bourdieu that common sense theories of learning are purveyed from a thoroughly bourgeois point of view and with respect only to what is commonly accepted as high culture. Privilege requires and underwrites appropriation of the "proper" (de Certeau) possibilities of producing knowledge. Bourdieu insists that in French class culture, at least, the production and acquisition of culture is reserved by the haute bourgeoisie for the haute bourgeoisie.

Key Issues, Key Silences

It is not common for theorists of learning to turn a critical eye upon their naturalized assumptions about subject/world relations and the *telos* of their

---

[12] Working class folks have what he says is

> the exact opposite of the Kantian aesthetic. Whereas ... Kant strove to distinguish ... disinterestedness, the sole guarantor of the specifically aesthetic quality of contemplation, from the interest of reason which defines the Good, working-class people expect every image to explicitly perform a function ... and their judgments make reference, often explicitly, to the norms of morality or agreeable-ness. Whether rejecting or praising, their appreciation always has an ethical basis. (Bourdieu 1984: 5)

theories. Psychologists and educational researchers who employ common theories of learning engage in experiment-based investigations into what they assume are individual mental processes of knowledge acquisition. So proper research on learning mostly consists of empirical studies of *mechanisms* of learning – not much help in considering subject/world relations and *telos*. I turned to philosophers, historians, and sociologists for examples and insight because their critical social historical accounts help identify dilemmas and issues concerning subject/world relations and conceptions of *telos* in dualist versions of everyday life and learning. They point out three difficulties that conventional learning researchers could address, but customarily do not.

First, separation and distancing from the everyday is central for learning in the logical operator and social zone conceptions of learning with respect to everyday life discussed to this point. Processes of learning are configured in the binary politics of which everyday life is one pole, making learning (as the acquisition of knowledge) a movement toward the other pole. Both Shapin and Bourdieu argue that epistemological characterizations of learning with respect to everyday life end up – perhaps more aptly, *begin* – with high cultural production, so theorizing about learning becomes a matter of stipulating privileged directions – paths, progressions, stages of knowledge accumulation, cultural capital, or expertise – that should lead to the production of monks and saints, artists, and philosophers, scientists, professionals, and experts.

Second, this notion of learning as a process of moving away from ordinary knowledge or mundane social zones toward the attainment of high cultural knowledge and identities, where more is better and only the exceptional are extraordinary, is the *only* process that meets the criteria for "learning" in these polarized accounts.[13] Such insistent singularity easily solidifies into the

---

[13] Harry Collins, sociologist of knowledge recently observed that this way of theorizing learning results in a one-dimensional approach by psychologists and philosophers to the acquisition of "expertise." I would characterize Collins as engaged in a critique of a logical operator view of high cultural knowledge/expertise. He argues that:

> Psychologists and philosophers tend to treat expertise as a property of special individuals. These are individuals who have devoted much more time than the general population to the acquisition of their specific expertises. They are often said to pass through stages as they move toward becoming experts ... This approach is "one-dimensional." (Collins 2013: 253)

He goes on to argue that psychology and philosophy are silent about other sorts of expertise, one of which he calls "ubiquitous expertise" – for example, the fluent mastery of a language by native speakers. His critical objection to (what I would call) logical operator arguments in part echoes those here: assumptions about a singular *telos* of learning as only movement away from the ordinary toward high cultural achievement, and a recognition that a huge hole follows with respect to questions about learning when the object is culture with a small "c." However, disappointingly, the alternative he espouses is the other familiar epistemological account – he is

reification of "learning" as a unique knowledge-acquiring mental process in and of itself. This reified conception of learning is inevitably deployed as one pole in common distinctions between learning and other things: learning and doing, learning and teaching, learning and applying knowledge, and, centrally, learning and knowledge production. For if knowledge to be acquired is produced elsewhere than in learners' activities, by high cultural knowledge producers, those in acquisition mode progress by absorbing and reproducing it. Doing, teaching, applying, and producing knowledge are in their own ways conceived as matters of not-learning.

Third, divides between producing knowledge and reproducing knowledge (for which both Shapin and Bourdieu provide vivid illustrations), permeate Western cultural and educational assumptions. Widespread belief underwrites distinctions between teaching and research, elaborated in notions that teaching is only a matter of reproducing knowledge, and that creativity cannot be taught; that learning is a matter of internalizing existing knowledge and reproducing culture (produced elsewhere) only to apply it. As a result, common sense distinctions turn knowledge into something that can either be created *or* reproduced (but not improvised nor conceived dialectically in ways that would challenge the very idea of a dualist divide between subject and world).

Beyond these issues, we can also consider questions that logical operator and social zone versions of everyday life and learning are not just uninterested in addressing critically, but are arguably *unable* to address. Four issues stand out, interesting in part in anticipation of the third account of everyday life and learning as praxis. First, where might we encounter the *telos* of learning-to-do, the *telos* of engaging in making everyday life in its complicated, messy, never entirely centered sense. Without the binary and hierarchical polarization of logical operator and social zone accounts of everyday life with respect to learning, the very existence of a one-directional, cumulative, commanding *telos* of learning is suddenly in question. Second, given the exclusive conception of learning as a process of rising toward elite realms to become "authentic intellectual agents" (Shapin 1991), where shall we turn for conceptions of learning when projects of learning engage culture with a small "c" rather than a capital "C"? Third, even accepting conventional understandings that learners are engaged in moving away from everyday knowledges or zones toward cultural pinnacles of various sorts, the only way to make that movement is in everyday ways. Again, the question does not seem to come up: How is it, *in*

on his way to a social zone conception of everyday life and a learning as a matter of immersion by the learner in a *group of experts in a knowledge domain*. My thanks to Rodrigo Ribeiro for calling my attention to this paper.

everyday practice, that all that moving away and "progressing toward" comes about?[14] Finally, assumptions about personal trajectories – as paths to mastery, to excellence, to becoming experts – assume that theorists are talking about the acquisition, but not the production, of knowledge. Are such distinctions possible? Plausible? Creating knowledge certainly involves learning. Surely the reverse is also true?

How does the third account of everyday life and learning deal with these issues?

Everyday Life and Learning as Praxis

It was not difficult to imagine an *epistemological* conception of learning in relation to the logical operator and social zone conceptions of everyday life (all about distinctions among kinds, qualities, and locations of knowledge). But it may be easier to accept uncritically claims that everyday life is indeed a social matter than to insist on a *social* conception of learning processes and practices. It would be easier to slide instead into another sort of dualist account, still holding on to common sense notions of learning as a container of mental processes of knowledge acquisition and storage. Then when discussing everyday life one would just get more rigorous about a socio-logical conception of something like groups, institutions, practices – i.e., schools. This is the most common, but still contradictory, way of taking up notions of "situated learning," or gesturing at a bit of social context around, say, cognitive accounts of learning. But social practice theory does not couple a social account of ongoing everyday life with a concept of learning as mental exercise. Rather, everyday life and learning are conceived as historically, dialectically, constitutive of each other. Everyday life and learning both make and are made in the medium of participants' partial participation in ongoing, changing social practice (that is an anthropological view of culture – all culture – as culture with a small "c.") Questions of boundaries and divisions, differences in power, in value, and the complex, conflictual relations separating categories or social zones, "high" and "low" facets of social life assumed and justified in epistemological terms in those accounts of zones and logical operators, are all assumed to be made through historical political processes, in practice.

---

[14] Schools are surely everyday social zones mystified as "not everyday," and understood as sites for purveying and acquiring non-everyday knowledge in non-everyday locations. But, in contradictory ways, schools are also contexts of everyday activity, about which we might note both their everyday existence and their claim to separate learners from their everyday knowledge and ordinary contexts. These assumptions about schooling make it all too easy to treat "learning" – in abstract terms – as if its very meaning is confined to institutional and ideological elaborations of schooling.

In this account, learning is not movement away from the everyday, but persons in their relations with each other moving into and through their social lives conceived as social, relational, historical processes. Knowledge, or rather knowing, is subsumed with many other things in the everyday production of ongoing practice. Salient questions about learning with respect to everyday life (and vice versa) focus on the ubiquitous, heterogeneous, changing relations of participation in everyday life. It is through such relations that practices, participants, and ways of participating change – learning in/as practice.

Processes of boundary-making that separate locations, participants, and practices conceived as proper to "knowledge production" from sites of learning naturalized as a matter of "knowledge reproduction" require political-economic and cultural analysis in order to explain differentiations of subjects, practices, institutions and historical forces.[15] If contemporary debates designate expertise, research and development, or entrepreneurship, as sites of "knowledge production," reserved in ideological and structural terms for privileged classes or institutions, they are nonetheless produced in historically political, economic and cultural relations and practices – not by an epistemologically-constituted world. Further, just as the third account of everyday life with respect to learning argues that learning is only possible in everyday relations and practices, it argues that there is no way to engage in knowledge production other than in everyday ways.[16]

The notion of *telos* in the first two accounts refers to putative "knowledge accumulation" via individual mental application and individuals' intentions to move toward expertise or other high cultural knowledgeabilities. But this does not capture processes of learning in changing relations of participation in ongoing changing practice. This requires something more complex than a singular *telos* of progressive knowledge accumulation. Changing participation

---

[15] If the epistemological issues of social existence are social in their constitution, epistemological issues must be *subsumed* within the social ontology and not the other way around. Most especially when we explore issues of learning and knowing as part of ongoing practice it does not make sense to ignore these radically counter-intuitive relations. Reversing the customary relations between social ontological and epistemological inquiry is one of the central projects in developing a theory of learning in/as practice.

[16] STS work has provided powerful arguments against an exclusively epistemological reading of everyday life (and learning). Since Latour and Woolgar's initial *Laboratory Life* (1979) one of the critical contributions of STS has been to investigate processes of "knowledge production" at sites of the sorts of practices located at the "high" poles in the first two versions of the epistemological everyday as in fact a matter of day-to-day social practice. This body of research encourages a pursuit of different understandings of learning with respect to everyday life, for several reasons. Chapter 1 raised the question: if the work of science is done in everyday ways, what does this do to our conception of "the everyday" everyday? STS raises questions about what would happen if we stopped ratifying bourgeois epistemological arguments that mystify political-economic differences and dominant ideologies by assigning them to differences among minds, knowledges, places and processes of producing knowledge and insisted on analyzing even the latter in terms of their production in practice.

in changing practice may be about knowledge and its accumulation – but more often it is not. These considerations lead to different material-social-historical conceptions of moving, changing social participation, and a notion of "trajectories of changing practice."

Inquiry into issues of learning focused on participants' changing participation in daily life disrupts notions of a single direction, a single process, or a single locus of change. Dreier makes this evident while laying out his account of what is involved in persons' conduct of everyday life:

The everyday life of a person reaches across several social contexts with different social practices. Ordinarily it contains social contexts and practices such as family homes, workplaces, schools, and other regular, temporary, occasional and one-off contexts and practices. In these different contexts a person faces different demands and takes part on different social positions in relation to different co-participants . . . In conducting her everyday life she must coordinate and negotiate it with the various others she is engaged in relations to at different times and places across the day . . . Its ordinariness allows her to build particular routines into its conduct and provokes her need for various kinds and degrees of variation. Furthermore, persons develop a self-understanding about themselves as the person who leads this particular life the way she does. A person's self-understanding is ordinarily based on her commitments to specific others in rich, concrete social relationships, to specific places and sense of place, to specific activities and organizations of rhythms of life. (Dreier 2015: 2)

Everyday life approached as active and multiple pursuits raises questions about how to characterize a variety of different and related changing practices that produce learning-in-practice. When we consider learning with respect to everyday life (and vice versa) in these terms we must ask how people take part differently in different contexts, face different demands in relation to different coparticipants, in different places, and in varied and changing organizations of rhythms of life, opening both theoretical questions and new lines of ethnographic inquiry. A concept of "*telos*" is not adequate for analyzing learning as movement across contexts, engaging with others in practices of various sorts, or for capturing changing knowledgeability-in-practices – processes of becoming different while also participating in reproducing practices.

Further, participants change in and through their changing participation in changing practices – including, of course, producing and changing knowledgeabilities. Practices also require (and help to produce) arrangements for participation, and some of these are institutional arrangements. Participants are engaged in producing their lives, participating in practices in ways that at the same time produce and reproduce them. Part of reproducing practices involves producing participants, and such arrangements might be called institutional trajectories for changing participation.

Indeed "changing trajectories of participation," and "trajectories of changing participants with respect to particular practices" mark a conceptual shift to a material, social analytic version of everyday life and learning. Learning in practice is to be found in relations among different sorts of trajectories of practice, of participants, and of participation. Salient questions include issues of access to participation, different ways of participating, inclusion and exclusion, and partial, including peripheral, participation. Also salient are questions about differences among participants in practice and their conflictual cooperation (Nielson 2007; Axel 2009), intergenerational relations and questions about how practices are produced and reproduced at the same time while not being reducible to one or the other. These are different aspects of changing participation and changing participants. All of these questions are *at one and the same time* questions about changing participants, about changing participation, and about changing practices. They need, above all, substantive formulation with respect to each other.

Conclusion

Pervasive practices with respect to theorizing learning distort our collective ways of recognizing and inquiring in broad and searching theoretical/empirical terms into processes of learning that are inescapably part of the fabric of everyday practice. It seems especially important to call attention to persons collectively engaged in practice in their different ways, changing those practices in the course of engaging in them (as well as not), or engaging in practice to change the conduct of their everyday lives, or to change themselves.

Is the everyday world not "really" as those epistemologically dualist premises claim? The argument that makes best sense to me is laid out in Chapter 2 ("The Problem of Context and Practices of Decontextualization"). That is: What is learnable is in part shaped by ideological–historical institutionalized arrangements. Much living is done in their name. Conventional theorists can describe this world, but those descriptions cannot explain the processes that *produce* it. The learning of everyday life is not in fact brought about by such invocations, and must be analyzed in other terms – practice theory being one serious resource in this effort.

7   Situated Learning
Historical Process and Practice

* * * * *

In talking about relations between theoretical practice and ethnographic inquiry in the Introduction, I emphasized the iterative character of research as learning that makes new projects preambles to old projects. The present chapter, written for *Learning and Everyday Life*, begins with a critical look at *Situated Learning*, asking how it does (and does not) hold up as a preamble to the central argument here. The chapter is framed around a question: *How [are we] to weave together the production of persons in their everyday lives and the generation in practice of the historical processes and practices that make the world as we are part, and take part, in it?*

A first step involves decentering studies of learning so as to explore learners' changing practice in the complex world that in part makes them what they are. In order to focus on the situated production of everyday life the chapter takes up Gramsci's approach to praxis in relation to Dreier's work on the conduct of everyday life. Gramsci did not have a lot to say about "the person," conceived in relational, dialectical terms as "the ensemble of social relations" (Thomas 2009: 275). He had much to say about the necessity of transforming everyday practice, bringing coherence into alternative world views now a fragmentary part of common sense, in order to bring about revolutionary change in everyday life. He had much less to say about how the incoherences – contradictory common sense – (laid down in long historical struggles, and heavily defended through hegemonic practices) are *produced* in everyday life. On the other hand, the production of everyday life is the central question for those engaged in studies of the conduct of everyday life

I made brief earlier attempts at a critical retrospective look at *Situated Learning*. This included a talk at the Copenhagen Business School in 2003 and an epilogue in Amin and Roberts 2008: 283–96). In the present context especial thanks to Ole Dreier and Gillian Hart. Working with Dorothy Holland on the *History in Person* project and her careful reading and substantive suggestions have much improved this chapter. Years of discussion with Paul Duguid, reading his work, and his readings of mine, have influenced the argument in many respects. Danish colleagues Tove Borg and Charlotte Hojholt persuaded me that on a key point I was wrong headed, which sparked revision of previous drafts and provoked new ideas. I am very grateful for their help. I would never have started this project without the encouragement of Ana Gomes and her colleagues and students at the UFMG in 2011. Without many long discussions with Ana about our work, and her extraordinary reading of this chapter in 2014 I never could have finished it.

(e.g., Dreier 2008; Schraube and Højholt 2015). The question is, do they engage with those hegemonic practices and historical divisions (and, if so, how).

The introduction to the essays as a whole outlines several interrelated issues that have shaped this work: first, a theoretical problematic – dialectical, relational Marxism, with its historical and philosophical development. Exploring this problematic is an open-ended project. It is also in part a process of articulating a critique of conventional theorizing. Just saying "no" to mainstream theory is a never-ending obligation that in the last decades has changed its language and even its location (e.g., from the argot of educational psychology, to neurobiology and behavioral economics) without changing theoretical assumptions or hegemonic intentions. But the effects of advice to "just say no" are well known. Opposition to common sense theory takes that theory as its predicate and does not itself produce an alternative. Effort to envision an alternative world view (in dialectical Marxist terms) is a long, slow process of trying to change ethnographic practice in response to changing theoretical understanding and vice versa. Traces of my engagement in this process are most clearly visible in this chapter.

* * * * *

"We are all apprentices to our own changing practice" (Lave 2011: ix). In that spirit, this essay is intended to reconsider *Situated Learning: Legitimate Peripheral Participation* (Lave and Wenger 1991), based on changing practice over the quarter century since it was published. The chapter as a whole has a single-minded focus on the situated character of practice, what this might mean, and how changing understandings of theory of practice might shape ethnographic inquiries. The determination to pursue changing conceptions of learning in/as practice here has hinged on two points. The first is a realization that the most important theoretical "move" of *Situated Learning* might not be its argument about the situated character of learning-in-practice, but rather its insistence that this implies and requires decentering inquiry into learning. After all, learning is always only part of changing practice in a changing world. Second, perhaps the most acute critique of *Situated Learning* in the years following its publication has been Duguid's argument that the book did not locate collective landscapes of possibility for learning-in-practice in the political-economic, historical, institutional relations of which they are part. Together these two points pose the problem of how to weave between and together the production of persons in their everyday lives and the generation in practice of the historical processes and practices that make the world as we are part, and take part, in it. The answer involves a better understanding of dialectical method.

The Argument of the Book

It matters how we read *Situated Learning*. For the book is often cited as the source of two concepts, "situated learning as legitimate peripheral participation" and "communities of practice." But when excised as simply things in themselves, as if they are *not* constituted as part of more comprehensive theoretical relations, concepts like "situated learning" easily travel as mere slogans, plugged into common sense, uncritical theoretical and analytical contexts. How concepts are taken up always matters for the analytic possibilities they support and the limitations they impose on the questions they frame. The uses to which the conceptual apparatus of *Situated Learning* has been put will illustrate this point. The book did work out a theoretical stance, a critical-theoretical account of learning; it derived analytic questions from theoretically constituted ethnographic accounts of apprenticeship. *Situated Learning* formulated a general question: How are we to understand learning as an integral part of ongoing social practice? The argument can be summed up in a short series of points: Learning is only a part of ongoing practice. Situated learning as legitimate peripheral participation makes inseparable participants' participation in practice and the practices in part embodied in changing participants. The practices of which participants are part are necessary conditions of possibility for learning. The object of analysis therefore needs to be a textured landscape of participation. Studies of learning as legitimate peripheral participation in communities of practice begin there. A coherent focus for such observations emerges from *decentering* the study of learning – "for to shift from the notion of an individual learner to the concept of legitimate peripheral participation in communities of practice is precisely to decenter analysis of learning" (Lave and Wenger 1991: 94). An historical, processual theoretical stance surely leads to an insistence on decentering analyses of learning.

Characterizing the book in these terms is already a step toward a deeper argument about analysis of practice in historical-spatial terms. For "decentering" was not so prominent a thread of argument at the time *Situated Learning* was published. Thinking back, the book was the third in a series of attempts to inquire into learning in all sorts of practices without having to cram and distort them into something resembling school arrangements in order to know what to look for and how to explain it. My research on apprentice tailors in Liberia was an attempt to find ways to address learning-in-practice in nonschool-centric terms. It started out from criticism of the dualist assumptions governing deeply-engrained common sense claims that some education, namely schooling is "formal" and everything else is "informal" education (Lave 2011). In this light *Situated Learning* could be thought of as an approach to ethnographic research as part of a theoretical problematic, social practice theory, with roots in Marxist theory of praxis. The book focused on how to inquire into ongoing practices, on the ground, empirically and theoretically. It was an attempt to develop questions to guide such research. Arguably much of the value of *Situated Learning* lay in the power of those questions to spark new lines of ethnographic inquiry.

Second, more specific comparative frameworks emerged, driven by the same concerns, toward the end of the ethnographic project in Liberia. I began to compare the practices of the tailors, as they assembled and rearranged arithmetic relations in different settings. One of these settings was a one-on-one experiment in which a series of problems were designed to probe the individual arithmetic prowess of the tailors and their apprentices, in spirit very school-like (a whole critical analysis of such experiments followed [Lave 1988]). But the ethnographic work in Liberia was intended to establish an even playing field for comparative research, one that did not treat Western, school-ish math as a gold standard against which to measure (and find wanting) all other practices. What would a less ethnocentric yardstick look like? This question led to one (futile) attempt to create such a basis for comparison (Lave 2011: 140–2).

Different conceptual frameworks generate different analytic questions. For example, the formal/informal model of education sends the researcher expect-antly looking for teachers, curricula, classes, exams and pupils on the one hand, and the absence of these things and/or evidence of replicative, limited, impoverished, incidental versions of same where "informal education" is the object of study. An analysis in these terms cannot be focused on anything except how it is or is not schooling. On the other hand, the experiments focused on different questions aimed at comparing problem-solving in cogni-tive experiments with problem-solving in Vai and Gola tailor shops. Questions in this context were things like: Is there such a thing as a "math problem" in a tailor shop that is similar to "math problems" in the experiments? What do processes for transforming relations of quantity look like? How are such relations generated? In relation to what else? Who, in practice, generates questions of quantity? (Experimenters? Tailors? Production processes? Cus-tomers?) If dealing with quantities seems effortful or inconvenient at particular moments, what happens? (In experiments? In tailor shops?) Questions of quantity often seemed to require inventive social circumvention in the tailor shops. How does this work? How are social strategies for problem solving in play? If they are not allowed in one case, but are frequent in another, how does that come about? Is "problem solving" (now in scare quotes) an end in itself or a means to other ends, or both at the same time, or neither? How, and how much, does it matter to the different participants in different settings?

Situated Learning proposed a third comparative framework. The idea of learning as legitimate peripheral participation in communities of practice was a way to speak about *relations* among participants, activities, identities, artifacts and communities of practice. The book proposed a way of inquiring into specific practices of learning-in-practice, formulating questions to guide research and practice that did not depend on school-centric assumptions about knowledge, power, their relations, and their effects with respect to learners learning. The book suggested questions to address to any particular practice as in part constituted through learning. Chapter 4 in *Situated Learning* set out a veritable handbook of questions intended to focus inquiry in directions that might illuminate how learning is part of ongoing practices. What structuring resources in community practice shape what/how learning is possible? What is the "learning curriculum"[1] – the "field of learning resources in everyday practices viewed from the perspective of learners" (1991: 97)? The notion of "structuring resources" for learning in practice pointed to questions about where widely varying possibilities for learning might be found. "Depending on the organization of access, legitimate peripherality can either promote or prevent legitimate participation" (1991: 103). What would one need to investigate in order to figure out which, and why? It seemed important to inquire into intersections and tensions between work practices and learning processes, as they made conflicting demands on apprentices for good and ill. This raised questions about how legitimate peripherality could be arranged/manipulated to prevent or circumscribe access to practices learners wanted to (learn to) participate in, the changing linguistic usage of all concerned, peers and practice as structuring resources, tensions among generations of practitioners and contradictory relations between producing a practice and reproducing it. Investigating these issues should produce accounts of learning situated in the everyday practices of which it is part.

Legitimate Peripheral Participation in Communities of Practice

In working out the core concepts in *Situated Learning*, "community of practice" was a way to give scope to an understanding of "practice" so as not to reduce social life to interpersonal transactions, interactions, and "problem-solving" activities. Similarly, learning as "legitimate peripheral participation of newcomers becoming old-timers" was intended to open out concepts like "learning" to broader historical, cultural and political relations and larger scopes of time and place.

The argument focused on movement, changing locations, and ways of participating, and pointed to questions about how knowledgeability changes in changing circumstances. In this view value (complexly, contradictorily, positive, and negative) is partly created by and for participants (differently) through their engagements in practice. "Identity" was a concept whose purpose was to insist that increasing knowledgeable skill is only a small part of the broader social being of newcomers becoming old-timers in practice.

---

[1] For critical studies of the relation between curriculum and learning see David Thornton Moore's work (1981, 1986).

One goal was to parse a community's day-to-day practice with respect to its involvement in producing "old-timers" from "newcomers," in such a way as to escape from abstract notions of the "universal person" or "individual," and to emphasize that participants exist in their relations with each other. Also, to get away from too-tight conventional assumptions that all "old-timers" (and no newcomers) are teachers and that all "newcomers" are (only) novices. "Old-timers" and "newcomers" left open just what, other than relative length of participation, differentiated participants from one another. The concept of "communities of practice" was likewise intended to move away from an abstract universal notion of group or social category. People are mutually engaged in *doing* things together. It is this doing, and its historical material production, that sustains for "next generations" the cultural practices that they make over and into their lives. Both old-timer–newcomer relations as well as relations among other situated participants embody tensions that help to generate the complexities of "legitimate peripheral participation."

"Legitimate peripheral participation" was intended as one indivisible idea. Or at least its parts should never be taken one at a time. In spite of this, the concept invited a polarizing vision of illegitimate, or central, or non- participation. Why it was hard to grasp as "a textured landscape of participation" had more to do with problems running through the book than with the three-part term itself. One problem was the notion of moving from peripheral to full participation. Care is required not to reduce that to merely a contrast between novice and expert (even if with reference to participation in whatever practice). Second, legitimate peripherality was the most problematic of the pairwise permutations of legitimate peripheral participation. Legitimate participation and peripheral participation were fairly straightforward concepts. But issues about accepting the unprepared as nonetheless legitimate participants pointed to ambiguities of power and to tensions over the changing possibilities for participation of newcomers becoming old-timers. Though acknowledged in discussing legitimate peripheral participation, perhaps it was not connected clearly enough to the analysis later of communities of practice, which took up just those issues. Taken together, these problems surely made it easier to dismember the concept of legitimate peripheral participation in simple abstract terms. The book should have made clearer that (and how) institutions and the forces and relations of production give some participants power over legitimate peripheral participation *indivisibly*.

Situated Learning tries to explain why "thinking," a partial, relational part of embodied engagement with things, participants, and events in practice – takes its salient character and qualities from its part in social practice. I am not certain the word "cognition" never appears in *Situated Learning*, but such was our intention – that, and the desire that every use of the term "participation" could be read twice – both as "a person participating" and as a "practice participated in." So legitimate peripheral participation describes the practice of persons with respect to communities of practice. Likewise, from the other side of this relation, communities of practice consist in part of their diverse participants. This ubiquitous double meaning is the key to our efforts to refuse to divide person from world:

[Legitimate peripheral participation (lpp)] is intended as a conceptual bridge – as a claim about the common processes inherent in the production of changing persons and changing communities of practice. This pivotal emphasis, via lpp, on relations between the production of knowledgeable identities and the production of communities of practice, makes it possible to think of sustained learning as embodying, albeit in transformed ways, the structural characteristics of communities of practice. (1991: 55)

The conclusion began: "[T]he concept of lpp obtains its meaning, not in a concise definition of its boundaries, but in its multiple, theoretically generative interconnections with persons, activities, knowing and the world" (1991: 121). One common problematic reading of the book merely relocates old dualistic divisions, acknowledging this new thing, situated learning, but then assuming it is just the other pole of general, non-situated, often "modern" or "advanced" forms of learning. But the argument of *Situated Learning* was emphatic. Learning is situated. There are no exceptions.

Ethnography and Theory

Situated Learning laid out five ethnographic examples, all contemporary. Two were about long-term practices of apprenticeship, those of the Vai and Gola tailors and Mayan midwives. These examples underlined and raised questions about the often gender-segregated relations of craft practice. One other ethnographic example explored methods of production characteristic of high technology labor (on a helicopter transport ship) and another examined production in conditions of manual labor with modest technological support (the butchers in the supermarket). The final example, Alcoholics Anonymous, raised issues about participation in collective healing, in practices interestingly different from more stereotypical medical/health practices (as also did the study of the Yucatec midwives). Different historical traditions, different arrangements of access to legitimate peripheral participation – it seemed important to disrupt a single unified stereotype of "apprenticeship."

The ethnographic examples captured some points in the theoretical argument in vivid terms, but not others. Most notably absent, from a contemporary perspective was close exploration of the varied practices of apprenticeship in historical terms. But all of the ethnographic examples pointed to peers and practice as structuring resources for learning. In all the examples motivation seemed to inhere in movement toward full participation in community practices in which apprentices also had a future and were developing identities. The accounts about the Yucatec midwives and Vai tailors showed how learning happens in the absence of didactic initiatives. The example of the Vai and Gola tailors showed that processes of tailoring and *simultaneous* learning processes were structured differently. This was a central analytic claim that took a long time to recognize. It was important in part because it drew into question common claims about learning through apprenticeship as merely a process of imitating masters at work. Further: "[D]issociating learning from pedagogical intentions opens the possibility of mismatch or conflict among practitioners' viewpoints in situations where learning is going on. These differences often must become constitutive of the content of learning" (1991: 113–14).

Two of the ethnographic studies were located in modern capitalist settings. In the military example issues of *access* to participation arose when huge numbers of participants took part for brief periods of time in a narrowly defined and repetitive series of tasks. The ethnographic account of butchers' apprenticeship in a supermarket explored the dark side of access by situating learning in alienated, commoditized relations in contemporary life. The meat department denied the apprentices legitimate peripherality to master butchers at their work. Apprentices were sequestered by management interested in extracting labor at the expense of facilitating learning. Apprentices learned more about conditions of labor in supermarkets than about butchering practices.

The Alcoholics Anonymous example helped to underline analysis of changing linguistic participation, including talk within and/or talk about the practice and occasions for war stories as diagnostic initiatives. Alcoholics Anonymous is not usually seen as a matter of apprenticeship, but it was not difficult to show that participation in the twelve-step program was a matter of legitimate peripheral participation, involving a gradual move by members toward more complex biographical accounts of contradictory processes of becoming non-drinking alcoholics.

Contradiction and Change

A community of practice is a set of relations among persons, activity, and world, over time and in relation with other tangential and overlapping communities of practice. (1991: 98)

Given common misreadings of "communities of practice" as homogeneous, shared, bounded groups (cf. Duguid 2008), it is worth turning to the book itself for an account of the argument: We imagined a community of practice as a nexus of ongoing cultural practice and as composed of its changing participants. A community of practice is a condition of possibility for learning. We argued that this implies that knowledgeability changes spatially, in motion, in participants' relations with diverse others, participating differently (Lave and Wenger 1991: 94–8). Possibilities for learning lie in those differences.

To speak of "knowledgeability" rather than "knowledge" implies that, whatever it is, knowledge is always partial and only partially in persons-in-practice. "Knowledge" in practice is not reducible to something distinct from its locations and its active situated production. It is not knowledge that produces social life or *is* social life but rather (a fundamental tenet of theories of praxis) it is the making and doing of social life that produces changing knowledgeabilities as part of ongoing practice.[2]

Communities of practice shape and are shaped by differences among changing persons, activities, and circumstances. There must frequently be specific conflicts over legitimate peripherality: whether, and how, someone may participate in peripheral ways that make less than a full contribution to ongoing activities, while preserving possibilities for learning to participate more fully. The notion of "legitimate peripherality" points to ambiguities and uncertainties that are common in struggles between newcomers' access to practice and sequestration from it. The butchers' example underlined common conflicts between masters and apprentices over whether apprentices should engage in short-term contributions of labor sequestered from arenas of masterly practice. (So did the ethnography of tailors' apprenticeship though those details were not included in *Situated Learning* [see Lave 2011].) Should apprentices be relegated to wrapping packages of meat (or working on the master's farm up country) or be included and take part in activity with peripheral participatory possibilities for learning that might not be immediately useful to the "boss"? Old-timers and newcomers have conflicting stakes in desirable scopes of access and control. Learning is always part of such problematic practices.

Further, "communities of practice are engaged in producing their own future" (1991: 57–8). So heterogeneous inter-generational relations, whether literal or metaphorical, are also constitutive of ongoing communities of prac-tice. Struggles for both continuity of practice and displacement of old ways pose a central contradiction in communities of practice with respect to legit-imate peripheral participation. For changing development of co-participants, and with it the production of a community of practice, also implies the displacement and replacement of old-timers (1991: 57). "Conflicts between masters and apprentices (or, less individualistically, between generations) take place in the course of everyday participation . . . Each threatens the fulfillment of the other's destiny, just as it is essential to it" (1991: 116).

---

[2] Further, since much takes place in the world in the name of knowledge assumed to be solid, nonreactive, and transmittable, or in the name of a knowledge society or knowledge economy, the social analyst's challenge is to come to understand how *these effects too* are created in practice – not to assume their existence *sui generis* (see Chapter 2 – The Problem of Context and Practices of Decontextualization).

For old-timers especially, "granting legitimate participation to newcomers with their own viewpoints introduces into any community of practice all the tensions of the continuity-displacement contradiction" (1991: 116). Resolutions to contradictions are inherently partial and unstable. This in part underwrites the claim that "practice" is necessarily *changing* practice, and that participation must require improvisation.

Situated Learning proposed that we pay attention to processes by which communities of practice are produced and produce themselves. Asking how and what continuity is being produced in contradictory processes of struggle and what and how displacements are being produced across "generations," is a useful way to focus attention on central and interesting questions: Just *what* complex practice is under production? How are changing participants in changing practices doing things together, in contradictory ways, in a changing world that is being produced and producing it too? These are both empirical and theoretical questions. Empirical and theoretical answers start with a relational claim – of situated practice. But crucial to this argument is the point that inquiry into situated practice with respect to learning requires decentering conceptions of learning through analytic methods that persist in asking *of what* are processes of learning a part?

Situated Learning, in Practice and Politics

Theoretical claims about learning are always a political matter whatever else they are. Our intention in *Situated Learning* was to lay out a critical alternative to conventional theorizing. The politics of common sense theory grows out of the ways it limits learning to institutional sites, processes of inculcation, and to state-mandated priorities. Such limitations are furnished (through laws, guidelines, teacher training, curricula, etc.) from the point of view of bureaucratic systems. We found conventional theory not only inadequate as a theoretical account of learning, but, taken uncritically, it naturalizes authoritarian methods and systemically unjust outcomes, with learners designated as the object of educators' attention, rather than being recognized as participants in their own right. We started instead from learners' perspectives, collectively, in their projects and practices, in their lives.

However, as the argument of *Situated Learning* was taken up in practice, it demonstrated an important old point: that theoretical arguments are always politically inflected, but they cannot determine the political ways in which they are taken up and deployed. This critical claim has often been ignored. This helps to explain why different readings of *Situated Learning* over the years have led in different directions. On the one hand they have been employed prescriptively as a "how to" manual for creating and "managing" communities of practice principally in corporate settings. Indeed, imposed from the top down, "communities of practice" enjoyed considerable *caché* over a period of years in the practices of corporate management, drawing especially on Wenger's consulting work and books (e.g., Wenger 1998; Wenger et al. 2002). It was taken up from corporate and educational establishment positions of power and drew lessons about management organization, possibilities for commoditized knowledge production and mandated creativity, encouraged in the belief that it would foster "regional economic drivers" and "incubators of entrepreneurship." "CoPs dominate the current literature, on economic creativity, organizational innovation, and local economic regeneration, as a key resource to tackle these challenges" (Amin and Roberts 2008: 13). When the organization of work practice (e.g., "communities of practice") is imposed from the top down it strips the concept of its critical character. Many who have taken up – in order to start up – "communities of practice" seem ignorant of the original development of that concept in *Situated Learning*, and have simply assimilated it to ahistorical, vernacular theory, unable to create other inspirations than visions of homogeneous informal work groups formed to mine "tacit knowledge" from them on behalf of corporate players in the "knowledge economy."

Paul Duguid coauthored an influential papers on the subject (Brown and Duguid 1991). He has been a leading critic of its various appropriations and misappropriations.[3] He once asked participants at a conference on communities of practice to quickly write down their understanding of the concept. The results included: "A group of people bound together by their interest in a common working practice," "social groups organized around a certain activity (practice)," and "groups sharing a same practice and oriented towards the resolution of common problems" (Duguid 2008: 1). He went on to argue that,

most noticeably, these accounts are "... preoccupied with groups brought together by their shared interests in a topic ... Papers also tend to make a lot of the purposefulness with which organizations create or manage communities of practice. So doing they tend to make communities of practice the outcome of management fiat, and not of practice. And many papers highlight the problems that such communities can be created to solve. In a significant proportion of the literature, then, the community of practice is seen as a useful, management-controlled, problem-solving tool. (2008: 2)

---

[3] Duguid observes that dilemmas with respect to power and control over participants, knowledges, and practices are unavoidable in settings where the installation of a community of practice has been mandated from above. Thus, for corporate managers wishing for control over employees in "communities of practice," contradictions of continuity and displacement present a double-edged sword: "Insist on conformity, and you inhibit learning and your organization might thus fall victim of the fragility of its own rules; encourage learning, and you encourage autonomy and might face mutiny in response to those own rules" (Duguid 2008: 7). He also points out that while improvisation and uncertainty are constitutive of changing practice, the *corporate* orthodox faith in Taylorism opposes improvisation as disruptive, while reading radical critiques of Taylorism with respect to improvisation as merely a gesture of opposition to Taylorism.

Mandated from above, the political relations involved in organizing communities of practice by fiat are erased from analysis. Top-down appropriations of situated learning resonate with neoliberal "invitations" to self-governance and can be recast in the interest of management engineering with the intent to control the production of commodifiable knowledge (or classroom productivity). And that is itself a political move whose effect is to reduce understandings of communities of practice to benign, pastoral, work groups. This results not in translating, but in transforming the conceptual relations of situated learning out of recognition. It is puzzling what the attraction of these ideas has been in the world of corporate management. Perhaps they provided a temporary, if fraught, resolution to contradictions between management and labor for true believers in "the knowledge economy" who faced the problem of establishing a supply line of commodifiable knowledge.

But conceptions of legitimate peripheral participation in communities of practice have been taken up in quite different circumstances by and for participants wanting to examine and consider changing their *own* ongoing practices. The conceptual work in *Situated Learning* offered resources to help make visible – to articulate – ongoing practices for learners' learning, often practices whose social, institutional, locations had been marginalized in various ways. Participants (with understandings already more complicated than orthodox characterizations of their practices) could examine their communities of practice to understand better how they did and did not provide conditions of possibility for learning and how those practices could be different and better.

Borg has described the work of occupational therapists under her direction in the setting of a neuro-rehabilitation hospital in Denmark, an institution dominated by biomedicine: "The understanding of rehabilitation, of professional initiatives and current biomedical research primarily has individualistic, non-relational and non-contextual focuses," she reports, while the occupational therapists' are supposed to prepare stroke victims to return home and take up their everyday lives again. The occupational therapists undertook a research project "concerned with changing and developing knowledge-in-practice" about their work. Together they drew on the argument and concepts from *Situated Learning* to help conceptualize what they were doing. It gave them a way to analyze and reconfigure their work with patients and with each other, a possibility for change that they wanted and needed (Personal communication October 2013; Kristensen et al. 2011).

Højholt's (2006) research concerns children caught up in fights between preschool teachers, primary school teachers, and parents over responsibility for children's problems as they move from preschool to the primary school. The adults treated the problems as a question of the child's learning (and/or learning disabilities) and made the child the center and object of blame. Using conceptualizations of communities of practice made it possible to steer people – for instance parents fighting with each other – away from formulating their conflicts as a matter of individual problem children, and instead raised possibilities for considering the problem to be problems of the community.

And it is interesting that the picture of (the problem) changes during these processes … to work with children's participation in communities requires reflections on how the children set up conditions for each other and on how the professionals arrange situations for the interplay among the children. But first of all it implies cooperation among the grown-ups … There is no universal model for such processes but [we must develop] a perspective about working with conditions for participation in communities. (Højholt 2011: 80ff)

Højholt observes that when they are asked, in effect, to examine their community of practice to get at the conditions of possibility for learning, parents begin to see their *own* conflicts as constitutive of problems for and by their children.

Production schools in Denmark take young people who have failed, or fallen out of, academic schooling and offer them a year or two of preparation for getting on with their lives (see Chapter 5). The director and other staff at the Kalundborg Production School did not seem to need to borrow ideas from *Situated Learning* – they already engaged young people in workshop-based processes of legitimate peripheral participation in the multiply related communities of practice that composed the school. What the conceptual and ethnographic argument could do was to translate their complex practice into positive theoretical terms relevant to that practice. Possibly this could make their highly effective but unorthodox practice more legitimate in the eyes of state bureaucracy, and more defensible in a variety of ways in educational contexts in which the state-authorized system of schools offered the only officially valued possibility.

Together these last three examples suggest ways in which the analytic and conceptual terms of *Situated Learning* have been useful to those reconsidering their own practices. First, it helped make it possible to resist influential common sense educational theory/ideology, by making the argument that conventional characterizations borrowed from school-based theory raise the wrong questions and suppress and mystify practices of learning in everyday life. Second, linking and giving meaning to conceptions of learning in everyday life as legitimate peripheral participation in communities of practice made it possible for some groups of practitioners to view their practices in usefully different terms. And, finally, the conceptual language of *Situated Learning* was useful in legitimating and defending ongoing practices employed so as to produce new forms of practice, "from below." In each of the examples, social location, marginalities of various kinds, and critical efforts by practitioners themselves were key in changing their practices.

Participants did not necessarily begin with a more direct and comprehensive grasp of situated learning assumptions and concepts than the management school gurus. So how is it that adult educators, occupational therapists and participants in Danish Production Schools seemed not to distort the theory in their versions of it? I think there is something different going on in their differently structured and differently located practices, because they are already critically engaged in changing their understandings of their own practices. They share the critical spirit of situated learning theory to begin with. The *conflicting* ways in which *Situated Learning* has been taken up make clear that there is no necessary relation between a theory and its political-ethical deployment.

The Question of Decentering

This extended review of the argument of *Situated Learning* has had several purposes: to sum up that argument, to clarify ways in which it invited misunderstanding, and to consider its political intentions and its subsequent political fortunes. At the beginning of the chapter I suggested that the idea of decentering inquiry into learning seems more important now than it did then. This idea, along with the references to historical contextual entailments of learning in practice, pop out as crucial in re-reading the book now – but also seem like black boxes – place holders for future theoretical work. *Decentering* the analysis of learning was a way to reject the convention that studies of learning are about only (1) a learner, (2) learning, and (3) something. Given a relational theory/method, the analysis of learning would require a broader contextualization of scope and focus than the process defined by those three decontextualizing elements.

It is really difficult (in practice) to do this, for reasons that suggest it is the relational theory that needs work. What follows are examples of inquiry into learning – taken to be a relational matter – which nonetheless fail to move beyond conventional disjunctive results. They succeed in rich descriptions of social contexts and relations – then stop at the conventional theoretical "line" between world and person. The analysis then reverts to conventional interpretations of learning as knowledge acquisition.

An example from Tim Ingold will help to make the point. There is no doubt that his approach is relational. He addresses questions about learning in a discussion of how each generation contributes to the knowledgeability of the next – a theoretical argument about the movement of knowledge across generations (Ingold 2001: 120). He gives both a powerful critique of cognitive theory and a brief account of his conception of learning as the "education of attention."[4] He affords complex scope to changing, collective material practices and clearly insists on the contextual production of occasions and possibilities for learning, that is, for educating the learner's attention:

In the passage of human generations, each one contributes to the knowledgeability of the next … by setting up, through their activities, the environmental contexts within which successors develop their own embodied skills of perception and action … But since the "taskscape" through which any person moves is constituted by the practices of all the others, each plays a part in establishing the conditions of development for everyone else. (2001: 142–3)

His discussion of "learning" focuses on the person engaged in the education of her attention: "the human being as a centre of awareness and agency" (2001: 142). The problem is that a theory centered on (1) a person (2) acquiring (3) skill has a *telos* of becoming *more* skillful, learning *more*. This reduces the field of relations to be analyzed to the learner, some knowledge, and "the taskscape." If the only context to be addressed is narrowly situated, glove-like, with respect to the learner's learning task, analysis must be limited to the increase (or lack thereof) in a learner's skill/knowledge. Bracketing off, setting aside, participants' multi-stranded changing participation in ongoing practice in this way has consequences: We can see them in Ingold's analysis. Deploying his theory of learning leaves him no choice but to move the discussion to tutors, novices, experts, and a question borrowed from J. J. Gibson, "what makes the knowledge of the expert superior to the knowledge of the novice?" There is a conventional logic embedded in this query that seems inescapable, reducing learning processes to the question of how *some thing* is learned, rather than about how learners in ongoing practice change in and through their participation.

Ingold was not alone – in *Situated Learning* we did a version of the same thing. "Textured landscapes of possibility" (Lave and Wenger 1991) are certainly broader than "taskscapes." This notion breaks down distinctions between learning and doing, between social identity and knowledge, and between education and occupation. At the same time, it suggests that intricately patterned relations among spaces, times, bodies, social relationships, and heterogeneous participants are key to everyday ways of producing work (in the broadest sense of the term), producing learning, and their inseparable

---

[4] He argues that, *pace* the claims of Sperber (1996) or Boyer (1994), evolutionary forces operate, not on genes or on inborn mental capacities, but on *developing lives*, through lifetimes. He ends up saying there is no evolution/history split – it is all evolution (2001: 143). It seems to me that there is no evolution/history split – but it is all history.

products. They are ubiquitous facets of ongoing communities of practice, both the content and the principle of effectiveness of learning. Our analysis was relational to a point, expanding the scope of what was to be learned from skills narrowly defined to landscapes of possibility for learning as a condition for changing knowledge-subsuming identities. So far so good. But we still took the issue "learning" to be one of producing mastery, increasing knowledgeable skill (e.g., 1991: 94–5), a centered analysis that assumes that the observer's eye is following the changing location of the stuff (knowledge?) the learner is supposed to be acquiring.[5]

There are both political and theoretical consequences of narrowing the relevant focus of analysis to a path or trajectory of knowledge "into" a person. Both are implicated in our characteristic failures to engage in fully relational analyses. Political consequences first: tunnel vision blocks out formative historical relations that produce persons, practices, and places. Thus, a conventional positivist theoretical stance edits and suppresses its own political entailments and effects. A general way to create possibilities for attending to them is to decenter the analysis of learning, beginning with the practices of which learning is a part. For the political–economic relations of which changing participation in changing practice are part are constitutive of all practices and processes of learning. Bracketing them out (via decontextualization practices) distorts the practice of learning and its meanings. The equation of "learning" with "acquiring more knowledge" should be seen, among other things, as a technique of political erasure.

Theoretically, the broader problem is the "weaving" problem of how to conceptualize relations between persons and world as part of each other and learning as a matter of changes in those relations in practice. Things may be their relations (from Ollman's account of philosophy of internal relations [1976]), but relations must be understood in dialectical terms. A first step is to consider, in dialectical theory, what sort of subjects are "persons in practice?" How does the answer to that question affect questions about those subjects' participation in the formative social divisions and struggles of which they are part?

---

[5] Learner-circumscribed contexts of learning ran deep in *Situated Learning*. For instance: (1) In *Situated Learning* references to historical process co-exist with a functionalist theory of social order (Lave 2008: 288–9). (2) We discussed two contradictions, on the one hand tensions between use and exchange value (clearly drawn from Marxist analysis of capitalist relations) and, on the other hand, contradictions of continuity and displacement in re-producing participation in communities of practice. The latter as well as the former could have been read in historically particular processual terms, but we did not do so at the time. (3) We employed an unrelational conception of situated activity in different contexts, missing the moving relations among them.

Persons Learning

The "person" learning may seem to have been erased in the course of exploring what it means to decenter analyses of learning in practice.[6] To be sure, landscapes of possibility for changing practice are interesting in their own right. But they matter here especially with respect to learning *because* they are vital to the production of persons, to the lives that persons are engaged in producing, and to analysis of their changing participation in changing practice.

Given the relational character of these concepts it is not surprising that different understandings of the constitution of landscapes of possibility lead to different conceptions of "the person" or "the subject."

This and the following section address the relational theories of persons-in-practice of critical psychologist Ole Dreier and political-historical theorist Antonio Gramsci. Critical psychology, especially Dreier's theoretical account of persons engaged in the conduct of everyday life, addresses, as constitutive, the movement of persons among the contexts of their lives. The issues of political and civil society, social classes, hegemonic projects, and political economic history saturate Gramsci's theory of praxis. These two complex nexes of theory and practice were not intended to speak directly to each other. But each works out issues that address the practical limits of the other. The tension between them lands us in the middle of the problem with which the chapter began – which is just where I want to be.

---

[6] Indeed, activity theorists have sometimes argued that social practice theory has no theory of the subject. A more accurate view, I think, would be that they address "the subject" differently: "Praxis" lies at the center of theory of practice, and so the subject is persons-in-praxis. Fritz Haug argues that Bertolt Brecht understands the individual as decentered, as "dividual." He conceives the "divisibility," which he observes in the individual, on the one hand, like Gramsci, "as membership in several collectives" (Brecht et al. 1998: 359), on the other hand as inherently conflicting: "The individual appeared to us more and more as a contradictory complex in constant development. Seen from outside, it may behave as a unity, and still it is a multitude full of fights, in which the most different tendencies gain the upper hand, so that the eventual action only represents the compromise" (Brech et al. 1998: 691) (cited in Haug 2007:150).

This stands in contrast to "the subject" as the central unit of analysis in Cultural Historical Activity Theory. Andy Blunden views "the subject" as *the* theoretical key for CHAT:

> By subject, I understand a self-conscious system of activity. A subject is therefore the identity of agency (or moral responsibility, the capacity to do something), "cogito" knowledge or understanding), and self-consciousness (or identity). Agency, cogito, and self-consciousness are however never in absolute identity with one another; the identity of agency, cogito, and self-consciousness is a process, never complete or fully adequate at any given point. The individual person is a limiting case of a subject, but in general, the individual-as-subject can only be the endpoint of a long-drawn-out, still-unfinished historical process. (Blunden 2007)

Dreier's 2008 book, and his long-term development of a theory of persons in the conduct of their everyday lives makes him an obvious choice. It might seem surprising, however, to introduce Gramsci into this discussion, for he, like other theorists of social practice, seems to "disappear" the subject. Peter Thomas (political theorist and historian of philosophy) published a monumental study of Gramsci's work in 2009. He notes that the concept of "the subject" "is noticeable in the *Prison Notebooks* by its almost complete absence. The term appears only fifteen times in over 2.000 pages" (2009: 396–7). He adds: "As Gerratana has pointed out, Gramsci's analyses operate with the much older and more ambivalent category of the 'person [*la persona*],' or more precisely, a particular reformulation of this category that is not easily assimilable to modern (epistemologically founded) discourses of the knowing subject that have often subsumed the older category" (2009: 396–97). However, there is an interesting argument about persons-in-practice to be found in Gramsci's theory of praxis, though he and Dreier would go about decentering the analysis of changing participants (with respect to learning) differently.

To begin with, both Gramsci and Dreier (also the cultural historical activity theorists), reject naive "ideologically humanist" assumptions about "*the individual*" as the repository of some abstract human essence, call it "human nature." Gramsci turns to the sixth thesis on Feuerbach to characterize human nature instead as "the ensemble of social relations" (Gramsci 1999: 133). He rejects another common un-relational conception of the individual "defined as a subject with a unitary and unifying essence." (Dreier also does this, though for different reasons.) Instead, Gramsci suggests that, as a unit of analysis, "the individual" (person) is only guaranteed to reveal incoherent fragments (of a complex collective life).

incoherently composed, or "bizarrely 'composite'." (Thomas 2009, paraphrasing Gramsci 1999: 324). The individual is not defined as a subject with a unitary and unifying essence, but a "living archaeological site" in which different levels of historical experience are "at work." (Gramsci 1999: 324). Furthermore, this "walking anachronism" finds itself in a present that is itself divided between different times and, crucially, different class hegemonic projects. For Gramsci, therefore the "human" is not to be explained rationally merely as an ensemble of historically determined social relations, but rather, as an ensemble of historical relations of *class struggle*. These social relations, rather than "human relations" founded upon an interiority-becoming-intersubjectivity, are instead conceived externally, as a *Kampfplatz* of competing hegemonies or relations of leadership that are ultimately determined by the 'necessity' imposed by the economic organization of a social formation and not the "freedom" of an "arbitrary" individual or even collective "consciousness." They impact upon the "subject" as the preconditions of its social activity and are in turn interiorised by it as its own particular "subjective" modes of being-in-this-particular-world. Only at this point, as a result of a complex series of mediations, can we begin to talk of a "subject" or "human essence," which nevertheless remains a type of heuristic shorthand for the processes it describes. (Thomas 2009: 394–5)

Differences between Gramsci and Dreier are of particular interest here. For Gramsci, the "incoherently composed person" is living in a present divided between different times and different class hegemonic projects. That is a world in which the "ensemble of historically determined social relations"

emerge, in the first instance, from the interests imposed by the world of production (relations of production) and which are then modified, "molecularly," in the struggle to impose them upon society as a whole in hegemonic relations between and within classes. In turn, these relation[s][sic] of production are ... grasped as "relations of force" between different class interests and projects whose conflictual dynamic is determinant; that is, it is their dialectical opposition and interpenetration that is constitutive [of those ensembles of historically determined social relations]. (Thomas 2009: 396)

So Gramsci does not view persons as simply participants in an ensemble of social relations, but in an ensemble of relations of historical struggle. For Gramsci these are class struggles. (For more recent scholars, the struggles involve other deep divisions and their articulations.)

Gramsci insists that historical divisions and the struggles they entail are part of the constitution of persons. In my view, however, he stops short of exploring how historical divisions and the struggles they entail are part of processes of producing persons *in practice*. Suppose we ask questions about historical societal divisions and struggles as they are part of, and encountered in, landscapes of possibility in practice. Each such inquiry is about the historical constitution of *practice* (through persons' engagements in the conduct of their lives). At the same time, it is a question about the constitution of persons *through their participation* in practice. Each may (perhaps must) be analyzed through the other. However, at the philosophical level at which Gramsci addressed the constitution of persons, those historical practices and processes seem to be lodged in "incoherently composed persons" but not in their everyday practices. It seems possible that, had he been able, he would have considered further what conceptions of persons-in-historical-struggles would require were they taken to be situated matters of everyday practice.

Persons-in-practice may well be archeologically inconsistent loci of their lived contradictions, of coherencies and incoherencies that make each other. But this seems too broadly drawn a characterization, perhaps a perspective on individuals *en masse*. Persons surely are not *only* registers of societal incoherence. What else? And how are partial coherences/incoherencies produced? An interesting question then is what is going on, in practice, as people produce their lives as they live them. This is Ole Dreier's question. From his stance in critical psychology Dreier has developed a theory of the person in practice, "in interplay with situations in and through her activities and participation," among and across the multiple contexts of her everyday life, in the course of conducting that life.

> We must . . . *fundamentally comprehend a person as a participant.* We cannot merely grasp her in her action or interaction with others, but must perceive her in the way in which she takes part in a social practice in a context which encompasses and carries her and due to which her activity gains particular qualities and personal capabilities. A participant has only a partial influence on what goes on in the context and she plays only a particular part in the emergence, maintenance, or change of the problems and outcomes of a social practice. She carries out only a particular part of the tasks of the social practice and she has only a particular, partial responsibility for its relationships and outcomes Still, the tasks and responsibilities of individual participants intersect and shape some aspects. Their different parts are not independent of each other or of the arrangement of the context and its social practice. The actions of particular persons therein are particular parts of this social practice. Their participation is a situated participation in the social practice in the context. (Dreier 2013a: 3, emphasis mine)

As part of the conduct of everyday life through multiple practices with multiple co-participants, he suggests: "Movements into and across diverse contexts and practices also enrich our understandings of them. They allow us to re-cognize widespread forces and arrangements and their impacts and meanings in their similarities and differences. Such recognitions across places *lend a chance of looking behind the veil of arrangements into how they hang together*" (Dreier 2013b: 7–8, emphasis mine). He addresses the implications of his work on "the conduct of everyday life" for persons learning and for conceptions of everyday life, beginning with the notion that persons in practice conduct their lives as they move among the contexts through and in which they compose them (e.g., Dreier 2008, 2013a, 2013b).

Neither Gramsci's nor Dreier's stance with respect to conceptions of "the person" precludes the formative concerns of the other. But Gramsci's is not a person-focused theory and Dreier's is not first and foremost a historical-societal theory. It is not easy to imagine a dialectical relation of Dreier's account of persons engaged in the conduct of their everyday lives as they move across contexts of everyday practice, with Gramsci's image of forces at work on "historically determined ensembles of relations" or his approach to subjects constituted as persons in and through historical struggles. Gramsci was not able to engage ethnographically with questions about how this comes about in and through everyday practice. In turn, it is not easy to address "persons" as living archaeological sites, which Gramsci sees as the effect of historical divisions, struggles, and their contradictions, while considering persons to be producing themselves as they conduct their everyday lives.

I am struck by both Gramsci's and Dreier's open-ended gestures when they reach the partial limits of their deepest concerns. These feel like invitations to take "next steps" in theorizing learning in practice in dialectical terms. Dreier gives colloquial recognition to the challenge of encompassing historical struggles when he considers how it is possible "to address and learn about overall social and political issues in the conduct of everyday life." He goes on:

It would be absurd to claim that it only becomes possible to see and comprehend them by leaving the everyday and entering the institutions of privileged knowledge and power. Rather, the literal meaning of "overall" is that something is all over . . . [O]verall issues are present in everyday life and gain meaning in it for us . . . [so] that persons may engage in them in various ways in and from their everyday life – from below, as it is called. . .Of course, the real challenge of grasping comprehensive issues is to understand how they hang together and what they hang together with. (Dreier 2013b p. 7)

He argues that inquiry that follows persons moving across contexts "allows us to re-cognize widespread forces" and their effects.

The structure of a society is. . .sedimented in the arrangement of social contexts and practices. . . To view *a structure as an arrangement* means to grasp it as *being ordered for purposes, interests and forms of practice* and as relying on certain experiences and ideas. A structure is then viewed in a less abstract way and is not only overarching: *it becomes visible in relation to the situated, embodied participation of persons moving within it.* (Dreier 2013a p. 4, emphasis mine)

It seems likely that he would agree that societal structure (however he conceives it) must also matter in particular ways in the constitution of persons-in-practice as well as in those arrangements.

Gramsci addresses situated practice through the mediations of which participation in practice could conceivably be a part:

[Economic processes] impact upon the "subject" as the preconditions of its social activity and are in turn interiorised by it as its own particular "subjective" modes of *being-in-this-particular-world.* [So that,] Only . . . as a result of a complex series of mediations, can we begin to talk of a "subject" or "human essence," which nevertheless remains a type of heuristic shorthand for the [historical, hegemonic] processes it describes. (Thomas 2009: 394, emphasis mine)

This chapter asks how might we weave between and together the production of persons in their everyday lives and the generation, in practice, of the historical processes and practices that make the world as we are part, and take part, in it. A dialectical approach would insist that we must analyze, as constitutive of each other, historical practices and processes and the formative conduct of everyday life as they *are* each other and make each other at the same time.

We have been considering the difficulties of doing this in theory. It is at least as difficult in practice, an observation that might seem familiar after the discussion of practices of decentering research. Geographers Ekers and Loftus, introducing a recent book on Gramsci, propose that "Gramsci's method demands of us that we refine concepts in relation to historically and geographically situated practices" (2013: 18). That acknowledgement of the importance of situated practice marks a boundary at which they and their colleagues for the most part turn back to broad political economic institutional issues without reconsidering them *as* situated practices. Likewise, the critique of *Situated Learning* from which this chapter sets out reflects similar limitations, for it did not locate collective landscapes of possibility for learning-in-practice in the political-economic, cultural, institutional relations of which they are part; without a dialectical method we did not know how to do this.

Dreier would probably agree that we have marked fairly similar limits to our partial social-historical analysis of persons engaged in the conduct of their everyday lives, without breaching the conventional limitation of analytic scope with respect to communities of practice. It looks like common conventions have stopped all of us – Gramscian political theorists, critical psychologists, as well as social practice theorists – from considering how specific historical processes and the spatially broad and complex articulations of which they are composed both produce and are re-produced (and changed) in participation in changing practice. The question is still how we can get at complex relations between specific historical processes as they produce, and are produced in, ongoing practice.

A case could be made that the Center for Contemporary Cultural Studies in Birmingham during the 1970s was a crucible in which the "sides" could not escape each other, but were locked in intense interplay (in Gramscian mode) (Lave et al. 1992). They were engaged in critical rethinking of Althusserian and Gramscian concepts around the articulation of modes of production, but as the articulation of the production of class and race (Hall 1996). At the same time, Paul Willis, writing his dissertation amongst the historians, political theorists and sociologists at the CCCS, produced *Learning to Labour: How Working Class Lads Get Working Class Jobs* (1977), a complex analysis in Gramscian terms of the cultural production of incoherent persons, together, in particular landscapes of practice. Willis insisted that the lads' community of practice was a condition of possibility for their precarious, profane, uncertain, creative engagement in the cultural production of their everyday lives. He explored the "double articulation" of working class cultural material and meanings that the lads worked and re-worked in practice as they moved among the shared contexts of their lives (as Dreier might also insist). Willis asked how articulations of class with racial and gender relations were incoherent – in their persons and practices. Their counter-cultural practices gave them, by his analysis, a partial understanding of the nature of their practices, beliefs, future, and fate. While it was also precisely the articulation – making and giving meaning to – their relations (as classed, raced, and gendered persons) working *through each other* in their lives, that profoundly limited their ability to do so in practice.

Dialectical Theorizing

In that spirit, the concept of dialectic requires clarification. There are many forms, logics, and practices of "dialectic" (see Warren's *The Emergence of Dialectical Theory* (2008); Haug (2007). It is important to consider which dialectical theory is under discussion. This seems especially urgent because there is a stereotype that reduces the meaning of "dialectic" to a single formula (implying that the question is unnecessary). It may sound familiar: there is a contradiction between a thesis and its antithesis; it is transcended through their synthesis, which then becomes part of new contradictory thesis/antithesis relations. This has in it a principle of movement from one to the next. That movement (in this highly reductive account) is "upwards." Such a process of transcendence is assumed to be a teleological one, quickly pinned on Hegelian idealism, a matter of Geist, spirit ascending toward some final resolution.

But the concept of dialectic in social practice theory, based in philosophy of internal relations, is quite another kettle of fish. This philosophical problematic conceives of things as their relations, in and of a world of historically constituted social processes and practices. Material, historical, political processual – *relational* being is at the core of Marx's theory of praxis (and social practice theory). In a very abstract sense the relations of which things are composed are all together the totality of all that exists. But that totality of all relations is composed of all *particular* relations. What matters most to me as an ethnographer, not a philosopher, is that the crucial effect of a premise of an infinitely relational world is to make equally definite the *partial* character of all relations and our attempt to grasp and analyze them.

Ollman (1976, 2003) explains dialectic in relational philosophical terms and discusses its implications for social analysis. He helps us to grasp this way of conceiving of the world by distinguishing the idea of Relation with a capital "R" – the complex relation we would like to analyze (situated learning, for example) from the relations of which it is composed. But if conceptions of praxis or learning are their relations, we need to be able to speak of "relation" with a lower case "r" to designate the relations that constitute a Relation. Praxis, or learning (understood as always situated) is not just a thing or indeed a single Relation. Ollman famously cites Pareto's observation about Marx's concepts:[7] "Marx's words are like bats: one can see in them both birds and mice" (Pareto 1903: 332). Marx pulled apart and examined relations that composed his concept of Value, or Labor, or Praxis differently at different times, thus exploring different partial multiple relations. Stuart Hall (2003) in his essay on Marx's 1857 introduction to the *Critique of Political Economy,*

---

[7] Network theory – separate unitary objects, and (separately) their connections, does not a dialectical theory of relations make!

analyzes a famous example of the production/consumption Relation as its multiple relations. Analytic questions that emerge from such an exercise include: How are production and consumption each part of the other, and how are they part of their own past and futures? How are they produced, as they produce each other? How do production and consumption, or learning and labor, or persons in ongoing practice, or disciplinary and interdisciplinary projects work *through* each other? Each of those relational foci of inquiry imply many other relations (and questions).

This is also what makes the concept of articulation of dimensions of social life through deep historical struggles so important for ethnographic inquiry. "Articulation" has a complex history and has been construed in profoundly different ways – e.g., by Althusser, Laclau, Hall, and Gramsci, among others (cf. Hart 2007). Hart shows how Hall understood the articulation of race and class *in practice*. He

> reworked the conception of articulation to argue that the workings of race and forms of racism cannot be read off economic structures: "One must start ... from the concrete historical "work" which racism accomplishes under specific historical conditions – as a set of economic, political and ideological practices of a specific kind, concretely *articulated* with other practices in a social formation. (Hall 1980: 338) in Hart 2007: 89, her emphasis added.) ..." [T]here is no "racism in general." Instead it needs to be shown *how* race comes to be inserted historically, and the relations and practices that have tended to erode and transform – or to preserve – these distinctions through time,... as active structuring principles of the present organisation of society and the forms of class relations ... Race is thus, also, the modality in which class is 'lived', the medium through which class relations are experienced, the form in which it is appropriated and "fought through." ... Racism is also one of the dominant means of ideological representation through which the white fractions of the class come to "live" their relations to other fractions, and through them to capital itself." (Hall 1980: 341 in Hart 2007: 89)

So how does such a theoretical problematic account for relations of change? In practice. In practice as persons are situated in motion in participation in the world. Their multiple relations, once in motion are in contradiction with one another, as persons, practices, and/or needs produce and are produced as themselves and their opposites, now and then, old and new at the same time. Contradictory relations are *problematic*. They are not problems that can be solved, or that have complete, stable solutions. Contradictions are dilemmas that can only be resolved for now. For a quick homely example think of de la Rocha's account of dieters who both want to lose weight and who do not want to be hungry. That sounds like the dieters have two independent goals in life, until they try to act on either one, and find them in agonizing contradiction with one another. Resolutions to contradictions are inherently unstable, and involve tensions and improvisation, in conflicting processes and practices.

All of this together should both underline the historical processual character of human being and make plain the impossibility of a teleological claim for this dialectical theoretical stance. In turn, this should make plain that critical political judgment is unavoidable when deciding which struggles across deep historical, political-economic and cultural divides are crucially important for inquiry and analysis. The partiality and contradictory character of social relations make social analysis always also political in character and create the responsibility to articulate, analyse, and deal carefully with one's own position and its political intentions and effects as well as others.

Within a historical relational theoretical problematic, based in Marx's theory of praxis, at the core of Gramsci's philosophy of praxis; a problematic drawing on a dialectical theory based on philosophy of internal relations, some questions become more significant than others with respect to learning as situated practice. Assumptions about persons, the world, and most especially their relational existence, leads to a focus on questions about everyday life, historical process and practices, heterogeneous landscapes of possibilities for struggle over persons' collective and changing access to participation in changing practice. In this view learning, learners, ongoing practices, and the conduct of everyday lives in movement among contexts historically forged in struggles, are always but never only political-economic ones. These are to be understood as being made in practice, in relations that compose their Relations.

Afterword
Learning Together – New Challenges and Ethnographic Scenarios

Ana Maria R. Gomes

Federal University of Minas Gerais (Belo Horizonte – Brazil)

Jean Lave's experiences in Brazil present a sequence of contacts and exchanges that happened at different moments of our country's history since the 1960s. More recently, the work from which the present book emerged has encompassed activities that began with Lave's visit to Minas Gerais in April, 2011. She came to UFMG as a guest of the Program "Cátedra de Humanidades, Letras e Artes" of the Instituto de Estudos Avançados Trans-disciplinares (Advanced Transdisciplinary Studies Institute – IEAT/UFMG).[1] This visit marked twenty years since the publication of her most well-known book, *Situated Learning: Legitimate Peripheral Participation.* She was invited to UFMG after she received the CAE/AAA's *George and Louise Spindler Award* in 2008. The issues raised by *Situated Learning* caught our interest and were eagerly debated in Brazil as well as many other countries and the book has been translated into nine languages, with different interfaces to varied fields of knowledge.

Our histories have crossed through common interests and shared concerns about our different historical circumstances. The UFMG group took up the learning theme as a possible way to bring together a number of diverse people working on different, widely dispersed, ethnographic projects. Notwithstanding that most of us had a history of research and work in schools, all of us had some other distinctive aspect of his or her activity that led us to become involved in something further than what was going on in schools. Our shared, but at the same time different, positions toward the field led us to move carefully and reflexively around our own circumstances as ethnographers, and around the way each of us addressed his/her own field relations and ethnographic project (cf. Velho 2006). The idea of focusing on the relations between learning and culture was central to our work as to Lave's as well. Progressively it appeared as a way to bring us together, to work around relations among

---

[1] Cf. www.ufmg.br/ieat/2011/09/jean-lave.

different themes – youth and sports, Amerindian people and education projects, children and urban metropolis, music and dance, *quilombos* and other related subjects regarding Afro-Brazilian communities, among others.

Lave had her first contact with indigenous people in a small community in Western Maranhão in the 1960s, and when she came back to Brazil in 2011 indigenous peoples themselves were the center of attention – indigenous youth had begun attending universities, urged forward by a new legal framework that creates the conditions for developing specific projects at all levels of education.[2] They were also urged on by a new epistemological and political scenario that centers diversity within the human sciences debate, such that Amerindian thought is brought into dialogue with other philosophies and encouraging comparative consideration of diverse ontologies (cf. Viveiros de Castro 1996, 1998, 2002/2013; Lima 1999). These priorities open up perspectives and possibilities for new knowledge practices in the university. Likewise, the presence of indigenous peoples in universities raises new forms of interaction between indigenous and non-indigenous worlds. The challenge, launched by Isabelle Stengers as a "cosmopolitical proposal," is to build ways of being together, or engaging in "experimental togetherness," asking "the question of who is entitled to speak and on what grounds, when we are facing problems that concern everyone" (2002: 248).

In Brazil today, indigenous peoples are granted the right to their "own learning processes," as is made clear in the legal text, which attempts to establish in juridical terms a recognition of this right beyond the mere acceptance of the existence of a different system of knowledge.[3] This assertion implies the possibility of keeping alive not only the "body of knowledge" that each indigenous tradition carries, but also indigenous ways, methods and procedures for the (re)production of such knowledge (cf. Carneiro da Cunha 2009).

After the main changes introduced by the Constitution in 1988 and by the new National Education Law (LDB 9394/1996), pedagogical proposals for indigenous schools sprang up and have been implemented in different places, while research projects have been developed to produce a deeper understanding of the new reality. The advent of such schools implemented within indigenous territories is, on one hand, closely linked to historically established ideas of (Western) school-based social organization and its cultural and economic dynamics. Today these affect almost all indigenous peoples in Brazil

---

[2] Constitution of the Federative Republic of Brazil, 1988. The term *indígena* (indigenous) is used in legal texts and refers to a juridical definition called the "principle of indigeneity" (*princípio ou instituto do indigenato*) to refer to the anteriority of this component regarding the Brazilian state. This principle is common to all Brazilian normative and legal texts where the Amerindians are referred to as "indigenous people."

[3] Law of Guidelines and Bases for the National Education, established on 12/20/1996 – LDB 9394/96.

and in different parts of the world (Anderson-Levitt 2003). On the other hand, "schools" and "classes" have taken countless shapes, inspired by a novel and inverse idea of "school pacification" developed by different indigenous communities in their villages. The evocative title of the seminar held at USP in 2013 – *Políticas Culturais e Povos Indígenas: a escola e outros problemas* (Cultural Policies and Indigenous Peoples: the school and other problems)[4] – hints at the wider scope of the issues. The idea of school as a problem, something that has to be changed by the Ameridians, echoes the idea of a process of "pacification" but in the reverse sense. "Pacification" is usually applied to non-indigenous peoples' actions intended to "civilize" their indigenous counterparts. Here it is inverted to refer to the process of the adaptation of "white people" and their institutions as led *by* indigenous peoples, in order to "civilize" whites from an indigenous perspective (cf. Albert and Ramos 2002).

All this has led to profound (re)considerations and has had implications that go well beyond issues associated with so-called "indigenous schooling education." The development of "indigenous schooling" now ongoing in Brazil offers urgent reasons for exploring broad horizons on learning. We have found the social theory of practice especially valuable and within it questions about, and understandings of, learning in practice. This perspective often resonates with Amerindian peoples' approaches to learning and has potential to advance productive collaboration among non-indigenous and indigenous persons of Brazil as they explore learning practices and educational policies regarding indigenous schooling, as well as broader transformations in standard Brazilian education.

Revisiting the Issue of Learning

The encounter with Lave, first through her books, and then in moments of joint work in Brazil and in other countries, unveiled convergences with our local efforts, expressed in the meeting at IEAT/UFMG.[5] Together we invested in a project to comprehend and take part in the huge changes regarding the fight against poverty and social inequality going on in Brazil then, and this generated a potential scenario for exchange and collaboration that rapidly turned into the proposal for the present book. This joint effort came to life as a window on Lave's recent reflections, and offered our research group further opportunity for a dialogue around the concepts and proposals we encountered

---

[4] Cf. Carneiro da Cunha, Cesarino, 2015.
[5] After her visit to UFMG, some encounters took place in the United States, during the AAA Annual Meetings in 2012; there were other meetings in Mexico, with the DIE-Cinvestav team of researchers, Elsie Rockwell and colleagues, in 2013. And two workshops developed in Brazil and Denmark in an ongoing collaboration between Brazilian and Danish researchers.

in *Situated Learning* as they have been elaborated and taken in new directions here.

As a way to open up directions connected to the development of Lave's ideas in the chapters of the present book, I will explore ongoing trajectories in the course of our research in the Anthropology and Education group that were based on Lave's inspirational work, illustrating new problematics for the study of learning. The concepts of legitimate peripheral participation and communities of practice provided us with an initial framework for research projects in widely different empirical arenas while at the same time addressing common questions. In addition to sharing certain guiding questions, each different field of research helped us generate other interfaces, thus building an enriched scenario in terms of possible articulations among issues and among researchers. The idea is not to produce comparative research, but to produce a shared research scenario that promotes a closer collaboration among researchers who are involved in those different subjects and often involved in different social movements. As a common reference, it could provoke an opportunity to produce reciprocal understandings of our different subjects, and thus contribute to the creation of new and necessary possibilities of working and living together, in different instances and situations – academic projects as one among many.

The reading of *Situated Learning* continues to bring about conceptual shifts vis-à-vis standard modern Occidental approaches to education. Lave's ideas open up new perspectives for investigation of oft-explored yet still complex and little understood issues of "learning" and "knowledge." In one of her seminars, Lave revisited a seminal moment in her field research in Liberia that led to a fundamental difference in the way it became possible for her – and then for all who read her book – to see what was before her eyes.[6] In order to see learning happening among apprentices in tailor shops, it was not enough to be there, gazing at what was taking place – although she did that repeatedly, to the point of exasperation to herself and to the people welcoming her. The latter, faced with what must have seemed the interminable troubles of the researcher and the questions she asked, kindly tried to assist her and make something visible. To repeatedly ask improper questions of interlocutors in the field is inevitable – yet it is from those errors that researchers at times manage to create new visibility. What happened in the tailors' shop, however, was the attempt to direct the researcher's vision by virtue of normally unsaid directives as the tailor remarked loudly to his apprentice that "the fly always goes on the front of the trousers" (an explanation clearly prepared so that the researcher

---

[6] The episode she narrated brings to mind Gregory Bateson's formulation (1972, p. 276) about the fundamental act in the process of knowing, which is to establish distinctions: to identify "a difference which makes a difference."

could register *something*). The absurdity of the tailor's comment encouraged Lave to move away from overt questioning and redirect her attention to matters of practice that shape and support tailoring achievements. That which supported people's learning was already happening, before Lave's eyes, but she lacked the lens to "see" it.

A reconfiguration of Lave's gaze was required – and this led to a conceptual shift that more than thirty years later Lave provoked/revitalized in her audience at UFMG by means of the account she offered in her lecture. That is, after months in those tailors' shops she started to see *people as themselves sources of information and learning for each other*. Not only what they said to each other (though this was also a necessary part of the picture), but what they actually did for each other, with each other, individually and collectively.

One of the key concepts here that Lave introduces in her work and develops in this book is that of "access." If learning takes place, it is because of the peculiar ways people *grant access* to one another (Lave and Wenger 1991: 100). Lave highlighted this idea in order to explain how learning is possible; access one to the other, to the very manner of acting and of being involved *in practice* creates the possibilities for learning. Granting access is facilitated by specific gestures, the use of objects, sentences and discursive inflections, expressive moods and emotions, previous information (cultural background) that is evoked, demonstrated, and unveiled in the specific environment, and peculiar dispositions, at times expressed bodily. Practices in different domains may be widely or variably accessible, or relatively sequestered, with consequences for learning processes.

The idea of access is fundamental as a central aspect of understanding participation in practice. In *Situated Learning*, Lave set out from the notion of "participation" and articulated key concepts of legitimate peripheral participation in communities of practice. She takes up both of these ideas in the last of the essays here, problematizing the latter idea almost to the point of discarding it because of the prevailing way it has been misunderstood.[7] At the same time, she reasserts an idea of shared practice more specifically assumed as legitimate peripheral participation as the privileged focus of inquiries into learning.

Regarding legitimate peripheral participation, as Lave remarks, the three terms cannot be dissociated. Their combined conceptual impact is at least twofold. First, teaching is not a uni-directional process, but rather involves people interacting and learning from/with one another (as much or more from their *different ways of participating* in some common practice as from their commonalities). And secondly, the focus of observation is not the mental

---

[7] See the section "Situated Learning, in Practice and Politics" in Chapter 7.

formulations people make "while" they practice (although this is also part of the picture), but rather the way they participate in practice with one another. In other words, it is the common *participation* in practice, made possible by *access to it*, which, in its turn, makes changes in one's own form of participation possible. And it is this very change in the form of participation in practices over time and space (forms themselves in constant processes of change) that Lave proposes to call learning. This is the central conceptual displacement, which establishes, for the (participant) observer, a new scenario – one that becomes, simultaneously, visible and describable.

Exploring Connections between *Participation* and *Access*

Reading *Situated Learning* once again under the light of the work encompassed in the essays in this book was, thus, a driving force which has allowed our research group to launch the project of a progressive reassessment, in search of a new way to question how it is possible to learn – understanding "learning" in the sense it has for G. Bateson (1979) as part of a vital process halted only when one dies.

The common issue in the ethnographic inquiries of our Anthropology and Education research group is an idea that may be generically named *learning culture*. As a strategic starting point (considering our backgrounds of schooled experience), we tried to focus on cultural practices in which discourse was not the central dimension – as it has to be in, for example, what is called verbal arts – even if it has to be taken into account in an appropriate way for each setting under inquiry. This intentional focus meant that discursive practices would be registered as part of a larger set of practices. At the same time, the symbolic dimension of the whole set of practices would be of central importance in the different ways it would emerge from our interlocutors in different settings.

Addressed in this way, a central feature of learning culture, as we understand it, is the mode of *access* provided for learners. This perspective has brought insights for our research approach to practices: on the one hand, those practices found extensively in Brazilian society such as soccer; and, on the other hand, practices that have a deep imprint on specific groups, as in the case of Afro-Brazilian religions, or the practice of hunting and cultivating the fields among indigenous peoples. Some of our other projects are associated with life in large Brazilian metropolises, such as the daily routines of children and teenagers from different social classes, and even the movement of children through the city. Addressing participation and access in these challenging domains required that we decenter the processes of learning, as Lave argues in the last essay here, by focusing on broad relations involved in the production of practices and practitioners, of which learning is part.

Learning is a central issue in the interface between anthropology and education (culture, whatever the definition, must be learned). So, we try to explore learning processes with a properly anthropological approach, in order to destabilize the hegemonic way it has been (de)limited (cf. Gomes 2000; Gomes and Faria 2015). In such a hegemonic scenario, as Lave warns, many conceptual elements are taken for granted and other important aspects of learning omitted (cf. Lave 2011). Our project instead turns to questions of who engages in the practices and how.

Our current focus emerged initially from the study of everyday practices of playing soccer, assumed as a kind of emblematic case in Brazilian society. Soccer is a common practice, widespread in Brazil, and its reproduction is assured by ubiquitous mechanisms (albeit present differently) in all Brazilian social segments, from various places for playing the game with diversified purposes, in private and public spaces, watching on TV or in videos, using videogames, even incorporated into advertising. Nevertheless, though we know that it is possible to learn soccer in Brazil, we know very little about how soccer is learned – in a situated way, in Brazilian contexts. Therefore, instead of focusing on *problems* of learning (or the so-called learning disabilities), which guide much research on education and other disciplines, we turned our gaze to practices such as young peoples' interactions during games and their exchanges with more accomplished players. These are constitutive settings in which we know that learning does take place. At the same time that these are very familiar practices for almost all Brazilians, the specific learning processes involved are, and remain, almost completely unknown to us.

The idea of *access* also allowed us to bring together different investigations, conducted in three different Brazilian settings: the study on soccer in a suburban neighborhood of a big city; research on everyday participation and ritual practices of people of different ages in a *terreiro* of *Umbanda* (site for celebrations of this Afro-Brazilian religion); and ethnographic studies exploring the changing practices of boys hunting and working in the fields in an indigenous territory in central Brazil (Gomes et al. 2012). The starting point for each of these investigations was the assurance that learning had already taken place effectively. Expert practitioners exist in all three domains and novices are continually advancing in their own practices. The three sites all illustrate successful learning practices in different communities of Brazilian society. As we have found, the modes of access to these practices and therefore the participation within them, also varies. However, the common focus on access itself provides a fruitful comparative framework for understanding the diversity of ways that learning can proceed. Revisiting these three settings with attention to the access issue, we explored different aspects of ongoing learning processes. The differences helped us to explicate the idea of "changing participation in ongoing changing practices" (Lave), and gave us a well-articulated framework for learning, both as a general process and as specifically emergent in each setting. For instance, turning again to focus on soccer: it appears as a practice available to all, although it has a clearly masculine emphasis (Faria 2008). So access is in one sense society wide, but at the same time there is also the risk of exclusion from certain venues for practice, especially by gender and class, an image that reproduces inequalities of Brazilian society in the dynamics of who can play with whom on which playing fields. Another constant feature of this practice is that peer interactions are more prevalent than the interactions between masterful players and apprentices, with an effect that dissolves clear boundaries between those who know and do, and those who cannot yet perform as they would like, or do not yet know enough. Nevertheless, we can say that the mastery of practice is continuously scrutinized by players themselves and boundaries are laid down and emphasized (even if fluid) through the endless public situations in which they participate in daily watching, talking, and concretely playing soccer. A young boy kicking the ball continuously against the wall (a common image in Brazil) is all about increasing mastery: the boy does not perform in the way he wants, but he knows enough to produce the situation of (auto) training that can lead him to learning, to perform better.

Hunting practices among Xakriabá people are also geared for boys but, in sharp contrast with soccer, the visibility of hunting practices is almost exclusively restricted to a particular world of selected male practitioners (Silva 2011). The intimate contact with the forest and its animals in all their complexity can barely be surmised by those excluded from it. In agricultural fields (roça) in the same communities, something different happens. There is still a perception that the practices are eminently masculine yet there is a greater presence of women at work, especially under current circumstances because most young men leave their indigenous lands for months each year in a transitory migration process in which they become low-income informal agricultural workers. It is noteworthy that in both hunting and farming configurations the interactions that characterize learning situations are clearly defined between adult masters and children who are in different positions in the process of learning. Access is provided in a stepped, progressive way for youths as they mature in their own practices in these domains. In the case of hunting, this progression is part of activities that enlarge the circulation of the boys over a much broader range of the indigenous territory, beyond the domestic environment. This circulation becomes itself a process of constituting male identities and domains of practice. It is assured by a very interesting alternating composition of groups of boys, youths and adult men of different ages, who are differently skilled practitioners.

The intensity and great sense of intentional convergence of the practices in the *terreiro* de *Umbanda*[8] call our attention to a third mode for reproducing communities through access that makes learning possible (Bergo 2011). Here, learning is similar to "picking up leaves" (Goldman 2005), a long and patient process of immersion in the *terreiro*'s life and activities, designed to collect precious information. Unlike soccer, where much information is evinced and overtly manifested, and one can watch and learn, in *Umbanda*, what one sees, and what provides learning, is never clearly advertised. Through the process of collecting and reflecting on bits and pieces of knowledge and practice persons reach by inference their place and understanding within the religious community. This movement combines participation and access in routinized ritual moments, as well as in the everyday life of community members.

A *gira* (round), a public moment par excellence of previously characterized and well-codified ritual, is overtly offered to a wider audience once a week. In this event a hierarchy of positions is clear, yet the *terreiro* is thought of as a place of *continuous learning for all*, because, unlike the previous practices referred to, religious practice is projected on a cosmic horizon, whose infinite amplitude prevents full mastery. In this domain, it is the "saint time" (*tempo de santo*, i.e., how long someone has been initiated) that defines who is more advanced in learning, regardless of participants' ages. Accordingly, the interactions that provide learning, and learning itself, are oriented in different directions depending on participants' current levels of understanding and accomplishment. This process rearticulates members according to their different identities (by gender, age, generation, position in the group), depending strictly on the *terreiro*'s internal processes. In this reorganization, the *socius* is redefined and expanded continually, involving human participants and entities received in the moments of trance; in a very broad sense – *everybody has to learn*.

This aspect of the *Umbanda* practice is similar in some ways to perceived differences among actors in a hunt. In hunting it is the most expert who have the power to act while less advanced participants observe. In hunting we also have an expanded *socius* and interactions at different levels, generating shifting positions between animals, humans, and nonhumans. According to Goldman, the idea of "picking up leaves . . . refers to the fact that knowledge and learning are under the sign of two *orixá, Ossaim* and *Oxóssi*, the master of the plants and the hunter, because to learn is, above all, searching and capturing, and doing this, of course, involves some risk" (2005: 107).

Focusing on issues of *access* helped us to address questions about the regulation of different forms of participation. It led us quickly to do away

---

[8] "Terreiro" is the site, the religious place or temple where activities are developed collectively.

with oppositions such as schooled/nonschooled, formal/informal education, and even institutional/non-institutional, for the varieties of access are clearly many. In fact, the school, and students' participation in conventional classes, are often involved as part of our research context; but they are only a part of the wider landscape of practices we are now analyzing. The focus of our research begins with a practice of interest – playing soccer, for instance. We found five different contexts for participating in soccer in the neighborhood we studied. School was one of them, allowing us to revisit or reframe research in this setting by means of lines of inquiry that emerged from our wider focus on those landscapes of practice. We addressed school activities within a larger investigation of how practices are produced across contexts and are implicated in questions of learning through access across these settings.

Finally, we can say that access is a political issue. It was already present in *Situated Learning,* particularly evident in the case of the butchers' apprenticeship. But it has taken on greater importance here within the more recent discussion Lave is developing about everyday life. Access to practices, as a *sine qua non* condition for learning, is at the heart of discussions such as those regarding affirmative action policies implemented in Brazil over the last twenty years – but already threatened by recent political restrictions directed at social programs. At the same time, it is a central aspect of many contemporary discussions about changes and new configurations in urban life (Monte-Mor 2014a). Many Amerindian groups are progressively involved in what can be called "extensive urbanization" (cf. Monte-Mor 2014b) especially with respect to the so-called public services apparatus – health and education – being implemented and spread out into their territories and villages. Everyday life in its typical or "traditional" guise is being intensively changed by the presence of professionals, objects, procedures, etc., involved in these apparatuses.

"Research on Apprenticeship; Research as Apprenticeship" – Toward New Challenges and Ethnographic Scenarios

In her most recent book, *Apprenticeship in Critical Ethnographic Practice* (2011), Lave offers an exercise developed over thirty years, as she describes her activities since the beginning of her research with Vai and Gola tailors in Liberia. In this book, Lave returns to crucial moments during this long ethnographic project to show how limiting school-centric assumptions about learning did, and for the most part still do, deeply affect many approaches to research on learning.

In response to the same issues, we are trying to develop a more appropriate theoretical framework to reflect the intensive and extremely diverse set of experiences across the many different indigenous schools in Brazil. Two different cases, part of our current activities, illustrate this diversity. The Xakriabá are a people whose lands lie in a very dry region of northwest of Minas Gerais (between biomes called *cerrado* and *caatinga*). They had contact and engaged in struggles with the colonial process from the beginning of the eighteenth century. The Yanomami are a people from the equatorial forest of Amazonia (in the state of Roraima) and are considered a recent contact group.

In the two cases, we believe it is important to understand the previous experiences and practices that are concerned with school and/or written culture in a much deeper and more critical way. This has led us to keep up a continuous review of our premises during the many initiatives and projects we are engaged in (from undergraduate indigenous teachers' course, to actions involving cultural production and environmental issues). Taking the same period – the last twenty years – we could say that the Xakriabá have set out to create schools in every village and for all levels. Recently, young people have begun to reject seasonal agricultural migration, in order to look for an opportunity to attend universities. They have now an entire school system that is part of their communities' everyday life, as all children attend school regularly. This massive attendance, happening along with many other changes in the landscape of Xakriabá villages (including the introduction of electricity, the monetarization of many internal activities, the consumption of industrial products on a daily basis, and so on), has implications neither anticipated nor yet clear for all aspects of daily life: they are actually a dense and incisive novelty.

The Yanomami, during the same period, have been trying to build an educational proposal, counting on the collaboration of many different partners (national and international NGOs and universities). So far it has not been possible to reach a clear and plausible design. Nowadays, even though many Yanomami teachers have regular contracts provided by the state agency, there is no shared educational project able to promote common or continuous educational initiatives. Each region or village seems to have different arrangements regarding the indigenous teachers' positions, their activities, and relations with their communities and the actual practices they are engaged in. The development of diverse intercultural research in the territory, in collaboration with many different local people in a variety of villages – youth and elders, men and women – seems to be leading in the direction of an educational proposal that can build dialogue in and with the Yanomami contemporary world in all its complexity.

The two cases direct our concerns toward a different time and space: the Xakriabá became in scarcely a single generation one of the most schooled indigenous people in Brazil – more schooled even than the average rate for the regional population where they live in Minas Gerais. Despite all the tentative projects, the Yanomami are still trying to make sense of an (im)possible process of schooling, with very specific dynamics and conditions that emerge in a variety of configurations across the diverse contexts of their land in Amazonia. In both cases, learning and schooling should be considered as part of a broader set of ongoing processes related and connected by the indigenous themselves, as they encompass them in their own terms: educational policies, cultural policies, territorial and environmental issues, or political economic local and national struggles.

Those scenarios re-affirm strongly the idea that, as ethnographers, we are apprentices of our own ongoing practices. This is the challenge this book addresses to all of us. At the same time the book can be seen as a meaningful message concerning Lave's specific contributions for the next generation of ethnographers. This communication among generations becomes even more important as we realize that it happens in a moment where our indigenous interlocutors have become not only our readers (Strathern quoted in Lave 2011: 6). Indigenous and non-indigenous are beginning to work together, searching for a more symmetrical endeavor in which the borders between researcher and researched are blurred or are marked by a circulation in both directions, so that we are actually exchanging positions in different shared scenarios (cf. Silveira, Mortimer, and Gomes 2017). The book can be seen as a result, and at the same time as just one moment in a vital and interesting dialogue that we insist/persist in keeping alive and always in motion.

References

Aadal, Lena, Marit Kirkevold, and Tove Borg. 2014. "Neurorehabilitation analysed through 'situated learning' theory." *Scandinavian Journal of Disability Research* 16, no. 4: 348–63.

Albert, Bruce, and Alcida Rita Ramos, eds. 2002. *Pacificando o Branco: Cosmologias Do Contato No Norte-Amazônico*. São Paulo: Editora Unesp/IDR.

Amin, Ash, and Joanne Roberts. 2008. *Community, Economic Creativity, and Organization*. Oxford: Oxford University Press.

Anderson, John Robert. 1990. *The Adaptive Character of Thought*. Hillsdale: Lawrence Erelbaum Associates.

Anderson-Levitt. Kathryn M. 2003. "A world culture of schooling?" In *Local Meanings, Global Schooling*, edited by K. M. Anderson-Levitt. New York: Palgrave Macmillan.

Aretxaga, Begona. 2001. "Engendering violence: Strip-searching of women in Northern Ireland." In *History in Person: Enduring Struggles, Contentious Practice, Intimate Identities*, edited by Dorothy Holland and Jean Lave. Santa Fe: School for Advanced Research Press.

Axel, Erik. 2008. "Developing praxis in conflictual cooperation: A preliminary report from a construction site." In American Anthropological Association 107th Annual Meeting.

2009. "What makes us talk about wing nuts? Critical psychology and subjects at work." *Theory and Psychology* 19(2): 275–95.

Bailey, Thomas Raymond, Katherine L. Hughes, and David Thornton Moore. 2004. *Working Knowledge: Work-Based Learning and Education Reform*. New York: Routledge Falmer.

Barker, Roger G. 1968. *Ecological Psychology*. Stanford: Stanford University Press. "On the Nature of the Environment: Kurt Lewin memorial award address 1963." *Journal of Social Issues* 19: 17–38.

Barnes, Barry. 1973. "The comparison of belief-systems: Anomaly versus falsehood." In *Modes of Thought in Western and Non-Western Societies*, edited by Ruth Finnegan and Robin Horton, 182–98. Eugene: Wipf and Stock.

Bartlett, Frederic. 1958. *Thinking: An Experimental and Social Study*. New York: Basic Books.

Bateson, Gregory. 1972. *Steps to an Ecology of Mind: Collected Essays in Anthropology, Psychiatry, Evolution, and Epistemology*. Chicago: University of Chicago Press.

1979. *Mind and Nature: A Necessary Unity*. New York: Dutton.

170

Beach, King. 1993. "Becoming a bartender: The role of external memory cues in a work-directed educational activity." *Applied Cognitive Psychology* 7, no. 3: 191–204.

Becker, Howard S. 1961. *Boys in White: Student Culture in Medical School*. Chicago: University of Chicago Press.

Bergo, Renata Silva. 2011. "Quando o Santo Chama: O Terreiro de Umbanda Como Contexto de Aprendizagem Na Prática." Doutorado em Educação, Faculdade de Educação, Universidade Federal de Minas Gerais.

Bernstein, Richard J. 1971. *Praxis and Action: Contemporary Philosophy of Human Activity*. Pennsylvania: University of Pennsylvania Press.

Birdwhistell, Ray L. 2010 [1970]. *Kinesics and Context: Essays on Body Motion Communication*. Pennsylvania: University of Pennsylvania Press.

Blunden, Andy. 2007. "Modernity, the individual, and the foundations of cultural–historical activity theory." *Mind, Culture, and Activity* 14, no. 4: 253–65.

Bourdieu, Pierre. 1984. *Distinction: A Social Critique of the Judgement of Taste*. Cambridge: Harvard University Press.

Bourdieu, Pierre, and Jean-Claude Passeron. 1990. *Reproduction in Education, Society and Culture*. New York: Sage.

Boyer, Pascal. 1994. *The Naturalness of Religious Ideas: A Cognitive Theory of Religion*. Berkeley: University of California Press.

Brecht, Bertolt, and Werner Hecht. 1988. *Werke: Grosse Kommentierte Berliner und Frankfurter Ausgabe*. Aufbau.

Brinck, Lars. 2016. "Jamming and learning: Analysing changing collective practice of changing participation." *Music Education Research* 19, no. 2: 214–25.

Brown, John Seely, Allan Collins, and Paul Duguid. 1989. "Situated cognition and the culture of learning." *Educational Researcher* 18, no. 1: 32–42.

Brown, John Seely, and Paul Duguid. 1991. "Organizational learning and communities-of-practice: Toward a unified view of working, learning, and innovation." *Organization Science* 2, no. 1: 40–57.

Cain, Carole. 1991. "Personal stories: Identity acquisition and self-understanding in Alcoholics Anonymous." *Ethos* 19, no. 2: 210–53.

Carneiro da Cunha, Manuela, and Pedro Cesarino, (eds.). 2015. *Políticas culturais e povos indígenas*. São Paulo: Editora Unesp e Cultura Acadêmica.

Carraher, Terezinha Nunes, David William Carraher, and Analúcia Dias Schliemann. 1982. "Na Vida Dez, Na Escola Zero." *Caderna de Pesquisa São Paulo* 42 (August): 79–86.

　　1985. "Mathematics in the streets and in schools." *British Journal of Developmental Psychology* 3, no. 1: 21–9.

Carraher, Terezinha Nunes, and Analúcia Dias Schliemann. 1985. "Computation routines prescribed by schools: Help or hindrance?" *Journal for Research in Mathematics Education* 16, no. 1: 37–44.

Chaiklin, Seth. 1992. "From theory to practice and back again: What does postmodern philosophy contribute to psychological science." In *Psychology and Postmodernism*, edited by Steinar Kvale, 194–208. Thousand Oaks: Sage.

　　2003. "The zone of proximal development in Vygotsky's analysis of learning and instruction." In *Vygotsky's Educational Theory in Cultural Context*, edited by Alex Kozulin, Boris Gindis, Vladimir Ageyev, and Suzanne Miller, 39–64. London: Cambridge University Press.

Chaiklin, Seth, Mariane Hedegaard, and Uffe Juul Jensen, eds. 1999. *Activity Theory and Social Practice.* Aarhus: Aarhus University Press.

Chaiklin, Seth, and Jean Lave. 1993. *Understanding Practice: Perspectives on Activity and Context.* Cambridge: Cambridge University Press.

Cole, Michael. 1998. *Cultural Psychology: A Once and Future Discipline.* Cambridge: Harvard University Press.

Cole, Michael, John Gay, Joseph Glick, and Don Sharp. 1971. *The Cultural Context of Learning and Thinking: An Exploration in Experimental Anthropology.* New York: Basic Books.

Cole, Michael, Lois Hood, and Ray McDermott. 1994. *Ecological Niche Picking: Ecological Invalidity as an Axiom of Experimental Cognitive Psychology.* Laboratory of Comparative Human Cognition Rockefeller University.

Collins, Harry. 2013. "Three dimensions of expertise." *Phenomenology and the Cognitive Sciences* 12, no. 2: 253–73.

Collins, Harry, Rob Evans, Rodrigo Ribeiro, and Martin Hall. 2006. "Experiments with interactional expertise." *Studies in History and Philosophy of Science Part A* 37, no. 4: 656–74.

Cooper, Eugene. 1989. "Apprenticeship as field method: Lessons from Hong Kong." In *Apprenticeship: From Theory to Method and Back Again*, edited by Michael Coy, 137–48. New York: SUNY Press.

Costall, Alan, and Ole Dreier, eds. 2006. *Doing Things with Things: The Design and Use of Everyday Objects.* Burlington: Ashgate Publishing.

Coutinho, Carlos Nelson. 2012. *Gramsci's Political Thought.* Boston: Brill.

Coy, Michael William, ed. 1989. *Apprenticeship: From Theory to Method and Back Again.* New York: SUNY Press.

Crehan, Kate. 2002. *Gramsci, Culture and Anthropology.* Berkeley: University of California Press.

Cunha, Manuela Carneiro da. 2009. *Cultura Com Aspas e Outros Ensaios.* São Paulo: Cosac Naify.

2015. "Políticas Culturais e Povos Indígenas: Uma Introdução." In *Políticas Culturais e Povos Indígenas*, edited by Manuela Carneiro da Cunha and Pedro Cesarino. São Paulo: Cultura Acadêmica.

Cunha, Manuela Carneiro da, and Pedro Cesarino, eds. 2015. *Políticas Culturais e Povos Indígenas.* São Paulo: Cultura Acadêmica.

Dannefer, Dale. 1992. "On the conceptualization of context in developmental discourse: Four meanings of context and their implications." *Life-Span, Development and Behavior* 11, no. 2: 83–110.

Danziger, Kurt. 1994. *Constructing the Subject: Historical Origins of Psychological Research.* Cambridge: Cambridge University Press.

Datan, Nancy, and Hayne W. Reese, eds. 1977. *Life-Span Developmental Psychology: Dialectical Perspectives on Experimental Research.* New York: Academic Press.

Davydov, V. V., and L. A. Radzikhovskii. 1985. "Vygotsky's theory and the activity oriented approach." In *Lev Vygotsky: Critical Assessments*, edited by Peter Lloyd and Charles Fernyhough, 113–44. New York: Routledge.

De Certeau, Michel. 1984. *The Practice of Everyday Life.* Translated by Steven Rendell. Berkeley: University of California Press.

Deafenbaugh, Linda. 1989. "Hausa weaving: Surviving amid the paradoxes." In *Apprenticeship: From Theory to Method and Back Again*, edited by Michael Coy, 163–79. New York: SUNY Press.

Dilley, Roy M. 1989. "Secrets and skills: Apprenticeship among Tukolor weavers." In *Apprenticeship: From Theory to Method and Back Again*, edited by Michael Coy, 181–99. New York: SUNY Press.

Dow, James. 1989. "Apprentice shaman." In *Apprenticeship: From Theory to Method and Back Again*, edited by Michael Coy, 199–210. New York: SUNY Press.

Dreier, Ole. 1991. "Client interests and possibilities in psychotherapy." In *Critical Psychology: Contributions to an Historical Science of the Subject* edited by C. W. Tolman and W. Maiers, 196–211. Cambridge: Cambridge University Press.

1980. *Familiäres Bewusstsein und familiares Sein: Therapeutische Analyse einar Arbeiterfamilie [Family Being and Family Consciousness: Therapeutic Analysis of a Working-Class Family]*. (Texte zur Kritischen Psychologies Bd. 11). Frankfurt am Main: Campus.

1993. "Re-searching psychotherapeutic practice." In *Understanding Practice: Perspectives on Activity and Context*, edited by Seth Chaiklin and Jean Lave, 105–24. Cambridge: Cambridge University Press.

1994. "Personal locations and perspectives: Psychological aspects of social practice." In *Psychological Yearbook: University of Copenhagen – Volume 1*, edited by Niels Engelsted, 1: 63–90. London: Museum Tusculanum Press.

1999. "Personal trajectories of participation across contexts of social practice." *Outlines. Critical Practice Studies* 1, no. 1: 5–32.

2008. "Learning in structures of social practice." In *A Qualitative Stance: Essays in Honor of Steinar Kvale*, edited by Klaus Nielsen, Claus Elmholdt, Lene Tanggaard, Peter Musaeus, and Gerda Kraft, 85–96. Aarhus: Aarhus Universitetsforlag.

2008. *Psychotherapy in Everyday Life*. Cambridge: Cambridge University Press.

2011. "Personality and the conduct of everyday life." *Nordic Psychology* 63, no. 2: 4.

2013a. "Learning and everyday conduct of life." In *International Society for Theoretical Psychology Conference*. Santiago, Chile.

2013b. "The person and her conduct of everday life". Unpublished Manuscript.

2015. "Learning and conduct of everyday life." In *Dialogue and Debate in the Making of Theoretical Psychology*, edited by J. Cresswell, A. Haye, A. Larraín, M. Morgan, G. Sullivan, 182–90. Concord, ON: Captus University Publications.

Dreyfus, Hubert, and Stuart E. Dreyfus. 1986. *Mind over Machine*. New York: Simon and Schuster.

Drummond, Ariana de Franca. 2014. "Participação de Crianças e de Adolescents Nas Tarefas Domésticas." Doutorado em Educação, Faculdade de Educação, Universidade Federal de Minas Gerais.

Duguid, Paul. 2008. "Prologue: Community of practice then and now." In *Community, Economic Creativity, and Organization*, edited by Ash Amin and Joanne Roberts, 1–10. Oxford: Oxford University Press.

Duranti, Alessandro, and Charles Goodwin, eds. 1992. *Rethinking Context: Language as an Interactive Phenomenon*. Cambridge: Cambridge University Press.

Durkheim, Emile, and Marcel Mauss. 1903. *Primitive Classification*. Translated by Rodney Needham. Chicago: University of Chicago Press.

Eagleton, Terry. 2013. *The Illusions of Postmodernism*. Hoboken: John Wiley and Sons.

Eckert, Penelope. 1989a. *Adolescent Social Categories, Information, and Science Learning*. Mahwah: Lawrence Erlbaum Associates.

1989b *Jocks and Burnouts: Social Categories and Identity in the High School*. New York: Teachers College Press.

Eisenhart, Margaret, and Dorothy Holland. 1983. "Learning gender from peers: The role of peer groups in the cultural transmission of gender." *Human Organization* 42, no. 4: 321–32.

Ekers, Michael, Gillian Hart, Stefan Kipfer, and Alex Loftus, eds. 2013. *Gramsci: Space, Nature, Politics*. John Wiley and Sons.

Elkjaer, Bente, and Ulrik Brandi. 2003. "Organizational learning viewed from a social learning perspective." In *Blackwell Handbook of Organizational Learning and Knowledge Management*, edited by Mark Easterby-Smith and Marjorie Lyles. John Wiley and Sons.

Elyachar, Julia. 2005. *Markets of Dispossession: NGOs, Economic Development, and the State in Cairo*. Durham: Duke University Press.

Engeström, Yrjö. 2014. *Learning by Expanding*. Helsinki: Orienta-Konsultit, 1987. *Learning by Expanding*. Cambridge: Cambridge University Press.

Faria, Eliene. 2008. "A Aprendizagem Da e Na Prática Social: Um Estudo Etnográfico Sobre as Práticas de Aprendizagem Do Futebol Em Um Bairro de Belo Horizonte." Doutorado em Educação, Faculdade de Educação, Universidade Federal de Minas Gerais.

Favret-Saada, Jeanne. 1980. *Deadly Words: Witchcraft in the Bocage*. Translated by Catherine Cullen. Cambridge: Cambridge University Press Cambridge. http://library.wur.nl/WebQuery/clc/131010.

Fernandez, Nadine. 1996. "The color of love: Young interracial couples in Cuba." *Latin American Perspectives* 23, no. 1: 99–117.

2010. *Revolutionizing Romance: Interracial Couples in Contemporary Cuba*. New Brunswick: Rutgers University Press.

Fortes, Meyer. 1949. *The Web of Kinship among the Tallensi*. London: Oxford University Press.

Gamst, Frederick C. 1989. "The railroad apprentice and the 'rules': Historic roots and contemporary practices." In *Apprenticeship: From Theory to Method and Back Again*, edited by Michael Coy, 65–86. New York: SUNY Press.

Gay, John, and Michael Cole. 1967. *The New Mathematics and an Old Culture: A Study of Learning among the Kpelle of Liberia*. New York: Holt, Rinehart and Winston.

Gentner, Dedre, and Albert L. Stevens, eds. 2014. *Mental Models*. New York: Psychology Press.

Gladwin, Thomas. 2009. *East Is a Big Bird: Navigation and Logic on Puluwat Atoll*. Cambridge: Harvard University Press.

Goffman, Erving. 1964. "The neglected situation." *American Anthropologist* 66, no. 6.2: 133–6.

Goldman, Marcio. 2005. "Formas do Saber e Modos do Ser: Observações sobre Multiplicidade e Ontologia no Candomblé." *Religião e Sociedade* 25, no. 2: 102–20.

Gomes, Ana Maria R. 2000. "Produção e reprodução da cultura escolar: algumas delimitações para a análise da experiência dos professores indígenas Xacriabá." *Educação em Revista*, número especial.

Gomes, Ana Maria R. and Eliene L. Faria. 2015. "Etnografia e aprendizagem na prática: explorando caminhos a partir do futebol no Brasil." *Educação e Pesquisa*, 41: 1213–28.

Gomes, Ana Maria R., Eliene L. Faria, Renata S. Bergo, and Rogério C. Silva. 2012. "Learning and culture; learning [the] culture in Brazil." In *AAA/CAE-Annual Meeting*. San Francisco.

Gomes, Ana Maria R., Carlos Steil, and Isabel Cristina de Moura Carvalho. 2015. "Cultura e Aprendizagem." *Horizontes Antropológicos (Special Issue)*, Cultura e Aprendizagem, 44.

Goody, Esther. 1969. "Kinship fostering in Gonja." In *Socialization: The Approach from Social Anthropology*, edited by Philip Mayer, 51–74. New York: Routledge.

　　1980. "Questions and politeness: Strategies in social interaction." *Philosophy and Rhetoric* 13, no. 3: 210–13.

　　1982. ed. *From Craft to Industry: The Ethnography of Proto-Industrial Cloth Production*. Cambridge: Cambridge University Press.

　　1982. *Parenthood and Social Reproduction: Fostering and Occupational Roles in West Africa*. Cambridge: Cambridge University Press.

　　1989. "Learning, apprenticeship and the division of labor." In *Apprenticeship: From Theory to Method and Back Again*, edited by Michael Coy, 233–56. New York: SUNY Press.

　　2005. *Contexts of Kinship: An Essay in the Family Sociology of the Gonja of Northern Ghana*. 7. Cambridge: Cambridge University Press.

Goody, Jack. 1977. *The Domestication of the Savage Mind*. Cambridge: Cambridge University Press.

Gramsci, Antonio. 1992. *Prison Notebooks*. Translated by Joseph A. Buttigieg. Vol. 1–3. New York: Columbia University Press.

Graves, Bennie. 1989. "Informal aspects of apprenticeship in selected American occupations." In *Apprenticeship: From Theory to Method and Back Again*, edited by Michael Coy, 51–64. New York: SUNY Press.

Gray, Ann, Jan Campbell, Mark Erickson, Stuart Hanson, and Helen Wood, eds. 2007. *CCCS Selected Working Papers*. New York: Routledge.

Haas, Jack. 1989. "The process of apprenticeship: Ritual ordeal and the adoption of a cloak of competence." In *Apprenticeship: From Theory to Method and Back Again*, edited by Michael Coy, 87–105. New York: SUNY Press.

Hall, Kathy, Patricia Murphy, and Janet Soler, eds. 2008. *Pedagogy and Practice: Culture and Identities*. Thousand Oaks: Sage.

Hall, Stuart. 1996. "Race, articulation, and societies structured in dominance." In *Black British Cultural Studies: A Reader*, edited by Houston jr. Baker, Manthia Diawara, and Ruth Lindeborg, 16–60. Chicago: University of Chicago Press.

　　1980. "Race, articulation and societies structured in dominance." In *Sociological Theories: Race and Colonialism*, 305–45. Paris: UNESCO.

　　2003. "Marx's notes on method: A 'reading' of the '1857 Introduction'." *Cultural Studies* 17, no. 2: 113–49.

Hallpike, Christopher Robert. 1979. *The Foundations of Primitive Thought*. Oxford: Oxford University Press.

Hanks, William F. 1990a. *Referential Practice: Language and Lived Space among the Maya*. Chicago: University of Chicago Press.

1990b. Meaning and matters of context. Dean's Inaugural Lecture, Division of the Social Sciences, University of Chicago, May 16.

Haraway, Donna. 1988. "Situated knowledges: The science question in feminism and the privilege of partial perspective." *Feminist Studies* 14, no. 3: 575–99.

Hart, Gillian. 2007. "Changing concepts of articulation: Political stakes in South Africa today." *Review of African Political Economy* 34, no. 111: 85–101.

2002. *Disabling Globalization: Places of Power in Post-Apartheid South Africa*. Berkeley: University of California Press.

2014. *Rethinking the South African Crisis: Nationalism, Populism, Hegemony*. Athens: University of Georgia Press.

2016. "Relational comparison revisited: Marxist postcolonial geographies in practice." *Progress in Human Geography*: 1–24.

Hass, M. 1986. "Cognition-in-context: The social nature of the transformation of mathematical knowledge in a third grade classroom." University of California, Irvine.

Haug, Wolfgang Fritz. 2000. "Gramsci's 'Philosophy of Praxis.'" *Socialism and Democracy* 14, no. 1: 1–19.

2007. "Philosophizing with Marx, Gramsci, and Brecht." *Boundary 2* 34, no. 3: 143.

Hebdige, Dick. 1988. *Hiding in the Light: On Images and Things*. London: Routledge.

Hedegaard, Mariane. 2012. "A cultural-historical theory of children's development." In *Extending Professional Practice in the Early Years*, edited by Linda Miller, Rose Drury, and Carrie Cable, 193–210. Thousand Oaks: Sage.

Herzfeld, Michael. 2004. *The Body Impolitic: Artisans and Artifice in the Global Hierarchy of Value*. Chicago: University of Chicago Press.

Hojholt, C. 2011. "Cooperation between professionals in educational psychology." In *Vygotsky and Special Needs Education: Re-Thinking Support for Children and Schools*, edited by Harry Daniels and Mariane Hedegaard, 67–86. New York: Continuum.

Højholt, Charlotte. 2006. "Knowledge and professionalism – from the perspectives of children?" *Critical Psychology*.

Højholt, Charlotte, Wolfgang Maiers, Betty Bayer, Barbara Duarte Esgalhado, René Jorna, and Ernst Schraube. 1999. "Child development in trajectories of social practice." In *Challenges to Theoretical Psychology*, 278–85. North York: Captus University Press.

Holland, Dorothy. 2001. *Identity and Agency in Cultural Worlds*. Cambridge: Harvard University Press.

Holland, Dorothy, and Margaret A. Eisenhart. 1990. *Educated in Romance: Women, Achievement, and College Culture*. University of Chicago Press.

Holland, Dorothy, and Jean Lave, eds. 2001. *History in Person: Enduring Struggles, Contentious Practice, Intimate Identities*. Santa Fe: School for Advanced Research Press.

Holland, Dorothy, Ray C. Rist, Margaret A. Eisenhart, and Joe R. Harding. 1979. *The Veneer of Harmony: Social-Race Relations in a Southern Desegregated School*. New York: Academic Press.

Holland, Dorothy, and Debra Skinner. 2001. "From women's suffering to women's politics: Reimagining women after Nepal's 1990 pro-democracy movement." In *History in Person: Enduring Struggles, Contentious Practice, Intimate Identities*, edited by Dorothy Holland and Jean Lave, 93–133. Santa Fe: School for Advanced Research Press.

Holsoe, Svend E. 1984. "Vai occupational continuities: Traditional to modern." *Liberian Studies Journal* 10, no. 2: 12–23.

Holzkamp, Klaus. 1985. *Grundlegung Der Psychologie*. Frankfurt: Campus-Verlag.

   1987. "Critical psychology and overcoming of scientific indeterminacy in psychological theorizing." *Perspectives in Personality* 2: 93–123.

   1991. "Societal and individual life processes." In *Critical Psychology: Contributions to an Historical Science of the Subject*, edited by Charles Tolman and Wolfgang Maiers, 50–64.

Hutchins, Edwin. 1993. "Learning to navigate." In *Understanding Practice: Perspectives on Activity and Context*, edited by Seth Chaiklin and Jean Lave, 35–63. Cambridge: Cambridge University Press.

Ingold, Tim. 2001. "From the transmission of representations to the education of attention." In *The Debated Mind: Evolutionary Psychology versus Ethnography*, edited by Harvey Whitehouse, 113–53. New York: Bloomsbury.

Johnson, Norris B. 1988. "Temple architecture as construction of consciousness: A Japanese temple and garden." *Architecture and Behavior* 4, no. 3: 229–50.

   1989. "Japanese temple gardens and the apprentice training of priests." In *Apprenticeship: From Theory to Method and Back Again*, edited by Michael Coy, 211–32. New York: SUNY Press.

Jordan, Brigitte. 1989. "Cosmopolitical obstetrics: Some insights from the training of traditional midwives." *Social Science and Medicine* 28, no. 9: 925–37.

Keller, Charles M., and Janet Dixon Keller. 1993. "Thinking and acting with iron." In *Understanding Practice*, edited by Seth Chaiklin and Jean Lave, 125–43. Cambridge University Press.

   1996. *Cognition and Tool Use: The Blacksmith at Work*. Cambridge: Cambridge University Press.

Kerr, Clark. 1964. *The Uses of the University*. Cambridge: Harvard University Press. http://library.wur.nl/WebQuery/clc/435116.

King, Kenneth. 1977. *The African Artisan: Education and the Informal Sector in Kenya*. London: Heinemann.

Kondo, Dorinne. 1990. *Crafting Selves: Power, Gender, and Discourse of Identity in a Japanese Workplace*. Chicago: University of Chicago Press.

   1992. "Multiple selves: The aesthetics and politics of artisanal identities." In *Japanese Sense of Self*, edited by Nancy Rosenberger, 40–66. Cambridge: Cambridge University Press.

Kristensen, Hanne Kaae, Tove Borg, and Lise Hounsgaard. 2011. "Facilitation of research-based evidence within occupational therapy in stroke rehabilitation." *The British Journal of Occupational Therapy* 74, no. 10: 473–83.

Kvale, Steinar. 1977. "Dialectics and research on remembering." In *Life-Span Developmental Psychology: Dialectical Perspectives on Experimental Research*, edited by N. Datan and H. W. Reese, 165–89. New York: Academic Press.

   1992. ed. *Psychology and Postmodernism*. Thousand Oaks: Sage.

2008. *Doing Interviews*. Thousand Oaks: Sage.

Lancy, David F. 1980. "Becoming a blacksmith in Gbarngasuakwelle." *Anthropology and Education Quarterly* 11, no. 4: 266–74.

Lansky, Samy. 2008. "Na Cidade Com Crianças: Uma Etno-Grafia Espacializada." Doutorado em Educação, Faculdade de Educação, Universidade Federal de Minas Gerais.

Latour, Bruno. 1987. "A relativistic account of Einstein's relativity." *Social Studies of Science* 18, no. 1: 3–44.

2006. "Les 'Vues' de l'Esprit: Une Introduction à l'Anthropologie Des Sciences et Des Techniques." *Culture Technique* 14.

Latour, Bruno, and Steve Woolgar. 1979. *Laboratory Life: The Construction of Scientific Facts*. Princeton: Princeton University Press.

Lave, Jean. 1982. "A comparative approach to educational forms and learning processes." *Anthropology and Education Quarterly* 13, no. 2: 181–7.

1986. "The values of quantification." In J. Law (ed.) Power, Action and Belief: The New Sociology of Knowledge. Sociological Review monograph Vol. 32. 88–111. London: Routledge and Kegan Paul. 88–111.

1988. *Cognition in Practice: Mind, Mathematics and Culture in Everyday Life*. Cambridge: Cambridge University Press.

1991. "Situating learning in communities of practice." In *Perspectives on Socially Shared Cognition*, edited by Lauren Resnick, John Levine, and Stephanie Teasly, 63–82. Washington, DC: American Psychological Association.

1996. "Teaching, as learning, in practice." *Mind, Culture, and Activity* 3, no. 3: 149–64.

1996. "The savagery of the domestic mind." In *Naked Science*, edited by Laura Nader, 87–100. London: Routledge.

October 1996. "A Selvajaria Da Mente Domesticada." *Revista Crítica de Ciêncas Sociais*, no. 46: 109–34.

1997. "The culture of acquisition and the practice of understanding." In *Situated Cognition: Social, Semiotic, and Psychological Perspectives*, edited by David Kirshner and James Whiston, 63–82. Mahwah, NJ: Lawrence Erlbaum Associates.

1997. "Learning, apprenticeship, and social practice." *Nordisk Pedagogik* 17, no. 3: 140–51.

2001. "Learning in practice: The Kalundborg Production School." In *Danish Production Schools*, edited by Niels Jakobsen.

2008. "Situated learning and changing practice." In *Community, Economic Creativity, and Organization*, edited by Ash Amin and Joanne Roberts, 288–96. Oxford: Oxford University Press.

2011. *Apprenticeship in Critical Ethnographic Practice*. Chicago: University of Chicago Press.

2012. "Changing practice." *Mind, Culture, and Activity* 19, no. 2: 156–71.

Lave, Jean, Paul Duguid, Nadine Fernandez, and Erik Axel. 1992. "Coming of age in Birmingham: Cultural studies and conceptions of subjectivity." *Annual Review of Anthropology* 21, no. 1: 257–82.

Lave, Jean, and Etienne Wenger. 1991. *Situated Learning: Legitimate Peripheral Participation*. Cambridge: Cambridge University Press.

Situeret Læring: Og Andre Tekster. Hans Reitzel, 2005.

Lave, Jean, and Ray McDermott. 2002. "Estranged ~~labor~~ learning." *Outlines. Critical Practice Studies* 4, no. 1: 19–48.

Lave, Jean, and Martin Packer. 2011. "Towards a social ontology of learning." In *A Qualitative Stance: In Memory of Steiner Kvale,1938–2008*, edited by Svend Brinkmann and Claus Elmholdt et. al., 12–22. Arhaus: Arhaus University Press, 2008. [Spanish translation in Revista de Estudios Sociales, no. 40].

Lefebvre, Henri. 1991. *The Production of Space*. Oxford: Blackwell.

 1968 [1991]. *Everyday Life in the Modern World*. London: Continuum.

 1947 [1991]. *Critique of Everyday Life Volume 1*. Translated by Jason W. Moore. New York: Verso.

 1971 [2008]. *Critique of Every Day Life Volume 3: From Modernity to Modernism*. Translated by George Elliot. Verso. New York.

 1962 [2002]. *Critique of Everyday Life Volume 2: Foundations for a Sociology of the Everyday*. Translated by John Moore. New York: Verso.

Levine, Harold G., and L. L. Langness. 1983. "Context, ability, and performance: Comparison of competitive athletics among mildly mentally retarded and nonretarded adults." *American Journal of Mental Deficiency* 87, no. 5: 528–38.

Levi-Strauss, Claude. 1966. *The Savage Mind*. Chicago: University of Chicago Press.

Levy-Bruhl, Lucien. 1926 [1910]. *How Natives Think*. London: George Allen and Unwin.

Lima, Tânia Stolze. 1999. "The two and its many: Reflections on perspectivism in a Tupi cosmology." *Ethnos* 64, no.1: 107–31.

Link, Carol Ann Bartusiak. 1975. *Japanese Cabinetmaking: A Dynamic System of Decisions and Interactions in a Technical Context*. Urbana-Champaign: University of Illinois Press.

Malkki, Liisa H. 2001. "Figures of the future: Dystopia and subjectivity in the social imagination of the future." In *History in Person. Enduring Struggles, Contentious Practice, Intimate Identities*, edited by Dorothy Holland and Jean Lave, 325–48. Santa Fe: School for Advanced Research Press.

Marshall, Hannah Meara. 1972. "Structural constraints on learning: Butchers' apprentices." *American Behavioral Scientist* 16, no. 1: 35–44.

Marx, Karl. 1998. "Theses on Feuerbach." In *The German Ideology: Including Theses on Feuerbach and Introduction to the Critique of Political Economy*, 569–75. Amherst: Prometheus Books.

Marx, Karl, and Friedrich Engels. 2009. *The Economic and Philosophic Manuscripts of 1844 and the Communist Manifesto*. Prometheus Books.

McDermott, Raymond. (July 1, 1977). "Social relations as contexts for learning in school." *Harvard Educational Review* 47, no. 2: 198–213.

 1980. "Profile: Ray L. Birdwhistell." *The Kinesis Report* 2, no. 3: 1–16.

 2001. "The acquisition of a child by a learning disability." In *Understanding Learning: Influences and Outcomes*, edited by Janet Collins and Deirdre Cook, 269–305. Thousand Oaks: Sage.

McLaughlin, Stephen Douglas. 1979. *The Wayside Mechanic: An Analysis of Skill Acquisition in Ghana*. Boston: University of Massachusettes. https://eric.ed.gov/?id=ED186702.

McNaughton, Patrick R. 1988. *The Mande Blacksmiths: Knowledge, Power, and Art in West Africa*. Bloomington: Indiana University Press.

McNeil, L. M. 1986. *Contradictions of Control: School Knowledge and School Structure*. New York: Routledge.

Mehan, Hugh B., Alma Hertweck, and J. Lee Meihls. 1986. *Handicapping the Handicapped: Decision Making in Students' Educational Careers*. Stanford: Stanford University Press.

Minick, Norris. 1985. "Teacher's directives: The social construction of 'literal meanings' and 'real words' in classroom discourse." In *Understanding Practice: Perspectives on Activity and Context*, edited by Seth Chaiklin and Jean Lave, 343–76. Cambridge: Cambridge University Press.

1993. "Vygotsky and Soviet activity theory: New perspectives on the relationship between mind and society." PhD Dissertation, Cornell University.

Mitchell, Timothy. 1988 [1991]. *Colonising Egypt*. Berkeley: University of California Press.

Monte-Mor, Roberto. 2005. "What is the urban in the contemporary world?" *Cadernos de Saúde Pública* 21, no. 3: 942–8.

2014. "Extended urbanization and settlement patterns in Brazil: An environmental approach." In *Implosions/Explosions: Towards a Study of Planetary Urbanization*, edited by Neil Brenner, 109–20. Berlin: Jovis.

Moore, David Thornton. 1981. "Discovering the pedagogy of experience." *Harvard Educational Review* 51, no. 2: 286–300.

1986. "Learning at work: Case studies in non-school education." *Anthropology and Education Quarterly* 17, no. 3: 166–84.

2004. "Curriculum at work: An educational perspective on the workplace as a learning environment." *Journal of Workplace Learning* 16, no. 6: 325–40.

Mork, Sonja M. 2011. "An interactive learning environment designed to increase the possibilities for learning and communicating about radioactivity." *Interactive Learning Environments* 19, no. 2: 163–77.

Murphy, Patricia, and Robert McCormick, eds. 2008. *Knowledge and Practice: Representations and Identities*. Thousand Oaks: Sage.

Murtaugh, Michael. 1985a. "The practice of arithmetic by American grocery shoppers." *Anthropology and Education Quarterly* 16, no. 3: 186–92.

Murtaugh, Michael Francis. 1985b. "A hierarchical decision process model of American grocery shopping." PhD Dissertation, University of California, Irvine.

Mustafa, Hudita Nura. 1998. "Practicing beauty: Crisis, value and the challenge of self-mastery in Dakar, 1980–1998." PhD Dissertation, Harvard University.

Nader, Laura, ed. 1996. *Naked Science: Anthropological Inquiry into Boundaries, Power, and Knowledge*. New York: Routledge.

Nielsen, Klaus. 2005. "The workplace – a landscape of learning." In *Learning, Working and Living*, edited by Steinar Kvale, Elena Antonacopoulou, Peter Jarvis, Vibeke Andersen, Bente Elkjaer, and Steen Høyrup, 119–35. New York: Springer.

2006. "Learning to do things with things: Apprenticeship in bakery as economy and social practice." In *Doing Things with Things: The Design and Use of Everyday Objects*, edited by A. Costall and O. Dreier, 209–24. London: Routledge.

2007. "Learning as an aspect of changing practice." In *Paper, ISTP Conference*, 18:22.

2012. "Gender, learning, and social practice." In *Encyclopedia of the Sciences of Learning*, edited by Norbert Steel, 1340–2. New York: Springer.

2013. "Collaborative learning in the bakery (unpublished conference paper)".

Nielsen, Richard P. 1988. "Cooperative strategy." *Strategic Management Journal* 9, no. 5: 475–92.

Nissen, Morten. 1999. "Wild learning – the beginning of practice research about a project combining social work, staff training, and institutional reform." Working Paper. Network for Non-Scholastic Learning, Institut for Filosofi University of Aarhus.

Ollman, Bertell. 1976. *Alienation: Marx's Conception of Man in a Capitalist Society.* Cambridge: Cambridge University Press.

2003. *Dance of the Dialectic: Steps in Marx's Method.* Urbana-Champaign: University of Illinois Press.

2015. "Marxism and the philosophy of internal relations; or, how to replace the mysterious 'paradox' with 'contradictions' that can be studied and resolved." *Capital & Class* 39, no. 1: 7–23.

Olsen, Laurie M. 1995. "From nation to race: The Americanization of immigrants in the high school of the 1990's." PhD Dissertation, University of California, Berkeley.

Østerlund, Carsten. 1996. *Learning Across Contexts: A Field Study of Salespeople's Learning at Work.* Vol. 21. 1. Aarhus: Aarhus University Press.

Østerlund, Carsten, and Paul Carlile. 2005. "Relations in practice: Sorting through practice theories on knowledge sharing in complex organizations." *The Information Society* 21, no. 2: 91–107.

Packer, Martin. 2001. *Changing Classes: School Reform and the New Economy.* Cambridge: Cambridge University Press.

1985. "Hermeneutic inquiry in the study of human conduct." *American Psychologist* 40, no. 10: 1081–93.

Pareto, Vilfredo. 1903. *Les Systèmes Socialistes.* Vol. 2. Paris: V. Giard & e. Briere.

Parsons, Talcott, and Robert Fred Bales. 1956. *Family Socialization and Interaction Process.* Vol. 7. London: Routledge.

Pear, D. 1972. *What Is Knowledge.* Oxford: Blackwell.

Peil, Margaret. 1970. "The apprenticeship system in Accra." *Africa* 40, no. 2: 137–50.

Petersen, Kirsten, Lise Hounsgaard, Tove Borg, and Claus Vinther Nielsen. 2012. "User involvement in mental health rehabilitation: A struggle for self-determination and recognition." *Scandinavian Journal of Occupational Therapy* 19, no. 1: 59–67.

Petitto, A. L. 1979. "Knowledge of arithmetic among schooled and unschooled African Tailors and cloth-merchants." Unpublished PhD Dissertation, Cornell University.

Pokrant, Robert J. 1983. "Survival of Indigenous Tailoring among the Hausa of Kano City, Nigeria." PhD Dissertation, University of Cambridge. www.dspace.cam.ac.uk/handle/1810/250818.

Posner, J. K. 1979. "The development of mathematical knowledge among Baoule and Dioula children in Ivory Coast." Phd Dissertation, Cornell University.

Rancière, Jacques. 2004. *The Philosopher and His Poor.* Durham: Duke University Press.

Rehmann, Jan. 2013. *Theories of Ideology: The Powers of Alienation and Subjection.* Boston: Brill.

Ribeiro, Rodrigo. 2007. "The role of interactional expertise in interpreting: The case of technology transfer in the steel industry." *Studies in History and Philosophy of Science Part A* 38, no. 4: 713–21.

2013. "Levels of immersion, tacit knowledge and expertise." *Phenomenology and the Cognitive Sciences* 12, no. 2: 367–97.

De la Rocha, Olivia. 1985. "The reorganization of arithmetic practice in the kitchen." *Anthropology and Education Quarterly* 16, no. 3: 193–8.

Rogoff, B. 1990. *Apprenticeship in Thinking: Cognitive Development in Sociocultural Activity*. New York: Oxford University Press.

Rommetveit, Ragnar. 1978. "On negative rationalism in scholarly studies of verbal communication and dynamic residuals in the construction of human subjectivity." In *The Social Contexts of Method*, edited by Michael Brenner, Peter Marsh, and Marylin Brenner, 16–32. New York: St. Martin's Press.

1987. "Meaning, context, and control: Convergent trends and controversial issues in current social-scientific research on human cognition and communication." *Inquiry* 30, no. 1–2: 77–99.

1988. "On literacy and the myth of literal meaning." In *The Written World*, edited by Roger Säljö, 13–40. New York: Springer.

Rumelhart, David E., and James L. McClelland. 1987. *Parallel Distributed Processing*. Vol. 1. Cambridge: MIT Press.

Säljö, Roger. 1982. *Learning and Understanding: A Study of Differences in Constructing Meaning from a Text*. Vol. 41. Guttenberg: Acta Universitatis Gothoburgensis.

Säljö, Roger, and J. Wyndham. 1990. "Problem solving and academic performance and situated reasoning: A study of joint cognitive activity in the formal setting." *British Journal of Education Psychology* 60, no. 3: 245–55.

Saxe, Geoffrey B. 1988. "The mathematics of child street vendors." *Child Development* 59, no. 5: 1415–25.

2015. *Culture and Cognitive Development: Studies in Mathematical Understanding*. New York: Psychology Press.

Schank, Patricia, and Michael Ranney. 1992. "Assessing explanatory coherence: A new method for integrating verbal data with models of online belief revision." In *Proceedings of the Fourteenth Annual Conference of the Cognitive Science Society*, 599–604. http://morenumerate.org/downloads/SchankRanney 1992.pdf.

Schraube, Ernst, and Charlotte Højholt, eds. 2015. *Psychology and the Conduct of Everyday Life*. London: Routledge.

Scribner, Sylvia, and Michael Cole. 1973. "Cognitive consequences of formal and informal education." *Science* 182, no. 4112: 553–9.

Scribner, Sylvia, and E. Fahrmeir. 1982. "Practical and theoretical arithmetic: Some preliminary findings. Industrial literacy project," working paper No. 3.

Shapin, Steven. 1991. "'The mind is its own place': Science and solitude in seventeenth-century England." *Science in Context* 4, no. 1: 191–218.

1996. *The Scientific Revolution*. Chicago: University of Chicago Press.

Silva, Rogério Correa. 2011. *Circulando com os meninos: infância, participação e aprendizagens de meninos indígenas Xacriabá*. Belo Horizonte: Universidade Federal de Minas Gerais.

Silveira, Katia Pedroso, Eduardo Fleury Mortimer, and Ana Maria R. Gomes. 2017. "Science education and Maxakali tradition: Constructing relationships in search of a common world." *Creative Education* 8, no. 10: 1590.

Sims, Christo. 2017. *Disruptive Fixation: School Reform and the Pitfalls of Techno-Idealism*. Princeton: Princeton University Press.

Singleton, John. 1998. *Learning in Likely Places: Varieties of Apprenticeship in Japan*. Cambridge: Cambridge University Press.

Skinner, Debra, Jaan Valsiner, and Dorothy Holland. 2001. "Discerning the dialogical self: A theoretical and methodological examination of a Nepali adolescent's narrative." *Forum: Qualitative Social Research* 2, no. 3.

Smutylo, Terence S. 1973. "Apprenticeship in the wayside workshops of an Accra neighborhood." MA Thesis, University of Accra.

Sperber, Dan. 1996. *Explaining Culture*. Oxford: Blackwell.

Stallybrass, Peter, and Allon White. 1986. *The Politics and Poetics of Transgression*. Ithaca: Cornell University Press.

Star, Susan Leigh. 1989. "The structure of ill-structured solutions: Heterogeneous problem-solving, boundary objects and distributed artificial intelligence." In *Distributed Artificial Intelligence*, edited by Les Gasser and Michael Huhns, 2:37–54.

Suchman, Lucy A. 1987. *Plans and Situated Actions: The Problem of Human-Machine Communication*. Cambridge: Cambridge University Press.

Suchman, Lucy A., and Randall H. Trigg. 1991. "Understanding practice: Video as a medium for reflection and design." In *Design at Work: Cooperative Design of Computer Systems*, edited by Joan Greenbaum and Morten Kyng, 65–90. Boca Raton: CRC Press.

1993. "Artificial intelligence as craftwork." In Understanding Practice: Perspectives on Activity and Context, edited by Seth Chaiklin and Jean Lave, 144–78. Cambridge: Cambridge University Press.

Thomas, Peter D. 2009. *The Gramscian Moment: Philosophy, Hegemony and Marxism*. Vol. 24. Boston: Brill.

Thomas, Robert J. 1994. *What Machines Can't Do: Politics and Technology in the Industrial Enterprise*. Berkeley: University of California Press.

Toren, Christina. 1993. "Making history: The significance of childhood cognition for a comparative anthropology of mind." *Man*, 461–78.

Traweek, Sharon. 1988. "Discovering machines: Nature in the age of its mechanical reproduction." In *Making Time: Ethnographies of High-Technology Organizations*, edited by Frank Dubinskas, 39–91. Philadelphia: Temple University Press.

Velho, Otávio. 2006. *Trabalhos de campo: antinomias e estradas de ferro. Aula inaugural no Instituto de Filosofia e Ciências Humanas da Universidade do Estado do Rio de Janeiro*. Rio de Janeiro: UERJ.

Verdon, Michel. 1979. "African apprentice workshops: A case of ethnocentric reductionism." *American Ethnologist* 6, no. 3: 531–42.

Verran, Helen. 2001. *Science and an African Logic*. Chicago: University of Chicago Press.

Viveiros de Castro, Eduardo. 1996. "Images of nature and society in Amazonian ethnology." *Annual Review of Anthropology*, 25: 179–200.

1998. "Cosmological deixis and Amerindian perspectivism." *Journal of the Royal Anthropological Institute*, 4, no. 3: 469–88.

2002. "O nativo relativo." *Mana (UFRJ. Impresso)*, 8, no. 1: 113–48.

2013. "The relative native." *Hau – Journal of Ethnographic Theory*, 3: 469–502.

Warren, Kay. 2000. "Indigenous activism across generations: An intimate social history of antiracism organizing in Guatemala." In *History in Person: Enduring Struggles, Contentious Practice, and Intimate Identities*, edited by Dorothy Holland and Jean Lave, 63–91. Santa Fe: School for Advanced Research Press.

Warren, Scott. 1984. *The Emergence of Dialectical Theory: Philosophy and Political Inquiry*. Chicago: University of Chicago Press.

Wenger, Etienne. 1998. *Communities of Practice: Learning, Meaning, and Identity*. Cambridge: Cambridge University Press.

Wenger, Etienne, Richard Arnold McDermott, and William Snyder. 2002. *Cultivating Communities of Practice: A Guide to Managing Knowledge*. Cambridge: Harvard Business Press.

Williams, Raymond. 1976. *Keywords: A Vocabulary of Culture and Society*. New York: Oxford University Press.

Willis, Paul. 1981. "Cultural production is different from cultural reproduction is different from social reproduction is different from reproduction." *Interchange* 12, no. 2–3: 48–67.

2001. "Tekin' the Piss." In *History in Person: Enduring Struggles, Contentious Practice, Intimate Identities*, edited by Dorothy Holland and Jean Lave, 171–216. Santa Fe: School for Advanced Research Press.

Willis, Paul E. 1977. *Learning to Labor: How Working Class Kids Get Working Class Jobs*. New York: Columbia University Press.

World Bank. 2015. *World Development Report 2015: Mind, Society, and Behavior.*

Wortham, Stanton, and Catherine Rhodes. 2013. "Life as a chord: Heterogeneous resources in the social identification of one migrant girl." *Applied Linguistics* 34, no. 5.

Wymer, Norman. 1949. *English Town Crafts: A Survey of Their Development from Early Times to Present Day*. London: Batsford.

Index

dualism
    contextualization/decontextualization. *See*
        context
    mind/body 31. *see also* learning
    critique of, 25
    everyday life/exceptional, 114,
        122
    formal/informal, 62
    mental/social, 116
    philosophy/non-philosophy. *See* Lefebvre,
        Henri
    primitive mind/civilized mind, 19
    science/everyday, 21
Duguid, Paul, 93
    critique of *Situated Learning*, *143*

ethnography, 93, 139
everyday life, 7, 12
    common sense understanding, 117
    and learning as dialectaically constitutive,
        129
    as logical operator, 118
    and praxis, 129
    as social practice, 119
    as social zone, 118, 120–3

failure to learn, 35, 39
formal/informal education, 86
Fortes, Meyer, 62

Goody, Esther, 52–8
Gramsci, Antonio
    theory of the person, 150–1
    theory of the subject, 150

Hall, Stuart, 154–5
Herzfeld, Michael, 77

identity, 137
    as process, 34
indigenous peoples
    and education, 159
inferior other, 13, 23
Ingold, Tim, 115, 146

just plain folks, 13

Kalundborg Production School,
        145
    description, 105
    dilemmas, 109
    projects, 107
knowledgability, 141
Kondo, Dorrine, 73

learning
    and anthropology, 1
    conventional theories of, 84, 115
    and identity, 98
    mechanisms, 95
    and politics, 142
    in school, 96
    as social practice, 85
    as social production, 33
    telos of, 94
    theory of, 93
    transformative versus reproductive, 2
    transmission theory of, 69, 91
learning curriculum, 137
Lefebvre, Henri, 118, 120
legitimate peripheral participation, 108,
        135
Levy-Bruhl, Lucien, 20
Link, Carol Ann Bartusiak, 73

Mande Blacksmiths, 58–61
Marx, Karl, 84
    reductive understandings of Marxism, 6
    theory of praxis, 155
math, 15
    Adult Math Project, 13–14
McDermott, Raymond, 35
McNaughton, Patrick, 58–61
Mitchell, Timothy, 88–91

nonlearning, 39

old-timers/newcomers, 138
Ollman, Bertell
    theory of internal relations, 7, 148,
        155
ontological turn, 159

Packer, Martin, 93
participation
    and access, 132
person, the
    as ensemble of social relations, 150
    as historical, 157
    conflicts within, 151
    in dialectical terms, 148
    in practice, 151–3
phenomenological theory, 40
politics, 8–9
    and change, 79
    as relations. *See* Marx, Karl; theory of praxis
    of everyday life, 148
    of knowledge, 1
    of social categorization, 26